Orlando
With regards.

Party-Directed Mediation

Ordering Information

https://ucce.ucdavis.edu/survey/survey.cfm?surveynumber=443&back=none

Party-Directed Mediation
c/o Gregorio Billikopf
University of California
3800 Cornucopia Way #A
Modesto, CA 95358-9492

(209) 525-6800

Additional Free Resources

http://www.cnr.berkeley.edu/ucce50/ag-labor/7conflict/

Party-Directed Mediation
Helping Others Resolve Differences

(2nd Edition)

Gregorio Billikopf
University of California

PARTY-DIRECTED MEDIATION: HELPING OTHERS RESOLVE DIFFERENCES

© 2004, 2009 by *The Regents of the University of California*
Agricultural and Natural Resources
UNIVERSITY OF CALIFORNIA

All rights reserved.
First edition 2004
Second edition 2009
Printed in the United States of America
ISBN 978-0-615-24633-8

The first edition was published under the title *Helping Others Resolve Differences: Empowering Stakeholders*.

Cover design by Harrison Aquino. Cover illustration by Steve Svancara of On The Draw Graphics, Ltd. The views and opinions expressed herein are solely those of the author. On The Draw Graphics, Ltd., provided the illustration for the front cover of this book without making any representations as to the views and opinions expressed herein or to the validity of the contents of this book. The illustration first appeared in the February 2004 issue of *Dairy Herd Management*, "How to reconcile two workers who are not getting along: Consider new caucusing approach," and is used here with permission from the artist and Vance Publishing Corp. Back cover photo by iStockphoto.com/twohumans.

Hard copy edition. This hard copy publication may *not* be reproduced or distributed in part or whole—including any of its elements, such as text, photos, or other graphic elements—in any form or by any means, nor may it be stored in a database or retrieval system. Copies may *only* be made of the *special on-line edition* (see below).

Special on-line edition: University faculty, educators, government, consultants, or any interested person who wishes to adopt *Party-Directed Mediation: Helping Others Resolve Differences* as a text for their courses or seminars may obtain permission—at no cost—to make or distribute copies of the on-line edition of the book for course participants as long as (1) they download the book—or complete chapters—from the Web at http://www.cnr.berkeley.edu/ucce50/ag-labor/7conflict/; (2) the author and the University of California are credited; (3) no changes are made to the text; (4) this copyright notice is included; (5) there is no charge to students or participants for the materials (beyond the costs of duplication); and (6) the author's permission is requested via e-mail (send to gebillikopf@ucdavis.edu), including the requester's name, organizational affiliation, and the applicable course or workshop title. Individuals downloading the book for their own personal use—from the Web site above—need not request special permission.

To contact the author, write or call Gregorio Billikopf at the University of California (gebillikopf@ucdavis.edu, 209-525-6800).

The University of California prohibits discrimination or harassment of any person on the basis of race, color, national origin, religion, sex, gender identity, pregnancy (including childbirth, and medical conditions related to pregnancy or childbirth), physical or mental disability, medical condition (cancer-related or genetic characteristics), ancestry, marital status, age, sexual orientation, citizenship, or service in the uniformed services (as defined by the Uniformed Services Employment and Reemployment Rights Act of 1994: service in the uniformed services includes membership, application for membership, performance of service, application for service, or obligation for service in the uniformed services) in any of its programs or activities. University policy also prohibits reprisal or retaliation against any person in any of its programs or activities for making a complaint of discrimination or sexual harassment or for using or participating in the investigation or resolution process of any such complaint. University policy is intended to be consistent with the provisions of applicable State and Federal laws. Inquiries regarding the University's nondiscrimination policies may be directed to the Affirmative Action/Equal Opportunity Director, University of California, Agriculture and Natural Resources, 1111 Franklin Street, 6th Floor, Oakland, CA 94607, (510) 987-0096.

Contents

Preface **vi**
Acknowledgments **xiii**
About the Author **xiv**

Part I – Introduction **1**
Chapter 1 – Party-Directed Mediation Model Overview **3**

Part II – Pre-Caucus **9**
Chapter 2 – Empathic Listening **11**
Chapter 3 – Coaching during the Pre-Caucus **43**
Chapter 4 – Interpersonal Negotiation Skills **61**

Part III – Joint Session **111**
Chapter 5 – Mediating the Joint Session **113**

Part IV – Mediation Case Study **127**
Chapter 6 – Introducing Nora and Rebecca **129**
Chapter 7 – Rebecca's First Pre-Caucus **133**
Chapter 8 – Nora's First Pre-Caucus **141**
Chapter 9 – Rebecca's Second Pre-Caucus **153**
Chapter 10 – Nora's Second Pre-Caucus **163**
Chapter 11 – The Joint Session at Last **173**

Part V – Preventive Mediation **209**
Chapter 12 – Negotiated Performance Appraisal: Alternative and Preventive Mediation **211**
Chapter 13 – Negotiated Performance Appraisal Clips **237**

Appendices **265**
Appendix I – Cultural Differences? **267**
Appendix II – Contributions of Caucusing and Pre-Caucusing to Mediation **283**

Index **305**

Preface

We live in a troubled world with conflicts near and far. Interpersonal issues play a large role in many, if not most, conflicts.

This book is primarily directed to mediators, facilitators, leaders, and helping professionals who assist others in managing deep-seated interpersonal conflict. Many of its concepts can also be of value to those who are seeking to better understand or solve their own interpersonal discords. Some of its key principles may apply to the management of intergroup conflict.

The objective of this book is to make the *Party-Directed Mediation* approach more widely available to mediators. The

In Party-Directed Mediation, individuals are coached in a pre-caucus before the joint session.

approach is simple: (1) mediators listen to and coach each party separately in a *pre-caucus* (or pre-mediation) before bringing them together; and eventually, (2) when disputants do meet in a *joint session*, the contenders address each other rather than the third party. The burden of solving the conflict remains with those who are most likely to be able to do so: the contenders.

Parties gain the skills that will permit them to solve future conflicts without a mediator. Furthermore, Party-Directed Mediation is designed to allow individuals to save face and preserve dignity to a greater extent than allowed by more traditional approaches. Some ethnicities and cultures place a great value on *facework*, and so Party-Directed Mediation is especially effective for resolving multicultural conflicts. The need to save face, of course, transcends nationalities.

More traditional mediators bring the parties into a joint session without employing a pre-caucus. And in the joint session, contenders address the mediator rather than each other.

A number of reasons have been advanced to defend the traditional method. The lack of pre-caucusing is mostly born of the fear that the mediator may collude with one of the parties ahead of time. After all, in the traditional approach, mediators retain a position of power and can wield considerable influence over the parties by imposing solutions. They can often resemble arbiters more than mediators.

In Party-Directed Mediation, contenders learn how to negotiate for themselves, so concerns about favoritism and collusion are all but eliminated.

Mediators are beginning to recognize that the traditional method is fraught with challenges. In *When Talk Works*, Kenneth Kressel explains that it is a "common theme in the mediation canon" (1994, p. 25) to let parties tell their sides of the story in front of each other. Kressel goes on to share how destructive such an approach can be (for the full quote, see Appendix II in this book, pp. 289–290). The contenders end up insulting each other in front of the mediator, and neither is able to save face. Furthermore, the mediator fails to keep the parties psychologically safe.

It has been said that "there is no new thing under the sun" (Ecclesiastes 1:9 KJV). Since the publication of the first edition of this book in 2004, several models have come to my attention that make effective use of the pre-caucus, such as *victim-offender mediation*. Depending on the severity of the cases, victim-offender mediation may require months of pre-caucuses, as incremental steps are taken to prepare the parties to meet in a joint session. Two excellent books, Dudley Weeks' *The Eight Essential Steps to Conflict Resolution* (1992) and Mark S. Umbreit's *Mediating Interpersonal Conflicts: A Pathway to Peace* (1995), describe successful pre-caucusing.

Perhaps the contribution of Party-Directed Mediation is the more explicit organization of mediation around the pre-caucus and subsequent joint session. Furthermore, while a few authors suggest parties face each other during the joint session, in Party-Directed Mediation the facilitator moves away from the contenders, underscoring the fact that a mediator is present to facilitate a conversation between the parties rather than to decide who is right.

It takes a greater leap of faith to prepare individuals to negotiate for themselves and then to step away from the contenders, but this is precisely what strengthens the process and leaves no doubt that we are dealing with *mediation* rather than *arbitration*.

Another innovative contribution of this approach has been long-distance international mediation. Third parties can work with the help of less experienced co-mediators in another country. The seasoned mediator may listen in and assist from a different location because most of the difficult work is carried out during the pre-caucus. Much of the negative emotion is dissipated before the joint session.

The reduced level of contention between the disputants in the joint session of Party-Directed Mediation, furthermore, allows apprentice mediators to gain the needed proficiencies with more ease and under less stressful circumstances.

The original title of this book was *Helping Others Resolve Differences: Empowering Stakeholders*. The Party-Directed

More traditional approaches have parties address the mediator rather than each other.

Mediation approach was described in detail in that work, but had not yet been named. Also, the word *stakeholder* was incorrectly used as a synonym for *party*, or a contender involved in the mediation.

I am indebted to fellow mediator Jon Linden for suggesting the name of the new approach and for his pointed questions that forced me to clarify the model. Linden has an extensive mediation practice that includes work for the Special Civil Part of the New Jersey Superior Court Law Division and for the U.S. Equal Employment Opportunity Commission. It was a great satisfaction to me when Linden successfully incorporated principles discussed in this book in a workplace mediation.

Most of the chapters in the book have been restructured, and there is a new section on preventive mediation, based on the

Negotiated Performance Appraisal model. This approach may serve as an alternative conflict resolution model for superior-subordinate relationships.

Chapter 1 provides an overview of the Party-Directed Mediation procedure. We look at the philosophy as well as the general mechanics of this unique mediation approach. Chapter 2 focuses on one of the major skills needed by the mediator as well as the contenders: *empathic listening*. It is the type of listening that permits others to vent their frustrations and begin to hear themselves. Chapter 3 covers other preparatory steps carried out during the pre-caucus and describes a litmus test as to whether it is safe to proceed to the joint session in which the parties confront each other. Chapter 4 details tips on interpersonal negotiation skills. Chapter 5 prepares mediators for handling the joint session.

Chapters 6 through 11 introduce the reader to Rebecca and Nora, based on videotape transcripts of their pre-caucuses and joint session. Nora and Rebecca had been involved in a workplace dispute spanning over two decades.

Chapter 12 covers the Negotiated Performance Appraisal model, which is an excellent tool to improve interpersonal communication and thus avoid conflict escalation early on. The approach foments talking about things we often do not talk about. Chapter 13 contains transcripts of portions of several negotiated appraisals. Most of the skills required for successful Party-Directed Mediation are transferable to the facilitation of Negotiated Performance Appraisals.

Appendix I revolves around cultural differences. An understanding of these is vital when interacting with individuals from other cultures or mediating multicultural disputes.

Appendix II contains an article that was included in the first edition of this book: "Contributions of Caucusing and Pre-Caucusing to Mediation." It points out why so many mediators were resistant to the pre-caucus. The paper I presented at the 2005 Annual Meeting of the International Association for Conflict Management in Seville, Spain, has been incorporated into the main manuscript.

Our website (http://www.cnr.berkeley.edu/ucce50/ag-labor/7conflict/) includes audio seminars on both *empathic listening skills* and *interpersonal negotiation skills*—as well as chapters 2, 4, or any other chapters of interest—that can be downloaded and distributed at no cost to clients, students, or others (see p. iv).

Over the years, there have been many important contributions towards the resolution of conflicts. We shall incorporate some of the key principles in the context of Party-Directed Mediation. This book does not purport to displace other writings on the subject of mediation, nor is it a complete handbook on mediation. Rather, it introduces two models that have made positive contributions to the field and have helped empower affected parties. I began work on Party-Directed Mediation in the U.S. in January 1992 and work on the Negotiated Performance Appraisal model during a trip to Uganda in May 1996.

Party-Directed Mediation is especially effective for resolving intercultural as well as interethnic conflicts.

Party-Directed Mediation is designed to allow individuals to save face and preserve dignity.

It has been gratifying to know that papers on these models have been widely reprinted. International interest has been shown not only by the academic community (for courses in organizational behavior, conflict management, and human resource management) but also by women's shelters, attorneys, churches, and mediation centers.

Part I – Introduction

1
Party-Directed Mediation Model Overview

The two pillars of *Party-Directed Mediation* are (1) a preliminary meeting (i.e., pre-caucus, or pre-mediation) between the intermediary and each of the parties prior to the joint session and (2) a joint session in which parties speak directly to each other rather than through the mediator. Both of these supporting columns are somewhat controversial.

We intend to examine the nature of the controversy and suggest which types of conflicts lend themselves to Party-Directed Mediation. And perhaps just as importantly, which do not. Another objective is to clearly describe the model so intermediaries can apply it in a consistent, positive fashion.

The aims of the *pre-caucus* are to (1) permit parties to vent and reduce negative emotions and (2) teach contenders to negotiate more effectively. Armed with these skills, individuals are more likely to arrive at satisfying and enduring outcomes.

The initial focus of the pre-caucus is to attend to each party through an *empathic listening* posture. The third party hardly speaks, but lets the affected persons feel accompanied through their journey. This active listening approach was developed by Carl Rogers and is best described in his renowned book, *Client-Centered Therapy*. Empathic listening is not the same as asking good questions. While the third party's role is that of a listener, we ought not think the mediator is either distracted or detached from the process.

Before concluding the pre-caucus, mediators prepare contenders for the *joint session*. The responsibility falls on the intermediary to assure that each party (1) is truly ready to confront the other, (2) has acquired the requisite tools for

During the pre-caucus, parties can vent and reduce negative emotions.

Party-Directed Mediation Model Overview • 5

> *It may not be surprising that individuals who have been listened to and coached in a pre-caucus may go on to resolve their dispute without a mediated joint session.*

effective interpersonal negotiation, and (3) knows how to avoid dysfunctional behaviors.

As individuals become more capable negotiators, they handle discord more effectively. Certainly, when differences in opinion are brought to the table, they present opportunities to find more elegant, satisfying, and lasting solutions.

When the contenders arrive at the joint session, they speak directly to each other with minimal third-party interference.

Mediators underscore their reduced role in the joint session dialogue by sitting at a distance from the disputants.

Some situations may call for a different conflict resolution strategy, as it may not be psychologically safe to bring disputants together for a face-to-face confrontation. The safety of proceeding into a joint session is gauged during the pre-caucus.

The application of Party-Directed Mediation principles, then, depends on the degree to which (1) the case lends itself to them and (2) the contenders wish to acquire interpersonal negotiation skills.

Just as people today are more likely to ask for second opinions when it comes to their health and doctors' recommendations, there are those who wish to have a greater hand in solving their own disputes. Some cases—as in certain restorative justice programs—call for months of preparation as parties come together for a joint session in which they face and speak directly to each other. Yet, other situations are solved by individuals after a friend lends an ear so they gain the necessary confidence to approach and face the other party on their own.

In fact, people tend to sort out most of their differences without a mediator. It is not surprising that individuals who have been listened to and coached in a pre-caucus may go on to resolve their dispute without a mediated joint session. Certainly, one of the objectives of Party-Directed Mediation is to help people resolve future variances without outside help. At times, however, the assistance of a third party is crucial. Yet, in Party-Directed Mediation, the contenders retain most of the responsibility for conflict resolution.

Talk about empowering disputants sometimes elicits a negative—if not defensive—reaction among some mediators and scholars. This resentment is partly justified. In their fervor for empowerment, some have come to imply the inferiority of other approaches. Empowerment is not automatically the best mediation approach.

For instance, a year and a half after one of my sabbaticals in Chile, I received a threatening letter from a collection agency on behalf of the car insurance enterprise I had utilized. I was accused

When differences in opinion are brought to the table, they present opportunities to find more elegant, satisfying, and enduring solutions.

of not paying my last installment. Unfortunately, I had long since discarded proof of payment. This was the first and only note forwarded to me. It was difficult to deal with this situation from so far away.

You can believe I was relieved when one of my brothers, who lives in Chile, contacted the insurance agency and mediated between us. I hardly knew the people involved and had no interest in mutual validation, transformative opportunities, or the like. I simply wanted the problem to go away without having to pay twice.

I know mediators who are very gifted at seeing solutions that the affected parties simply cannot perceive. These skilled practitioners are able to discern potential agreements, know exactly when to speak, find the right tone of voice to use, recognize when humor would be helpful, and get people to agree. They are virtuoso artists within the profession. In my opinion, such skills and abilities will always be needed, especially in the resolution of certain types of conflicts.

There are other types of disputes, especially those of an interpersonal nature—involving people who will continue to live with each other, work together, or interact after the mediator goes home—that can greatly benefit from a style that empowers each disputant. This is when Party-Directed Mediation can play a key role.

The Party-Directed Mediation model is particularly useful in the resolution of deep-seated interpersonal discord as well as multicultural or ethnic clashes. While its primary focus is on contention affecting two individuals, some of its tools may be profitably applied to disputes among groups.

PART II – PRE-CAUCUS

The process of mediation can help contenders discuss issues, repair past injuries, and develop the tools needed to examine disagreements directly with each other. Preparing for such a conversation takes work. While there are hundreds of factors that can affect the successful resolution of a mediated conflict, in Party-Directed Mediation the *pre-caucus* is an essential pillar. Here, the mediator meets alone with each party.

Until recently, any private conversation between the third party and one of the contenders was perceived as suspect: mediator neutrality was considered compromised. Such fears assume a mediator-directed approach in which the third party wields much power and often acts as a quasi arbitrator. When the mediation process is understood—from its inception—as one in which the contenders retain control over the outcome, then less importance is given to the mediator's supposed neutrality.

The pre-caucus affords each party the opportunity to be heard and understood. Through it, participants can (1) vent emotions, (2) broaden perspectives, (3) feel the support of a third party, (4) discover blind spots, (5) prepare to negotiate, (6) increase their desire in resolving the conflict, (7) obtain hope, and (8) come to see the other party as a real person.

Finally, the pre-caucus helps answer an important question for the intermediary: "Can I safely bring the parties into a joint session in which they will converse directly with each other? Or will a more traditional approach be preferable?"

During the pre-caucus, individuals learn to hear themselves (and prepare to listen to each other during the joint session). Pre-caucusing is not about finding concessions, compromises, or solutions to the discord. Mediators have no clear clues as to how the conflict will be solved. There is no need for the intermediary to panic and wonder, "What did I get myself into this time?" Eventually, the disputants will find their own answers.

Generally, the pre-caucus (1) consists of a brief introduction by the mediator, (2) permits the party to speak and be heard through empathic listening, (3) challenges blind spots and prepares the individual for the joint session, and (4) helps harvest positive comments made by each party about the other.

Before mediators focus on listening, they briefly explain the issue of confidentiality and the mechanics of the mediation process, so participants do not feel surprised or lost. Parties may have questions about the process, also.

Each party must understand that the role of the intermediary is not to decide which of the contenders is in the right. For many people this is a difficult concept to grasp. Yet, little will be achieved as long as the parties are under the impression that they must defend the virtues of their own perspectives before an arbitrator. Participants, then, need to realize that mediation offers a unique opportunity to clarify their objectives and begin to comprehend each other's needs. Mutual understanding allows for more enduring solutions.

The preliminary conversation generally lasts less than five minutes. Let us move on to the empathic listening portion of the pre-caucus.

2
Empathic Listening

The Panama Canal evokes an adequate analogy for the listening role a mediator plays during the pre-caucus. As a youth, I traversed the canal several times on a freighter from the Port of Valparaiso in Chile to New York. Massive lock gates regulate the water levels in the canal so ships can move across the waterway. The water level behind a set of closed locks can be much higher than that of the next compartment through which a ship will sail.

Compare this scene to the state of mind of an individual involved in an intense conflict. Disparate water levels build pressure behind the closed locks. Open the lock gates, and the water gushes out—mostly in one direction. Likewise, an individual who has pent-up feelings of antagonism needs a

An individual who has pent-up feelings of discouragement or antagonism needs a release; otherwise, he or she is unlikely to be receptive to outside input.

release. Without a discharge, a contender is unlikely to either think clearly about the dispute or be receptive to external input—from the other party or the mediator.

The intermediary helps contenders open emotional lock gates. When they do, intense affect pours out. During this venting process, the pressure blocks other perspectives.

Only when the water has leveled off between the two compartments does it begin to flow evenly back and forth. The role of the mediator is to help parties empty the large reservoirs of emotion, anger, stress, frustration, and other negative feelings until each is able to think and see more clearly. Not until then can an individual consider the needs of the other. Perhaps we can think of it as *listening first aid*.

At one enterprise, the manager introduced me to one of the conflicting parties. As soon as we were left alone and began the pre-caucus, this individual broke into tears. A similar situation took place at a different organization. One of the managers began to cry, ostensibly because of pressing issues. Had these men come immediately into joint meetings with the other contenders, their feelings of vulnerability might easily have turned into anger and defensiveness.

I was once informed that the pre-caucus would be quite brief, as the person I was about to listen to was not a man of many words. Yet this individual spoke to me for almost two hours. By the time we finished, he felt understood and had gained confidence. During the joint session, he was able to speak and even laugh when it was appropriate. I have found the silent type will often open up during a pre-caucus—when there is someone who will truly listen.

People like to explain their own perspectives first, and this adds to the complexity of the mediation process. Certainly, both parties cannot speak and be heard at the same time. Although not the same as explaining one's position to an adversary, the pre-caucus does serve this need well. Each party can freely vent to the mediator before having to be receptive to other ideas.

The more entrenched and emotional the conflict, the more vital the listening role. It is impossible to know for certain, before the pre-caucus, exactly how deeply emotions are running. Lesser disputes will simply require shorter pre-caucuses. The process of listening so others will talk is called *empathic listening*.

Empathy, according to some dictionary definitions, means to put oneself in a position to understand another. Certainly, this is an aspect of empathy. I prefer to define empathy, however, as it is often used in psychology: the process of attending to another so the person who is speaking feels heard in a non-judgmental way. Empathic listening requires that we accompany others in their

Carl Rogers modeled the empathic listening approach in his book Client-Centered Therapy.

moments of sadness, anguish, self-discovery, challenge—or even great joy!

This approach to listening was championed by Carl Rogers, author of *Client-Centered Therapy*.[1] Rogers applied the method to therapy as well as human resource management.

Empathic listening skills are critical to the practitioner of Party-Directed Mediation. When an individual feels understood, an enormous emotional burden is lifted, stress and defensiveness are reduced, and clarity increases. Furthermore, the contenders will greatly improve their own negotiation skills as they master empathic listening.

Listening in Interpersonal Communication

We spend a large portion of our waking hours conversing and listening. When two friends or colleagues have an engaging dialogue, they often compete to speak and share ideas. Listening plays an important role in such stimulating exchanges. When it comes to empathic listening, we do not vie to be heard, nor do we take turns speaking. Rather, we are there to motivate and cheer the other person on.

Empathic listening requires a subset of proficiencies different from that used in conversing, and it is surely an acquired skill. Many individuals, at first, find the process somewhat uncomfortable. Furthermore, people are often surprised at the exertion required to become a competent listener. Once the skill is attained, there is nothing automatic about it. In order to truly listen, we must set aside sufficient time to do so.

Perhaps making time is at the root of the challenge. People frequently lose patience when listening to others' problems. Empathic listening is incompatible with being in a hurry or with the fast-paced world around us. Such careful listening requires that we, at least for the moment, slow down and suspend our own thoughts and needs. Clearly, there are no shortcuts to empathic listening.

Some of the dialogues in this chapter are video transcripts made possible by generous volunteers. It is my goal to give life to some of these clips, so as to illustrate what it means to listen empathically.

I challenge the reader to put aside any preconceived notions about effective listening. In order to more clearly illustrate empathic listening, I will include both positive and negative examples.

Effective listening and attending skills can be applied to all of our interpersonal and business relationships. We will become more effective listeners as we practice at home, in our business dealings, and in other circles. One of the greatest gifts we can give another is that of truly listening.

Different Approaches to Listening

One listening model involves a three-step process: (1) attentive listening, (2) asking diagnostic questions, and (3) offering a prescription, or solution. Slowly, or sometimes quite abruptly, people move from listening to prescribing. It is not uncommon for a helper (e.g., friend, listener, mediator) to focus on the third of these steps—offering advice—even when none is sought. At times individuals may utilize the first two steps. Perhaps most uncommon is an emphasis on listening alone.

Specific situations may call for different responses. When there is little time, or in dangerous situations, people may offer advice. For matters of a technical nature, the three-way process of listening, diagnosing, and prescribing is often preferable. After prescribing, it is helpful to take a step back and determine how the individual feels about the proposed solution. A related tactic involves going through the first two steps and then involving the party in examining alternative solutions. When the solution is owned by the individuals facing the challenge, as is often the case in deep-seated interpersonal conflict, a listening approach is most advantageous. This is where empathic listening fits in. Let us consider these phases in reverse order.

PRESCRIPTIVE PHASE

The majority of individuals may begin with intentions of listening but quickly transition into the diagnostic and prescriptive phases. People accustomed to solving problems often listen with this frame of mind. Others focus on sympathy. Sharing

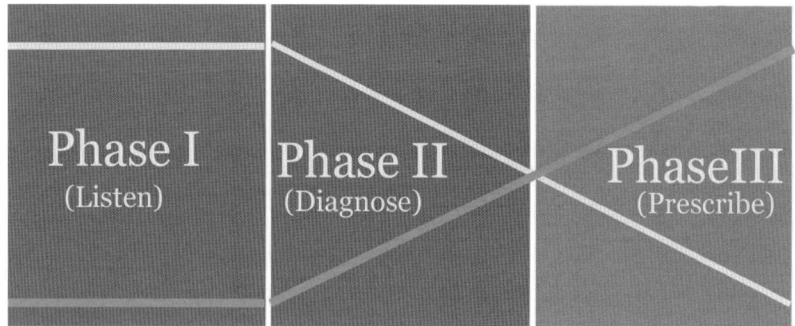

FIGURE 2–1

The listening process is often divided into three phases. In the first phase, the helper (bottom line) permits the person with the challenge (top line) to do most of the talking. Note that in the diagnostic phase, the helper begins to speak more. In the prescriptive phase, the helper ends up doing most of the talking. The third phase is often colored red as a warning that the parties are stepping into dangerous territory.

The role of the mediator is to help parties empty the large reservoirs of emotion, anger, stress, frustration, and other negative feelings until each is able to think and see more clearly.

a story of how a similar difficulty was faced is not much better. Nor is being quiet so a person will hurry up and finish. None of these is a helpful response to venting. Each reflects, among other things, a certain amount of impatience. When people are not paying attention we can often see it in their body language, as Nichols describes in *The Lost Art of Listening*: "The automatic smile, the hit-and-run question, the restless look in their eyes when we start to talk."[2]

It seems easy to solve other people's problems. Individuals habitually say, "If I were in *your* position, I would have . . ."

Perhaps. Maybe we would have solved the dilemma had we been in their place. Different personality types approach specific challenges in predictable ways, with foreseeable results. For instance, some people would not dream of confronting their friends, but instead would let irritations fester. Many others have trouble keeping their opinions to themselves.

Have you noticed that some of your acquaintances seem to repeatedly fall into the same types of predicaments, giving the impression they did not learn from experience? Each of us has different personality traits and skill sets that permit us to solve some challenges more easily than others.

Occasionally we think we would have solved a person's dilemma had we been given the chance to do so. Instead, when we find ourselves in the same predicament, we often feel just as unsure about how to proceed.

We are all too ready to give advice. Years ago, on the way home from a father-daughter date, I asked Cristina, my youngest, if I could give her some free advice. "I certainly don't plan to pay for it," she quipped.

On another occasion a young woman came to see me. Sofía could not perceive how giving the cold shoulder to Patricia—who had been her best friend at the university—was not only a cause of pain to Patricia but also a way to further escalate the growing conflict between the two.

"I no longer speak to Patricia when I see her," Sofía began. "Her cold attitude hurts. She never greets me, and that really upsets me. She used to be very kind. But you know, now, when she tries to come over and speak to me, I pretend I haven't noticed her and look away."

"How do you expect your friend to act in a warm way towards you if you give her the cold shoulder when she tries to speak to you?" I inquired, stating the obvious.

I should have kept the comment to myself. Sofía was upset by my counsel and avoided me for some time. A few weeks later she came to see me again. This time I listened empathically. Rather than stating the obvious, I was attentive while Sofía described, in full detail, the ache she was feeling, the history of the conflict, her suffering and hopes. Sofía felt heard and was able to take some preliminary steps towards resolving her challenge.

Our effectiveness as listeners is often lost if we solve the problem before the person we are attempting to help does. Some try unsuccessfully to disguise advice-giving tactics through such questions as "Don't you think that . . . ?" or "Have you tried . . . ?"

Aaliyah is very concerned about her grown daughter and has been openly disclosing her worries to her friend Shanise. Let us listen in on their conversation.

"These are the problems I have with my daughter," Aaliyah shares, anguish punctuating each word. "I want to seek her out, try and speak with her, try and have her understand, but she doesn't listen to me. [Pause] I simply don't know what to do. I feel incapable of helping her."

"If you could get her professional help, would she go?" Shanise proposes.

"Uh. As I was telling you, she doesn't listen to me. When I try and speak to her, give her advice, then she changes topics. That is the problem I have—that I seek her out but she doesn't listen to me," Aaliyah insists.

Aaliyah considers Shanise's contribution a distraction and momentarily loses track of what she was saying. Aaliyah eventually takes back control of the conversation. Because Shanise has been showing empathy to this point, Aaliyah forgives the interruption.

People such as Aaliyah seem to be asking for a solution when they say "I don't know what to do." Perhaps they even ask for advice, imploring, "What should I do?" The listener ought not rush in with a prescription. It is worthwhile, at least, to say something like "You are unsure as to how to proceed." It is a statement, not a question. If the person says something like "Exactly!" and continues to speak, then the helper has hit the mark. If, instead, the individual continues to ask for suggestions, the listener can help the person explore options.

In a listening skills workshop, John, one of the participants, shared some real concerns facing his enterprise. "Our top

The role of an empathic listener is to accompany another person and celebrate together the fact that the other can begin to unpack and analyze the difficulties being faced.

manager seems unsure as to how to proceed with such a delicate issue," John explained. "He simply doesn't know what to do about these two guys who won't speak to each other." After a while, I stopped the role-playing to give the listener some ideas on how to keep John talking. Interrupting me, John explained that he did not want to "play the listening game"—he simply wanted a solution.

This was an ideal opportunity to illustrate some vital points. When workshop participants listen to people with real hardships, everything they have learned so far in the seminar can fly out the window. Rather than analyze the quality of the listening, participants are all too often ready to suggest additional solutions.

Seminar participants were permitted to go around the table prescribing solutions. But not before being warned that they were entering the prescriptive phase, which I have labeled red for danger. Suggestions started flying.

"Obviously, John," the first participant began, "you must insist on having the supervisor speak with both individuals."

"What I would do instead . . . ," another piped in.

It soon became clear that, despite John's request for a ready-made solution, these suggestions were irritating him. John admitted he would have preferred to continue to think aloud with the support of the class participants.

Sympathy is quite different from empathy. It often springs more from our desire for normality than from our desire for helping. One of my favorite illustrations that contrasts sympathy with empathy comes from Alfred Benjamin's *The Helping Interview*: "When Lucy said, 'I'll never get married now that I'm [disabled],' what did you do? You know you felt terrible; you felt that the whole world had caved in on her. But what did you say? What did you show?"[3]

If Lucy were your seventeen-year-old daughter, niece, or younger sister—I often ask—what would you like to say to her? Some of the most frequent responses include:

- "Your internal beauty is more important than outward appearances."
- "I still find you beautiful."
- "If a young man cannot see your beauty, he is not worthy of you."
- "Modern medicine can work miracles, and perhaps you can recover beyond expectation."

Benjamin continues:
> Did you help her to bring it out; to say it, all of it; to hear it and examine it? You almost said: "Don't be foolish. You're young and pretty and smart, and who knows, perhaps . . ." But you didn't. You had said similar things to patients in the hospital until you learned that it closed them off. So this time you simply looked at her and weren't afraid to feel what you both felt. Then you said, "You feel right now that your whole

life has been ruined by this accident." "That's just it," she
retorted, crying bitterly. After awhile she continued talking.
She was still [disabled], but you hadn't gotten in the way of
her hating it and confronting it.[4]

In my opinion, many of these comments about her beauty and intelligence may be shared, but later, *after* Lucy feels truly heard and does not have more to say herself.

There are numerous ways we discount the needs of others, even when we think we are being good listeners. For instance, we may attempt to share our own stories of loss, disappointment, or success before the individuals we are listening to have had the opportunity to be heard. We may feel that sharing our own stories proves that we are listening, but instead, the other person feels we have stolen the show.[5] Once again, this is not to say there is no room to share our stories with others, but rather, we should hear them out first.

Some people confuse empathic listening with being silent. First attempts to listen empathically are often betrayed by facial and body language that says "Be quiet, so I can give you some good advice." Have you ever tried to speak to individuals who give no indication of what they are thinking? We do not know if they have lost interest or are judging us.

When people have deep sentiments to share, rarely do they expose their vulnerability by getting to the point right away. Ordinarily, the topic is examined through increasingly constricting circles. It can also be compared to an iceberg. Only an eighth protrudes at the surface, while the rest remains submerged in the ocean. When someone says, "I am worried because . . . ," and another responds "Don't worry so much," the worried person does not cease to be concerned. Rather, it becomes clear that the apprehension cannot be safely shared with such an individual. Likewise, when a person proceeds to give a suggestion before understanding the situation, individuals will frequently pretend to go along with the proposal simply to get rid of the problem solver.

Diagnostic Phase

Perhaps the greatest danger with the process of diagnosing is the natural tendency to move from listening, to diagnosing, to prescribing. Rarely do people reverse the process and return to listening after entering the diagnostic phase. It is much more likely that they will be swept up by the turbulent current that takes them to the prescription mode.

I do not wish to imply that the diagnostic process has no value. A useful advantage of the diagnostic process is that the listener can, at least at a superficial level, gain a better idea of what the challenge entails. Indeed, people frequently give too little attention to diagnosis. But in the process of empathic listening, the diagnosis needs to be carried out by the troubled person rather than by the listener. An emphasis on diagnostics betrays a perspective in which the intermediary is the provider of all wisdom.

Often, individuals listen and ask questions with the idea of confirming their own observations. A much more effective method, according to the authors of *Narrative Mediation*, is to be moved by a spirit of curiosity. Such an approach has been called a stance of deliberate ignorance. Instead of assuming that a certain experience is the same as another we have gone through or heard of, we listen with interest and curiosity. Inquisitive listeners, according to John Winslade and Gerald Monk, "never assume that they understand the meaning of an action, an event, or a word."[6]

Let us return to the conversation between Aaliyah and Shanise.

"My husband doesn't help me resolve my problem with my daughter," Aaliyah laments.

Shanise asks a couple of investigative questions: "What would he like you to do? Not to have any contact with her?"

"Well, we quarrel a lot because I tell him I'm a mother. [Pause] And he doesn't feel what I feel. And he doesn't want me to seek her out because, after all, she doesn't listen, and the situation will not improve. But I always seek her out. [Long pause] And I told her not to be wandering about aimlessly—to come to my home, but she won't, she says that . . . ," Aaliyah continues, a narrative born of a mother's pain.

The questions have helped Shanise understand the situation a bit better. Observe, however, that Aaliyah, after answering, returns to speaking about that which hurts her the most: her inability to help her daughter.

Here is an another example of an investigative question. Once again, we pick up in the middle of a conversation:

"So that is the challenge I've been facing with one of our engineers," says Raymond.

"In the morning or afternoon?" inquires Paul.

"I've been wondering if there's a pattern indeed—if this happens on Mondays, or if there is anything predictable in all of this," Raymond answers. "The truth is that I haven't found anything obvious."

"Have you sat down with him and spoken about your concern?" Paul asks.

This conversation follows a pattern. Paul asks a question. Raymond answers and then waits for Paul's next inquiry. Pauses become an excuse to interrupt. Paul has control over the conversation, and his worried tone betrays the responsibility he feels for solving Raymond's challenge. While Raymond may feel heard, such comprehension tends to be somewhat superficial. Raymond is not working as hard as he could to solve his own problem. Instead, he seems to be saying, "Go ahead, Paul. Be my guest. See if you can solve this mess. I dare you! I sure haven't been able to."

There are other types of questions, such as those that promote talking about feelings. Manuel tells his wife, Magdalena, that despite the international acclaim his work has received in New York, he is unsure whether they should remain in the United States or return to their native Argentina. While Magdalena has heard her husband in the past, her current focus is to let her husband vent:

"That is the problem: to stay or return to Argentina?" Manuel sighs.

Empathic listening requires that we accompany individuals in their moments of sadness, anguish, self-discovery, challenge—or even great joy!

"What is it that you really miss from Argentina?" Magdalena inquires.

"Well, that's what we were talking about recently . . . one misses the family . . . family relations . . . Sundays with the extended family and the kids . . . but I also miss my friends. I had a huge group of friends . . . ," Manuel continues speaking and sharing his concerns. Magdalena's question has permitted Manuel to examine his feelings.

When a question is asked to help someone take control of the conversation, it serves to *prime the pump*. Old-fashioned water pumps functioned through a lever and a vacuum. It took effort to make them start pumping water, but much less once the water started flowing. Prime-the-pump questions are especially useful to help individuals start speaking. Or take back control of the conversation, especially after an interruption (e.g., after the conversation stops when a third person momentarily walks into the room, when the conversation is being renewed after a few days, or when listeners realize they have interrupted or taken an overly directive approach to listening).

There are several types of questions, comments, and gestures that can help prime the pump. These may include, for example:
- Investigative questions
- Analytical comments
- Summaries of what has been heard
- Invitations for the person to say more
- Body language that shows interest
- Empathic comments

Empathic Listening

A mother tells of an experience with her young child: "Years ago one of our daughters asked me to come outside and play tetherball with her. She told me to sit down and watch as she hit over and over again a ball on a rope that wound itself around a pole. After watching several windings I asked what my part was in the game, and she said, 'Oh, Mom, you say, "Good job, good job," every time the ball goes around the pole.'"[7]

This is, essentially, the role of empathic listening—that of patiently accompanying another while they begin to unpack and analyze the difficulties being faced. In the child's game, success is measured by the ability to wrap the ball's tether around the post. In empathic listening, success is measured by the ability to help someone dislodge pain-soaked discourse and let it float to the surface. The speaker guides the direction of the conversation and is often surprised to find where the venting takes him or her.

I shall attempt to describe, in a more detailed way, how to accompany without interfering. There is a marvelously therapeutic power in the ability to think aloud and share a quandary with someone who will listen.

In contrast to the diagnostic approach to helping, the empathic mediator:

- Motivates the parties to speak without feeling judged
- Does not use pauses as an excuse to interrupt
- Permits the speaker to direct the conversation

If the intermediary earns their confidence through this process, individuals begin to:
- Speak more (easily 97 percent of the conversation)
- Control the direction of the account
- Increase self-understanding (first, by reviewing what is known, and later, by digging deeper)
- Consider options and choose a possible outcome

A warning is in order. Empathic listening is dynamic. It is not sufficient to have an interest in another; the mediator must also *show* it. And it is not sufficient to show an interest; the intermediary must *feel* it. The person being heard immediately notices if the mediator seems bored, distracted, or upset.

> During the process of empathic listening in the pre-caucus, it will often happen that people who feel listened to will begin to see how they may have contributed to the conflict.

In the words of Alfred Benjamin, "Genuine listening is hard work; there is little about it that is mechanical . . . We hear with our ears, but we listen with our eyes and mind and heart and skin and guts as well."[8]

Dangling Questions

An incomplete question gives the other person control of the conversation. Let us return to the Argentine couple.

"And the children . . . miss . . . ?" Magdalena asks, prolonging the word *miss*.

"And the children miss . . . much, especially the . . . affection of their grandmothers, cousins. Undoubtedly they miss the whole family structure . . . ," Manuel explains as he continues to uncover the issues that are troubling him.

Indications That We Want to Know More

There are many ways we can signal an interest in listening and learning more. One of the most typical is simply to say, "Tell me more." We could also say something like "How interesting!" or simply "Interesting."

Brief, empathic noises or comments such as "yes," "a-ha," and "mm-hmm" are also very powerful. Discourse analysis scholars sometimes call these expressions *positive minimal responses.* The key is not getting stuck with one monotonous, irritating technique.

Repeating a Phrase or Key Word

Another empathic listening technique is repeating, from time to time, one word, or a few, in the same tone of voice the speaker used. Aaliyah continues to share with Shanise the pain she is feeling because of her daughter:

"She moved and now lives in a nearby town with a friend," Aaliyah gestures with her left hand indicating the direction.

"Friend," Shanise repeats.

"Yes, but she won't last long. She doesn't work, and she won't be able to live there for free," Aaliyah continues. "She must contribute something, too."

A single pre-caucus may not provide sufficient time to listen empathically when a person has been involved in a prolonged hurtful conflict.

Empathic repetitions contribute to the process without overly interrupting. There are times when the conversational flow is briefly paused—usually the first time the technique is used—while the speaker reflects on the repeated words. But normally it happens in a very natural fashion. Speakers have the option of continuing what they are saying or further reflecting on the comment. Let us look at the technique as used by the Argentine couple.

"It's true that the cost of education in this country is high, but the possibilities are infinite," Manuel declares.

"Infinite," Magdalena repeats, using the same tone.

"Infinite . . . Infinite in the sense that if we can provide support for the children and motivate them to study . . . ," Manuel continues, developing his thinking.

Critics have accused Carl Rogers of being directive. They claim empathic responses reward the speaker for concentrating on topics the listener wants them to focus on. My research, however, shows that when a person is interrupted by an empathic listener—with a distracting observation or comment—the speaker makes it clear that it was an interruption. Unless the disruption constitutes a serious breach of trust, the party continues to speak and control the conversation.

Mekelle, a young African American professional, is telling Susan that her best friend, Palad, is angry with her because her fiancé is Caucasian. The conversation proceeds normally until Susan asks a question that distracts Mekelle.

"My friend Palad . . . it bothers me—as bright and perceptive as he is—he cannot see that in reality, if one were to educate more people . . . ," Mekelle explains, expressing her frustration.

"Yes," Susan adds, following the conversation.

"Then, he wouldn't feel the way he feels. You understand?" Mekelle asks a question that rather means "Are you listening to me? Are you following my logic?"

"Where is Palad from?" Susan interrupts. The question has no relationship to the anguish Mekelle is feeling.

"Palad is from Florida. He has lived several years in California. He's now living in Oregon," Mekelle answers. "But . . ." Having lost track of what she was saying, Mekelle waves her hand, as if to say "Let's get back to the topic." She continues "But . . . and it is only about Caucasian people. He only has problems with Caucasian people," Mekelle smiles. "If the person were from any other race it wouldn't matter, but when it's a matter of a Caucasian person . . ."

Mekelle has taken back control of the conversation, despite the interruption. People often regain control by using the word *but*. It is also common for individuals to gesture or move a hand meaning "As I was saying," or "Do not interrupt."

Empathic Listening • 31

Empathic listening permits those who own the problem to begin to hear themselves.

Some hand gestures, such as the flat hand with the fingers raised, often mean "Don't interrupt. I have more to say."

Empathic Sayings

An empathic saying is a longer comment, of a reflective type, given to let individuals know we are following them. We might say something like "At this moment you feel terrible," or "I can see you are suffering." When used sparingly, these expressions can be very potent.

A troubled youth approached me one day. "I hate life," he said. The loud, bitter comment filled the room. How I wanted to moralize and tell him that his own actions had placed him in the present predicament. Instead, I calmly stated, *à la* Rogers, "Right now, you are hating life." I was trying to truly comprehend and letting him know that I was listening.

"Oh, yes," he continued, but the anger lessened enormously. "Life, right now, is terrible!" With each subsequent exchange, the tension and volume of his voice subsided. This same youth soon recognized that he was not walking down the right path, without my having to say it.

In contrast, I observed a speaker—a therapist by training—who freely used the line "I can see you are hurting." As the conference Spanish-language interpreter, I was in a unique position to observe the audience. An older man told his heartbreaking anecdote, and the speaker used his line at what seemed the perfect moment. The participant stopped talking and leaned back. I could see in his eyes and body posture that he had felt empathy from the therapist. The man had been touched and now felt understood. I was impressed. It seemed to me, however, that with each subsequent use of "I can see you are hurting," the catchy phrase became increasingly artificial. The magic was gone. Fewer people were convinced of its sincerity, and the expression soon meant "Be quiet. I want to move on with my talk." The process had become mechanical and empty, rather than based on true empathy.

How do we know if the listening approach is empathic? Gerard Egan says, "If the helper's empathic response is accurate, the client often tends to confirm its accuracy by a nod or some other nonverbal cue or by a phrase such as 'that's right' or 'exactly.' This is usually followed by a further, usually more specific, elaboration of the problem situation."[9] And when we are off the mark, sometimes the speaker will say so. Just as likely, the person will be quiet and avoid eye contact.

Empathic Questions

In contrast to diagnostic questions, especially those analytical in nature, empathic queries go to the source of what the person is *feeling*. These questions regarding affect are very powerful, yet less dangerous. They promote talking rather than silence. In effect they are prime-the-pump questions. An example is "What are you feeling at this moment?" Or without completing the phrase, the listener may stretch out the word *feeling*: "You are *feel*-ing . . . ?"

The strength of empathic questions is that they help expose and dissipate negative feelings.

Body Language

One of the best steps, in terms of body language, is to invite the person to take a seat. By so doing, we let people know we are willing to listen—that we are not going to ration out time.

We may also show interest by occasionally leaning forward toward the speaker. Interest is reflected in facial expressions, head movement, gestures, and tone of voice. As with all of the techniques we have discussed, variety is critical. Otherwise, if we keep mechanically shaking our heads, we will soon look like the bobbleheads in the back windows of cars.

If we are truly interested in listening, our body language shows it. Our non-verbal communication also betrays us when we get distracted.

FIGURE 2–2

People who are interested in what others are saying will show it through their body language.

During a Negotiated Performance Appraisal, I had been listening attentively for quite some time. I had not yet said anything but must have shown intentions of interrupting. Before I could utter a word, the person who had been speaking said, "Excuse me for interrupting you, but . . . ," and she continued relating her account. This happened several times, proving what communication experts have told us all along: individuals signal their intent to interrupt before doing so.

Respecting Pauses

Silence makes people uncomfortable. Yet, one of the most important empathic listening skills is not interrupting periods of silence. When people pause, they continue to think about their troubles. By not interrupting, we are in essence offering the person a *psychological chair* to sit on; it is a way of saying "I am not going to abandon you."

The person who feels truly heard begins to speak more slowly and to pause more often. When individuals sense they will not be interrupted, they embark on an internal trajectory, every time deeper, wherein they commence to intensify the process of self-understanding and analytical thinking. Many listeners—who found it difficult enough to be patient when the other person was speaking at a normal speed—find this slower pace torturous. Yet, this is part of the gift of empathic listening.

How long can you endure a pause without getting impatient? Four seconds? Eleven seconds? One minute? Ten minutes? Often, the individual coming out of this pause will have undergone some serious reflective thinking.

A young professional reported that she had put this advice to work. After a mediation and listening skills seminar she called her boyfriend. He had been experiencing some tribulations. "I had to bite my lips several times," she reported. "But I managed not to interrupt him. After a long pause he asked me, 'Are you there?'"

The disadvantage of the phone is that fewer empathic responses are available to the listener. The young woman's boyfriend could not see the interest with which she had been listening. She responded, "Of course! I'm very interested." Once these words were pronounced, he continued talking, this time with even more enthusiasm and penetration.

To conclude this subsection, let us review two more clips from our friend, Mekelle. In the first one, she speaks of her desire to make a decision and resolve her difficulty. This comment comes after she has had a long time to vent her emotions.

"I know I must call Palad again and have another conversation with him," Mekelle resolved. "I haven't decided . . . yet . . . when

When we respect pauses by not interrupting, we are in essence offering the person a psychological chair to sit on; it is a way of saying "We are not going away."

> I will call him. [Long pause] Yeah . . . that's where I find myself at the moment . . . I'll probably find a moment to call him next week. I always like to plan this type of thing." And laughing, she adds: "I am not ready to speak with him at this moment."

Susan is accompanying Mekelle, and laughs when she laughs. "Not at this moment . . ."

"Right. Perhaps I should call him some day when I'm mad." Mekelle laughs again. "But, hmm . . . it's beginning to weigh on me . . . this lets me know I ought to call now."

In the second clip, Mekelle speaks about the gratitude she is feeling for having been heard.

"The really interesting thing to me is that I generally am not one to share my feelings. I tend to keep them buried and let other people tell me how they feel."

"Mmm," Susan listens.

After several false starts, Mekelle finally says, "This whole process . . . of realizing I'm still mad at him—because I didn't know I was still mad at him—is very interesting . . . to me, that is." Mekelle once again attempts to speak between her own pauses. Finally, asserting herself, and drawing out the word *mad* each time she uses it, she says: "I ask myself, 'Why, exactly are you mad? You know? Should you be mad? You could be disappointed. But mad? Especially since he didn't do anything to you.' By that I mean he didn't use offensive language, he didn't hit me." After another pause, she continues, "I feel he disappointed me. I want to ask him, 'How can you be so intelligent and think like that?'"

A person who uses the purely empathic listening approach will have to dedicate large blocks of time to it. Empathic listening, as used in Party-Directed Mediation, can easily last an hour or two. A single pre-caucus may not provide sufficient time to listen empathically when a person has been involved in a prolonged hurtful conflict.

Reconciling Empathic Listening with Our Belief Systems

Throughout the years, I have read numerous books about empathic listening. Some of its distinguished proponents suggest there is no such thing as *absolute truth*. My challenge, however, was the need to reconcile such a stance with the incredibly positive results obtained by the methodology. You see, I am a strong proponent of the existence of absolute truth, of right and wrong, of good and evil.

For instance, Rogers did not moralize, no matter how horrible his clients' comments were. Nor, to his defense, did he patronize people who felt troubled or tell them it was normal to feel a certain way. When a client said she really hated her mother and would be glad to see her dead, Rogers listened. Soon, his client would say, "Well, actually I don't hate her totally. I also really love her, and I wouldn't want her to be dead." Through several transcripts of Rogers' sessions with clients, this pattern is repeated. Each time, the client seems to make good decisions, backing away from hurtful, destructive approaches.[10] From my experience observing how poorly people listen, I suspect most would benefit from reading Rogers.

But returning to my dilemma, how could I reconcile my belief structure with being a good listener? Or how about situations involving people who are blind to the most basic common sense? For instance, how should I respond to individuals who say they are starving for the affection of family members or former friends yet are doing everything in their power to reject those persons?

On reflection, I arrived at these conclusions: (1) When people are truly heard, they will often come to their own correct insights. But if their assumptions are still faulty, (2) by the very process of truly listening, the helper will earn the right to *challenge blind spots*. There will be moments when listeners have the right—or, should we say, obligation—to speak their truth.

During the process of empathic listening in the pre-caucus, people who feel listened to begin to see how they have contributed to the conflict. For this mediation model to work, it is necessary to have confidence in the goodness of people. We must believe that individuals, when given the opportunity to reflect and reconsider, will find the path that is necessary to leave the darkness behind. Party-Directed Mediation does not function unless the parties are essentially good people. If this is not the case, other mediation models will be more effective.

EMPATHIC LISTENING • 39

We can let others know we are listening in a non-judgmental way by occasionally repeating one word, or a few, in the same tone of voice used by the speaker.

Goodwill deposits, earned through the listening process, are required before the mediator earns the right to challenge an individual. After listening, concerns may be calmly raised if it becomes necessary.

Despite all that has been said in this chapter, there will be times when the mediator's values are incompatible with those of one or more of the parties. Mediators should not suggest that people violate their own principles or belief systems, nor should

One of the greatest gifts we can give each other is that of truly listening.

anyone expect a third party to be amoral. Likewise, such a quandary may occur with empathic listening in general. If a friend tells me he is thinking of being unfaithful to his wife, and if he does not reconsider during the process of being heard, I think it would be a great fault on my part to keep silent.

There may be times, then, when empathic listeners may need to share their value systems. Often, people will seek the intermediary's opinion out of respect for the person's values. One of the leading experts on empathic listening and challenging, Gerard Egan, suggests that living by a value system may well be a prerequisite to properly challenging others,[11] a topic we will pick up in the next chapter.

SUMMARY

Through the process of being heard empathically, each party in a conflict will control the direction, pace, and final destiny of the exploratory expedition. The contenders in the discord will have to do most of the hard work. Yet, these individuals will not be left alone during their difficult voyages. Empathic listening permits those who own the problem to begin to hear themselves. And as they hear themselves, they become better equipped to hear others and solve their own disputes. The empathic listening approach permits the individuals being heard to sufficiently distance themselves from the challenge so as to see it with more clarity.

There is great therapeutic value in being able to think aloud and share a problem with someone who will listen. Good listeners have enough self-confidence to hear others explain their difficulties despite the absence of any apparent solutions.

Part of being a good listener may require consciously fighting to keep an open mind and avoid preconceived conclusions. Mediators may want to continually assess their listening style, making sure that they show interest, avoid being judgmental, and permit the person with the problem to do most of the talking. They should welcome long pauses.

Ultimately, the key is to have confidence in the process, knowing that the listener does not need to come up with a solution, but rather, should simply listen.

Chapter 2—References

1. Rogers, C. R. (1951). *Client-centered therapy: Its current practice, implications, and theory*. Boston: Houghton Mifflin.
2. Nichols, M. P. (1995). *The lost art of listening: How learning to listen can improve relationships* (p. 111). New York: Guilford Press.
3. Benjamin, A. (1974). *The helping interview* (2nd ed.) (p. 21). Boston: Houghton Mifflin.
4. Benjamin, A. (1974). *The helping interview* (2nd ed.) (p. 21). Boston: Houghton Mifflin.
5. Nichols, M. P. (1995). *The lost art of listening: How learning to listen can improve relationships*. New York: Guilford Press.
6. Winslade, J., & Monk, G. (2000). *Narrative mediation: A new approach to conflict resolution* (pp. 126–128). San Francisco: Jossey-Bass.
7. Clegg, G.M. (2004). The Finished Story. *Ensign*, 34(5), 14–16.
8. Benjamin, A. (1974). *The helping interview* (2nd ed.) (p. 44). Boston: Houghton Mifflin.
9. Egan, G. (1986). *The skilled helper: A systematic approach to effective helping* (3rd ed.) (pp.199–200). Monterey, CA: Brooks/Cole.
10. Rogers, C. R. (1951). *Client-centered therapy: Its current practice, implications, and theory*. Boston: Houghton Mifflin.
11. Egan, G. (1986). *The skilled helper: A systematic approach to effective helping* (3rd ed.). Monterey, CA: Brooks/Cole.

3
Coaching during the Pre-Caucus

Negative emotions can be dissipated as the parties feel heard during the pre-caucus phases of Party-Directed Mediation. While the mediator's empathic listening is crucial to preparing disputants for the joint session, it is not always sufficient. The mediator can play an active role by coaching individuals through some additional preparatory steps. These steps have been separated for conceptual clarity, although several points may arise at one time. The pre-caucus, then, is also a good time to:

- Prepare a list of topics to discuss
- Create distance from contentious feelings
- Validate identity projections
- Permit positive feelings
- Challenge blind spots
- Practice through role plays
- Improve communication skills

Prepare a List of Topics to Discuss

As mediators listen during the pre-caucus, they also take notes. Each topic of concern brought up by the parties is recorded (they often overlap considerably). These lists are a vital springboard for the joint session dialogue. Even sensitive matters need to be jotted down, unless a party requests otherwise. Even then, the mediator and the disputant may think of possible ways to broach the topic in the joint session.

Create Distance from Contentious Feelings

There seems to be a pattern in entrenched interpersonal conflict: each contender is overly distracted with the stress of the dispute, has difficulty sleeping, and is generally thinking of bailing out (of the workplace, marriage, or friendship). Individuals may be in denial about the negative effect of contention in their lives.

One manager claimed that he became angry and exploded but that his resentment was short-lived. He asserted that he did not hold grudges, no matter how disagreeable the encounter. Further into the pre-caucus, however, the manager admitted that a recent confrontation made him so furious that he was ill for a couple of days.

Mediators can help individuals visualize life without the tension created by destructive contention. John Winslade and Gerald Monk, in *Narrative Mediation*, argue that while people are theoretically free to say what they wish in a conversation, parties often feel their responses are influenced by the remarks of others. They see themselves entrapped within the conflict cycle.[1] Certainly, the results of numerous social psychology studies show that people often react in predictable ways to specific situations.

The authors of *Narrative Mediation* ask individuals how they might have felt forced by the dispute to do or say regrettable things. Or how the conflict affected them negatively in other ways. By placing the blame on the clash itself, mediators allow the parties to save face and slowly distance themselves from the conflict-saturated story. Parties can detach themselves from the

During the pre-caucus, mediators note the issues that need to be addressed by the parties during the joint session.

dispute long enough to consider if they want to keep feeding their negative feelings for each other.[2]

In *Crucial Conversations*, we learn that people are adept at creating defensive stories in milliseconds. As we entertain these narratives, they are likely to grow more clever and complex. Every emotional outburst, the authors argue, is preceded by such a story.[3] Part of the role of the mediator, then, is to help parties recognize the function that self-justifying and defensive stories play. They also help contenders look for alternative narratives—those which permit the existence of motives that are less hideous and perhaps even honorable.

Some years ago, I attended a meeting of soccer referees in which my supervisor pointed out problems that referees needed to avoid. I became defensive. I remembered very well what had happened during the game in question. In my opinion, I had made the right call. I raised my hand and began to support my decision. "We were not talking about you," the supervisor said calmly.

The authors of *Crucial Conversations* would explain that it was not the referee director who made me upset, but rather the story I told myself to justify my behavior. The very fact that I felt compelled to create such a story should have been a warning to me. The story permitted me to entertain defensive emotions, which resulted in my negative behavior: defending myself at the meeting when no one was attacking and thus running at "the sound of a shaken leaf."

Part of the role of the mediator is to help parties recognize the function that self-justifying and defensive stories play.

VALIDATE IDENTITY PROJECTIONS

Individuals attempt to cultivate an identity of how they like to be seen by others. One person may see herself as an intellectual; another may see himself as an outdoorsman, a scholar, a rebel, an athlete, a cowboy, or a free thinker. Such identity labels are part of a complex set of traits that a person might value.

An important part of mindful interpersonal communication, explains Stella Ting-Toomey, is the mutual validation of such *identity projections*, through a process of *identity negotiation*. Ting-Toomey suggests that people tend to build bonds with those who seem supportive of the identity they attempt to project.[4] Certainly, such mutual validation builds psychological intimacy.

Charles T. Brown and Charles Van Riper explain the broader concept this way: "Acceptance [requires] listening to the other to sense how he wishes to be heard. This confirms him and thus he tends to confirm us, and thus we are led to further self-confirmation. Self-acceptance and acceptance of the other are therefore interactive."[5]

Those involved in significant interpersonal conflict may go as far as denying contenders their most valued identity characteristics. When individuals have built a relationship at least partially based on affirming identity validation, it is not uncommon for one or both parties to want to take back such positive attributions.

For instance, one associate built her relationship with another by telling her that she was artistic. The affirmation was greatly valued by the recipient. Over the years, these two women continued to strengthen their friendship. After a contentious disagreement, the artist was told she really did not have much creative and artistic ability. And the women were not even fighting about art when the comment was made.

People who have felt hurt or manipulated in the past may be slow to accept validating projections from others. Such rejections may come across as guarded or even confrontational. Intermediaries help disputants exchange at least a small, tentative measure of validation.

Individuals attempt to cultivate an identity of how they like to be seen. For instance, a person may see herself as an intellectual; another may see himself as a cowboy. Such identity labels are part of a complex set of traits that a person might value.

Lack of validation normally plays a pivotal role in interpersonal conflict. Some of the most hurtful experiences are attacks on self-image or valued identity. They may take the form of a refusal to use the contender's name or to speak, greet, or look at the other person. When confronted about their passive aggression, the offender might say that there is nothing wrong. "I don't say anything bad to her. I simply don't look at her or speak with her. She just doesn't exist for me."

Individuals also project the personal qualities they wish to attain. When people's weaknesses are exposed, they may reason that it is not worth trying to pretend anymore.

Because friends, colleagues, and loved ones are more likely to have seen an individual's weaknesses, the person may first stop pretending with family, close friends, and associates at work. A key mediator role is to help the party who has crossed the line and stopped trying, so the person can put the best foot forward, cross back, and thus get a second chance at a relationship.

It is not easy to cross back. Some people prefer to show improvement through actions rather than words. Both are often required. A vital step is for the party to announce planned behavioral changes—no matter how positive the changed conduct—lest these be misunderstood.

A man who had been involved in a contentious relationship voluntarily began to make what he thought were positive changes. When they did not seem to make a difference, he tried other adjustments. During the pre-caucus, the other party explained that this individual seemed somewhat fickle, changing personalities from day to day.

PERMIT POSITIVE FEELINGS

In the process of meeting with the parties, the mediator can make a more informed determination as to whether to proceed with Party-Directed Mediation, use a more conventional style of mediation, or even recommend arbitration.

Under certain circumstances, more harm than good can result from permitting parties to speak directly to each other. It is not the purpose of mediation to simply provide a safe place for contenders to exchange insults. In order to empower parties, there must be some hope—an olive branch buried within the anger, frustration, and despair.

In *The Promise of Mediation*, the authors suggest that mediators watch for and recognize *transformative opportunities*.[6] That is, mediators should be alert for any sort of compliment, kind word, show of understanding, apology, or acceptance of an apology. Transformative comments help the disputants validate each other.

Contenders have probably had unproductive exchanges. Each party has taken the role of *victim* or *aggressor* or, most likely, has alternated between both. Each probably owes an apology to the other. Learning how to apologize and accept an apology is an essential interpersonal negotiation skill.

During a pre-caucus, an executive, almost as an aside, had something positive to say about the other party: "One thing I really value about the assistant manager is that he shows pride in his work—something I really admired in my father." The mediator suggested that the executive share these thoughts in the joint session, but was turned down. The challenge had been extended in a gentle way, permitting the executive to retain control. During the joint session, the executive did compliment the assistant manager despite his earlier refusal to consider doing so.

While a number of factors can affect the success of a mediated joint session, perhaps none is as telling as asking what one contender values in the other. This question is asked during the pre-caucus *after* the participants have had a chance to vent their frustrations. Individuals are more apt to see the good in their opponents after they feel understood by the mediator. It is not uncommon for the contenders to raise these positive issues on their own. The intermediary then asks permission to share the details with the other party.

From a psychological perspective, this matter is of transcendental importance. People involved in contentious interpersonal conflicts not only fail to validate each other but also tend to discount their adversaries and strip from them any vestiges of humanity. Failing to find a positive quality in another is a reflection of this phenomenon. Individuals who have such negative feelings must give themselves permission to allow others a measure of humanity. Without some degree of mutual respect, Party-Directed Mediation is destined to disappoint.

In the absence of this tiny light of hope, there is no point in proceeding to a joint session. And it is not enough to say that the other person "is always on time," "drives a nice car," "is attractive," or "doesn't smell." If there is nothing of significance that one person can value about the other, more harm than good can come out of the joint session.

COACHING DURING THE PRE-CAUCUS • 51

While a number of factors can affect the success of a mediated joint session, perhaps none is as telling as asking contenders what they value in the other.

Mediators often notice that one person tends to be nobler in terms of affirming the other. Years ago, I asked a party for the positive characteristics of his antagonist. When he claimed there was none, I shared the affirming remarks that had been made about him. I was surprised by his second refusal to find anything of value in the other person, especially after hearing something so positive about himself. Most people want to appear reasonable before the mediator.

"Well, if there is nothing positive you can say about the other person, there is no purpose in attempting a conflict management session together," I explained. I suggested a short break after which we could sit down and look at the alternatives. When we returned, the taciturn party had prepared, to my shock, a long list of positive attributes about the other disputant.

Since then, I have come to recognize that if one party seems to have nothing affirming to say about another, it might mean that I have not listened sufficiently. Such a person may require several pre-caucuses before they are ready for the joint session. This was the case with Nora and Rebecca, the subjects of the extended case study included later in this book. Some conflicts, such as the one between Nora and Rebecca, have spanned decades. Is it reasonable to think that after one listening session the adversaries will be ready to meet?

It is essential, before moving into a joint session, for each party to have something positive and validating to say about the other.

CHALLENGE BLIND SPOTS

Psychologists speak of *blind spots* as information individuals may not know about themselves. As a youngster, no one told me I was a terrible singer. When I found out, I was shocked. Now, I joke that I got rich because people paid me *not* to sing. Blind spots prevent us from seeing our own faults. We do not always notice how our actions may be contributing to our difficulties.

Conflict tends to enlarge our blind spots and reduce our ability to think rationally and creatively. People involved in disputes also tend to make false attributions. Contenders often excuse their own negative behavior, yet ascribe the worst motives for others' actions. As long as blind spots exist, we tend to blame everyone but ourselves for our predicaments.

During the mediation process, each party will face plenty of difficulties. Contenders will have to confront blind spots, beginning with the pre-caucus. If the mediator has listened to each of the parties with empathy, disputants will often recognize some of their faults on their own.

Furthermore, there is a certain amount of *psychological unfreezing*[7] that takes place when people are willing to see other possibilities. To use another metaphor, while they may not open the window blinds all the way, they begin to crack them and let some light in. As a result, after the pre-caucus the parties often begin to soften their stances towards each other.

Given enough time, such as in therapy, people can begin to see additional blind spots. Mediation seldom affords such opportunities. More complex Party-Directed Mediation, however, tends to be carried out over a longer period of time, and the time factor seems to work in favor of softening obdurate stances.

Just as in mediation, there are different approaches to therapy. Despite the similarities between some types of therapy and Party-Directed Mediation, these forms of intervention are not the same.[8] Therapists have specialized training and longer periods of time to work with clients. Blind spots may have to be considered sooner in mediation than in therapy.

So, what does it mean to challenge a blind spot? According to Gerard Egan, "At its simplest, confrontation is an invitation to examine some form of behavior that seems self-defeating, harmful to others, or both, and to change the behavior if it is found to be so."[9] Not everyone can challenge these blind spots. A listener must earn the right to do so,[10] by showing empathy and true concern.

Only after the party feels heard can a mediator introduce challenges. Under no circumstances should a person be challenged so the intermediary can feel better. Nor should the challenge be based on feelings of resentment the facilitator might be harboring. On the contrary, a mediator should only challenge a person for whom he or she has a positive regard. Furthermore, intermediaries must be willing to accompany the party through the painful process of examining dysfunctional behaviors.[11]

An example of a challenge is to ask a person to explore possible reasons why others react negatively to her. Another example—as discussed in the previous subsection—involves challenging one person to share positive qualities the other party may possess.

Egan suggests that it helps to "deliver challenges tentatively, as hunches."[12] I call this using the miniature toy hammer rather than the industrial sledge hammer. Gentle challenges invite reflection; overbearing ones, defensiveness. The power of the

Conflict tends to enlarge our blind spots and reduce our ability to think rationally and creatively.

miniature hammer is that it does not remove responsibility from the party involved in the dispute. In contrast, the industrial size is likely to act as a punishment in itself, permitting the person to discount the challenge as well as the challenger. People who have been effectively challenged may respond right away, after a few hours, or even months later.

A positive negotiation technique is to ask permission to pose a question.[13] The mediator, by using this strategy, lets the party know that the matter requires deep thinking and is not easy to answer.

Sara and her boss, Nick, have been involved in a dispute that has taken on major proportions. Among other things, Nick has complained that Sara is constantly threatening to leave the enterprise. The first time Sara used this tactic, Nick worked hard to please her. Now he feels great resentment towards Sara. Threats—both direct and veiled—can reduce a party's negotiating power.

Nick greatly values Sara's work, but he has reached the point where he would rather see Sara leave the business than be exposed to her constant threats. This might be a blind spot for Sara. Though she might vent her anger at length, it is doubtful she would ever realize—in spite of having an empathic listener—the dysfunctional nature of using threats as a negotiating tactic. Nick has given the mediator permission to share his concerns with Sara. We pick up the conversation after the mediator has listened to Sara for some time. It is not the first time Sara mentions that she would like to find another job.

"I'm so tired of working here, and I've told Nick that perhaps I should look for another job," Sara explains with a tone that betrays both resignation and angst.

Instead of directly reproving Sara for her use of threats, the mediator may acknowledge Sara's frustration and eventually broach the issue of negotiation techniques.

"Sara, may I share a negotiation concept with you?"
"Of course!"
"Part of my role is to prepare parties to face each other by first improving their negotiation skills. We can often obtain better

results if we know how to frame the matter at hand. Finding the right language so others will be receptive to what we say. People may stop listening when we use certain approaches. Nick told me—and he gave permission for me to share this with you—that he tunes you out when you threaten to quit. Threats are a hot button for him. But on the other hand, it is so important that you can express the stress and frustration you're feeling. We don't want to minimize these annoyances, such as when Nick asks everyone for advice except you. Would you like to spend a little time together finding just the right language to use so Nick is more likely to listen?"

The mediator has not given Sara any reason to believe she favors Nick's perspective in the overall conflict. She is simply inviting Sara to present her perspective in a clearer, more effective, and less threatening fashion. Once Sara comprehends that she must merely replace the unproductive tactic with a more positive one, the mediator (or a co-mediator) can role play Nick while Sara practices alternative ways of expressing her views. Together, they can try different approaches and find one that Sara feels good about and that fulfills her objectives.

The intermediary, as a careful listener, will often pick up on potentially problematic communication during the pre-caucus—even when the other party has not mentioned it. The mediator, then, also prepares parties to challenge each other during the joint session.

Regrettably, there are times when the third party needs to step in during the joint session. This is not the ideal, as the third party then risks the appearance of favoritism. Issues of defensiveness and saving face are paramount.

Practice through Role Plays

Role plays are powerful pre-caucus tools. After listening to a young woman, I asked her to imagine she was talking to a co-worker with whom she had been involved in several unpleasant exchanges. As she told her story, the tone of her voice was relaxed and friendly. As soon as she pretended that she was speaking to her colleague, her comportment changed instantly.

Coaching and modeling effective interaction styles is an ongoing task for the mediator.

Her body language, the tension in her voice, and the rough words that she spoke surprised me. The transformation was alarming, but it permitted me to offer some helpful suggestions.

At one enterprise, a manager's angry outbursts were well known. Martin had minimized the seriousness of his problem. A co-mediator played the role of the other contender. "Martin," she began. "When you get angry at me, shout at me, and use profanity, I feel very bad."

"Well, I'm so sorry I used bad language and was angry at you," Martin began nicely. "But . . ." And then Martin began to excuse himself and to place conditions on controlling his anger. I interrupted. "An apology with a qualifier or a 'but' is not a true apology; it is merely a statement of justification," I explained.

In total frustration Martin turned to me, raised his voice, and said, "Look, everyone has his style. Some people deal with disagreement this way or that. I'm an expert in intimidation. If I can't use intimidation, what can I do so I don't get run over? Am I supposed to just sit here and tell the other guy how nice he is and not bring up any of the areas of disagreement?"

As previously mentioned, one of the purposes of the pre-caucus is to coach individuals on how to present their perspectives in a way that they will be listened to. So, I calmly responded to his anxious query, "I am so glad you asked, Martin. That's why I'm here."

When mediators have done their work during the pre-caucuses, the joint sessions can be very positive. Martin's case was one of the most difficult I had ever encountered. Yet, once the joint session began, the two managers did most of the talking. They were extremely cordial, attentive, and amicable, showing understanding for each other. I had no need to interrupt as they negotiated, other than to ask for clarification in noting what they had agreed on. Although these individuals did not completely solve their dispute on that occasion, they continued to make progress after the mediator left.

Improve Communication Skills

Coaching and modeling effective interaction styles is an ongoing task for the mediator. The objective is to enhance the interpersonal negotiation skills of the parties involved.

The lack of effective negotiation skills is often the culprit when people experience interpersonal conflicts. Chapter 4 is a primer on the subject titled "Interpersonal Negotiation Skills." That chapter—or the corresponding audio seminar by the same name—may be downloaded from http://www.cnr.berkeley.edu/ucce50/ag-labor/7conflict/ and distributed at no cost to clients, students, or others (see p. iv).

Mediators can suggest that clientele familiarize themselves with these materials before the joint session. Parties are likely to identify dysfunctional communication styles in other people. Instead, they can better take advantage of these tools by introspectively considering if there are behaviors that they can improve *themselves*.

Intermediaries may also need to coach individuals on how to formulate questions, ask for clarification, reflect on what has been said, properly frame ideas, avoid defensiveness, and adequately challenge others.

SUMMARY

After some of the emotional stress is dissipated, intermediaries can continue to help the contending parties prepare for the joint session. Listening with empathy is a powerful tool to help reduce negative emotions, but there are other techniques that also help create a sense of distance between the parties and the dispute.

All of these tools can help the involved parties see more clearly and begin to recognize their own faults and their contributions to the conflict. With good measures of tact and gentleness, mediators can help parties begin to see blind spots in their communication styles and negotiation tactics.

The mediator also listens to each party with the idea of eventually teaching the person how to express viewpoints in the best positive light. Only after individuals are able to (1) effectively put forth their ideas and (2) listen attentively and analytically to other points of view will the parties be empowered to negotiate successfully in the joint session.

If the parties have been able to distance themselves from the conflict enough to see some good in each other, they are ready to move on to the joint session. If in doubt, holding another set of pre-caucuses may save time in the long run.

One of the functions of the mediator in the pre-caucus is to help parties capture the essence of their conflict by making a list of issues that need to be addressed during the joint session.

When the parties are well prepared, the mediator is unlikely to be required to take an overly active role in the joint session.

Chapter 3—References

1. Winslade, J., & Monk, G. (2000). *Narrative mediation: A new approach to conflict resolution.* San Francisco: Jossey-Bass.
2. Winslade, J., & Monk, G. (2000). *Narrative mediation: A new approach to conflict resolution.* San Francisco: Jossey-Bass.
3. Patterson, K., Grenny, J., McMillan, R., & Switzler, A. (2002). *Crucial conversations: Tools for talking when stakes are high.* New York: McGraw-Hill.
4. Ting-Toomey, S. (1999). *Communicating across cultures.* New York: Guilford Press.
5. Brown, C. T., & Van Riper, C. (1976). The role of speech in human relationships. In K. Giffin & B. R. Patton (Eds.), *Basic readings in interpersonal communication: Theory and application* (2nd ed.) (p. 166). New York: Harper & Row.
6. Bush, R. A. Baruch, & Folger, J. P. (1994). *The promise of mediation: Responding to conflict through empowerment and recognition.* San Francisco: Jossey-Bass.
7. The unfreeze-change-freeze model is based on the theory that people must unfreeze their attitudes before they are able to change, as shown by K. Lewin (1947/1951) in Frontiers in group dynamics. In D. Cartwright (Ed.), *Field theory in social science: Selected theoretical papers* by Kurt Lewin (pp. 188–237). New York: Harper & Row.
8. Bradshaw, W. (1995). Mediation and therapy. In M. Umbreit (Ed.), *Mediating interpersonal conflicts: A pathway to peace* (pp. 237–250). West Concord, MN: CPI.
9. Egan, G. (1986). *The skilled helper: A systematic approach to effective helping* (3rd ed.) (p. 219). Monterey, CA: Brooks/Cole.
10. Benjamin, A. (1974). *The helping interview* (2nd ed.). Boston: Houghton Mifflin.
11. Eisenberg, S., & Delaney, D. J. (1977). *The counseling process* (2nd ed.) (pp. 100–112). Chicago: Rand McNally.
12. Egan, G. (1986). *The skilled helper: A systematic approach to effective helping* (3rd ed.) (p. 200). Monterey, CA: Brooks/Cole.
13. Rackham, N. (1999). The behavior of successful negotiators. In R. J. Lewicki, D. M. Saunders, & J. W. Minton (Eds.), *Negotiation: Readings, exercises, and cases* (3rd ed.) (p. 348). Burr Ridge, IL: Irwin.

4
Interpersonal Negotiation Skills

The very thought of negotiating is intimidating, yet we are all experienced negotiators. The process of taking turns in a conversation, or of deciding who says hello first, involves tacit negotiation. Some types of negotiation may be almost subconscious, such as holding a door open for another to pass through. It is one thing to negotiate, another to be a skilled negotiator.

Wherever choice exists, there is a potential for disagreement. Such differences, when handled properly, can result in richer, more effective, creative resolutions and interaction. But, alas, it is difficult to consistently turn conflicts into opportunities.

As we put into practice effective interpersonal negotiation techniques, we gain confidence in our ability to find agreement and overcome challenges. This confidence can be contagious.

When I was about thirty years old, I climbed Half Dome, in Yosemite National Park, without much difficulty. The view from the top was spectacular. Twenty years later, I took two of my adult children to the summit. The second climb took a lot more faith, but I knew that since I had succeeded once, I would certainly be able to do it again. Mind would triumph over matter. There were times when doubts crept in. But Andrea, my oldest daughter, kept cheering us on: "We can do it, team!"

When we put negotiation skills into practice in our lives, we know that eventually we will conquer fear, make it to the peak, and find success. Negotiation is not about making it to the top alone, but rather, in tandem with the other person with whom we were in disagreement. Just as with climbing Half Dome, there will be challenging and difficult moments; but, oh, how worthwhile the results!

The good news about conflicts is that there are simple and effective tools to generate positive solutions and strengthen relationships damaged by disputes. Do not let the simplicity of the concepts obscure the challenge of carrying them out consistently.

Effective dialogue entails as much listening as talking. When disagreements emerge, it is easy to hear without listening. While effective two-way exchanges will happen naturally some of the time, for the most part they need to be carefully planned. Certainly life gives us plenty of opportunities to practice and improve.

Experiences can give us the confidence to climb ever-more-difficult heights in the future. Let us begin, however, by discussing why differences can be so challenging.

Fighting Words: How Did We Get Here?

Two grown men appear to be conversing normally, then suddenly break into a fight. The taller one hits the other twice, hard. The shorter of the two is now bleeding from the side of his mouth. They exchange further insults, and the taller man walks away only to return an instant later. He creeps up on the shorter man, again lands a couple of punches, and then leaves satisfied.

These men knew each other, and something was eating at them. Despite the apparent calm before the physical attack, their anger had boiled much earlier. Why did their disagreement turn into an act of violence? Why was the taller man compelled to come back and hit his acquaintance again? Many of us have observed, read about, or heard of situations worse than this. The world around us can, at times, erupt into violence.

Good people occasionally do and say things they later regret. I once spoke to an individual who hungered for a kind word from his wife, yet refused to take the initiative to say something nice to her. I could read the concern in his eyes. Another person took offense where none was intended. A youth talked about feeling elated after taking revenge on a friend. Only later, when he arrived home, did he begin to feel guilty about what he had just done. Why is it that people can so easily fall into the gutters like deviant bowling balls instead of rolling straight and true down the lanes?

Sam and Porter

Sam and Porter have allowed feelings of resentment and antagonism to build over the years while they have worked at a dude ranch. I have been acquainted with these men for a long time and know them to be caring, concerned, and giving individuals—when they are not around each other.

Today, Sam and Porter are among those leading a group of trail riders on a weeklong ride through parts of the majestic Rocky Mountains. As usual, each is trying to show off his riding skills and understanding of horses. Lee, one of the ranch guests, asks an innocent question about snaffle bits. Sam is the first to comment on Lee's query. Porter disagrees with Sam, however, by saying, "Those who have spent enough time around horses recognize . . ." With these words, Sam is excluded from the club; his opinion has lost any value, if it ever had any. Everyone around is embarrassed for the two men.

Effective dialogue entails as much listening as talking.

Sam is losing face in front of the people he is trying to impress. He attempts to protect his reputation. "Porter, that's funny," Sam quips. "Since when are *you* the big cowboy?" Several riders laugh. But Sam's moment of glory is short lived. If Sam's objective is to save face, the last thing he wants to do is to get into a verbal exchange with Porter. Sam has little chance of succeeding. Porter knows all the buttons to push to get a reaction from him.

In the heat of battle, it is difficult to realize how others may be seeing us. Worse, we do not care, for we are invested enough in the contest to feel we must minimize our injuries. We want to make sure the other guy is hurt as badly as we are. If the ship is going down, well, it better take both of us. Such attitudes only serve to escalate the conflict to the next level.

Back on the trail, the cowboys' subtle attacks are becoming increasingly direct. When Sam desperately makes a flippant comment, Porter loses no time in grinding his face against it with calculating and dripping sarcasm: "I'll try to remember that next time I ride my mule."

One gets the impression of Porter as a cool and calculating provocateur. He never raises his voice. He does not have to. His verbal skills are superior to those of Sam. The lion tamer in a cage with a lion. The angry lion is roaring for the crowd at the circus.

During a lull in the action, Sam manages to refocus and brilliantly deals with the matter at hand rather than his quarrel with Porter. Several of the riders are observing and seem impressed. But Sam soon succumbs to the conflict and makes a snide comment about Porter. Sam may be a lion, but Porter verbally squashes him like a mouse and leaves him twisting and turning in pain for exhibiting such insolence.

Another lead rider attempts to smooth things over but only manages to make matters worse. Sam begins to address the riders who are close enough to listen, and ignores Porter. But frustration has taken its toll. Sam's voice is cracking and betrays deep emotions as he recounts past injuries and the history of the conflict. Sam is now using some profanity, which is out of place for the culture of the group. In the process of speaking, he continues to provide Porter with ammunition. From the beginning, it has not been a fair match.

The more Sam attempts to defend his hurt ego, the faster the quicksand engulfs him. Porter's tone of voice remains cool and calculating. The lion tamer knows the lion will jump at him, and he is trying to provoke the spectacle.

Sam's next comment takes everyone by surprise. He announces that he has been offered a job at a dude ranch in the Green Mountains of Vermont, where he will be better appreciated.

And that is what Sam has wanted all along—just a little appreciation. Porter mocks him instead. The lion is ready to pounce on the lion trainer. He is roaring and angry. The crowd watches in amazement. Has the lion tamer gone mad? Sam, flushed, stands on his stirrups to speak. None of us had ever heard him use such degrading language. Sam yanks on the reins of his mount and rides back to a different cluster of riders who had not heard any of the conversation.

The lion attacks the lion tamer, and the lion tamer wins. But wait. Did he really win? Are lions always defeated, and do lion tamers always win? In the short run, both of these men lost the respect they desired. It is hard to measure the long-term losses.

In most conflicts, the people involved suffer from a momentary (and sometimes *not*-so-fleeting) inability to think about consequences. They are willing, in a flash of anger, to pay any consequence if need be. Pride displaces prudence.

The origins of conflict can be so many and varied that it would be impossible to catalogue them all. Common sources of conflict include disagreement, perceived lack of fairness, jealousy, misunderstanding, poor communication, and victimization. Several factors may play a role in any given conflict.

Contention

When disagreement is poorly dealt with, the outcome can be *contention*. Contention creates psychological distance between people through feelings of dislike, bitter antagonism, competition, alienation, and disregard.

When faced with problems, the human brain is capable of taking large amounts of data, quickly analyzing it, and coming up with the best solution. Unwanted options are discarded. This is fine when it comes to making quick decisions under time constraints.

Unfortunately, we are often eager to accept the first solution that seems to work rather than the truly creative one. While some decisions may require careful consideration and even agony, we make others almost instinctively.

Our best solution becomes our position or stance in the matter. Our needs, concerns, and fears play a part in the process of establishing our position.

Misunderstanding and dissent arise when our solutions are at odds with other people's positions. Several foes combine to create contention:

- Our first enemy is the natural desire to *explain our side first*. After all, we reason, if they understand our perspective, they will come to the same conclusions we did.
- Our second enemy is our *ineffectiveness as listeners*. Listening is much more than being quiet so we can have our turn. It involves a real effort to understand other perspectives.
- Our third enemy is *fear*. Fear that we will not get our way. Fear of losing something we cherish. Fear we will be made to look foolish or lose face. Fear of the truth—that we could be wrong.
- Our fourth enemy is the assumption that *one of us has to lose* if the other is going to win—that differences can only be resolved competitively.

Four Weak Solutions

We are often too quick to assume that a disagreement has no possible mutually acceptable solution. Certainly, talking problems through is not so easy. Confronting an issue may require (1) exposing ourselves to ridicule or rejection, (2) recognizing we may have contributed to the problem, and (3) willingness to change.

When involved in conflict, we often enlist others to support our perspective and thus avoid trying to work matters out directly with the affected person. Once we have the support of friends, we may feel justified in our behavior and fail to put much energy into resolving the disagreement.

Sympathetic co-workers and friends usually tend to agree with us. They do so mostly because they see the conflict and possible solutions from our perspective. After all, they heard the story from us.

Whether dealing with family members, friends, acquaintances, or associates at work, sooner or later difficulties will arise. We usually do not find ourselves at a loss for words when dealing with family members and other people with whom we have extended contact on a regular basis. Communication patterns with those closest to us are not always positive; they often fall into predictable and ineffective exchanges.

With virtual strangers we often put forth our best behavior. Out of concern for how others perceive us, we may err in saying too little when things go wrong. We can suffer for a long time before bringing issues up. This is especially so during what could be called a "courting period." Instead of saying things directly, we try to hint at problems.

Although it is easier to sweep problems under the psychological rug, eventually the mound of dirt becomes so large we cannot help but trip over it. Honeymoons tend to end. At some point, "courting behavior" gets pushed aside out of necessity. After the transition is made, it can become all too easy to start telling spouse, friend, or co-worker exactly what has to be done differently.

It is good to be perceptive of how others react to us while, at the same time, refraining from taking offense. We can find constructive outlets to dissipate stressful feelings (e.g., exercise, music, reading, service to others, or even a good night's sleep). It

Our friends and sympathetic co-workers often tend to agree with us when we tell them about a conflict we may have had. They are apt to see the conflict from our perspective. After all, they heard the story from us.

is not helpful to appear unaffected while resentment builds up within and eventually explodes.

Unresolved conflict often threatens whatever self-esteem we may possess. Few people can boast of self-esteem that is so robust that it cannot be deflated by conflict. By finding others who agree with us, we falsely elevate our self-esteem. But we only build on sand.

As our self-esteem is depleted, we become less able to deal with conflict in a positive way. A constant need to compare ourselves to others is a telling sign that something is amiss and that our self-esteem is weak. It is easy to confuse self-esteem with pride.

Self-esteem is built on a firmer foundation as individuals learn to deal effectively with conflict. In Spanish there are two related words: self-esteem is *autoestima*, while false self-esteem is *amor propio* (literally, "self-love"). As we learn to successfully negotiate through conflicts, our self-esteem and confidence are strengthened.

It takes more skill, effort, and commitment—and in the short run, more stress—to face disagreement directly. Instead of effective dialogue, we often gravitate to less helpful approaches to conflict management. We fight (or compete), yield, avoid, or find a weak compromise.

Fighting It Out

A man sat in his train compartment looking out into the serene Russian countryside. Two women joined him. One held a lap dog. The women looked at the man with contempt, for he was smoking. In desperation, one of the women stood, opened the window, took the cigar from the man's lips, threw it out, and closed the window. The man sat there for a while and then proceeded to re-open the window, grab the woman's dog from her lap, and throw it out the window. No, this story is not from today's news; instead, it is a scene from Fyodor Dostoevsky's nineteenth-century novel, *The Idiot*. The frequency and seriousness of workplace, domestic, sports, and other types of violence seems to be ever on the rise.

The objective of competition is for one person to get his or her way. At least it seems so at first. In the long run, both parties often end up losing. It does little good, for instance, to secure a spectacular contract for a new facility, if the small profit margin forces the contractor out of business before completing the job. Once people are caught up in competitive negotiation, it is often hard to step back and see clearly enough to work through difficulties in a collegial manner.

Competition tends to focus on a particular episode, rather than on long-term viability—on the present goal, rather than on the long-term relationship. A retired supervisor bragged that his subordinates learned he was "not always right—but always the boss." Although he might have obtained compliance from his winning-focused tactics, I doubt he got much in terms of employee commitment. Losers often hold grudges and find ways of getting even.

Should a business try to obtain a good price for raw materials? Or negotiate the best possible deal when buying a new piece of equipment? What about one-time situations involving people who will never see each other again? Hidden in these questions are deeper issues. Surely, there are times when people bargain with the idea of getting the best possible results. In some cultures, merchants are offended if you pay the asking price without bargaining.

We have all heard the story about a man who was running late for a job interview. He rudely cut off a woman who was waiting her turn to park. They shouted at each other, and he hurried off to his appointment. The man was relieved to see that his interviewer had not arrived yet and that he had made it on time. His contentment was short lived. The interviewer turned out to be the woman he had cut off in the parking lot! At times, then, people incorrectly assume they are dealing with a one-time situation.

Yielding

Yielding involves unilateral concessions at the expense of the submissive party. People are most likely to yield when they perceive there is little chance of winning or when the outcome is more important to the other person.

In some situations, yielding can be a virtue, but not always. A person who continues to yield sometimes stops caring. I do not see any harm in occasional yielding during a business transaction, or a balanced yielding between spouses, or even the frequent yielding obedience of a child to a parent or teacher. There are two specific types of yielding that are troublesome: (1) saying *yes* today and living with frustration or resentment tomorrow and (2) repeatedly agreeing to go along with a weak solution in order to avoid disagreement. In these instances, yielding is not a virtue. When people stop caring, they often withdraw physically or emotionally.

It takes more skill, effort, and commitment—although in the short run, more stress—to face disagreement directly.

Avoidance

Avoidance weakens already fragile relationships. Sending someone else to deliver a message is one particularly damaging form of conflict avoidance.

Silence is sometimes confused with avoidance. I have observed numerous situations in which a person was asked a question, and when the listener did not respond, the questioner walked away angrily. In at least some of these cases, it seemed that the listener was about to answer but was not given enough time to reflect and respond.

Among the many reasons for remaining silent is not knowing how to answer without increasing the conflict spiral or hurting someone. Yet silence can hurt. Suggesting that the conversation be continued later, under less emotional circumstances, is effective, unless it is viewed as another form of avoidance. There are individuals who use the expression "We'll see" when they mean "I don't want to talk about this." They have no intention of conversing about the subject later.

Compromise

Mutual concessions in which both parties yield are compromises. Some compromises involve an arrangement somewhere between two positions; others alternate the beneficiary. An example of the former is paying something less than the original asking price but more than one had hoped for. An instance of the latter may involve taking turns using one computer. While some issues lend themselves well to compromise, many others do not.

Compromise takes a measure of goodwill, as well as trust and maturity, but not much creativity. Compromise often involves lazy communication and problem solving, and the term has acquired a negative connotation. While mutual concessions may take place at any time in the negotiation process, too often they occur before the challenge is sufficiently understood or more creative solutions are considered.

You may have heard the classic tale of two siblings who argued over who would get an orange. They compromised and split it in half. One ate her half and threw away the peel; the other, who was cooking, grated the peel and discarded the rest.[1]

When we are involved in a conflict, toward which of these methods do we tend to gravitate? Are we likely to fight it out, yield, withdraw, or look for a compromise? We develop techniques for interpersonal relations and conflict management in our youth. As we mature, we need more effective approaches.

Next, we consider behaviors that lead to more positive interpersonal relations and reduced discord.

Interpersonal Relations

Interpersonal skills play a critical role in the development and maintenance of trust and positive feelings in our dealings with others. They are the building blocks for successful interpersonal negotiation.

Social Rituals

The most basic unit of wholesome human interaction is the *stroke*—a verbal or physical way to acknowledge another person's value and existence. A *ritual* is a mutual exchange of strokes—a sort of reciprocal validation of each person's worth promoting a sense of trust between people. The term *stroke* connotes intimate contact, as when an infant is caressed, squeezed, or patted.[2]

People generally do not go around patting or caressing other adults (except in the sports arena) but they may shake hands, wave, or say hello. Most stroking takes the form of verbal communication and body language. Examples include waving, smiling, a glance of understanding, saying hello, and even sending a card or flowers.

Between spouses, touch is an important way to show care and liking. Physical strokes among friends and associates may include placing a hand on another person's shoulder, elbow, or back. While some people do not mind, others feel these gestures, unlike the handshake, can be inappropriate.

A young woman reported that an acquaintance mistook her friendly pats on the back—intended to convey thanks for a job well done—as romantic interest. Similarly, when a woman threw water at a man and grabbed him by his shirt, he confused the horseplay with a show of sexual interest.

People may resent physical strokes, not necessarily because they are sexual in nature, but because they often represent a show of superiority. Dexter, a supervisor, frequently tended to place his arm around Laurie's shoulder. The day Laurie put *her* arm around Dexter's shoulder, he was visibly uncomfortable. As a result, Dexter stopped the annoying practice.

In terms of physical strokes, we may have widely differing feelings about them depending on the situations and persons involved. From one individual, we may find these gestures comforting, yet we resent the same kind of stroke coming from another.

The need for personal validation is so great that people may prefer negative attention to being ignored. Try to imagine how awkward it would be to meet a friend you have not seen for a few weeks and not greet the person through either gesture or word. From an Argentine folk song, I like the saying, roughly translated, "When two people like each other well, from four kilometers away they will greet each other."[3] The opposite of a stroke is the "cold shoulder" treatment.

Some verbal strokes may be neutral or uncommitted, such as "I see." Others show more care or interest: "I heard your daughter is getting married. That's exciting!" Body language and tone of voice play important roles in the intensity of stroke exchanges.

Generally, when individuals know each other well, have not seen each other for a while, or are responding to a catastrophe or other special circumstances, a more forceful stroke is expected.

At times, the intensity of a stroke may make up for its brevity. For instance, we may realize special circumstances call for a longer stroke exchange, yet we may not be able to deliver at the moment. A neighbor may enthusiastically welcome a friend returning from a vacation, "Hey, I'm so glad you're back! You'll have to tell me everything about your trip this evening. I've got to be running now, before the store closes." This stroking validates the neighbor's existence while simultaneously acknowledging more is owed. A drastic change in ritual length or intensity among people, for no apparent reason, may affect a person's self-esteem or raise suspicion that something is wrong with the other party.[4]

Strokes help maintain goodwill in relationships. Without them, conflict may surface or escalate. When discord has landed, these strokes—even eye contact or other subtle ways to show validation—tend to be eliminated. Part of the reconciliation process requires that these mutual validation gestures be resumed, which may often mean swallowing pride.

Conversational Skills

Once the basic ritual is over, people may either go their own ways or engage in a longer conversation. Poor conversational skills hinder interpersonal relations and thwart the resolution of conflicts. So, what makes a person difficult to talk to? Poor conversationalists are interested in only one topic, tend to be negative, talk excessively about themselves, resort to monosyllabic answers, talk too much, or are overly competitive (that is, they can top anything you say).

Some conversations are much more animated than others, involving some interruption, exchange of stories, and description of experiences. In *The Lost Art of Listening*, Michael Nichols says, "Talking and listening is a unique relationship in which speaker and listener are constantly switching roles, both jockeying for position, one's needs competing with the other's. If you doubt it, try telling someone about a problem you're having and see how long it takes before he interrupts to tell you about a problem of his own, to describe a similar experience of his own, or to offer advice—advice that may suit him more than it does you (and is more responsive to his own anxiety than to what you're trying to say)."[5] While this competition to share ideas and feelings can be invigorating at times, all too often both parties feel discounted and dissatisfied.

Some claim they can simultaneously listen while they work on the computer, read a newspaper, or attend to other business. Certain individuals are better at multi-tasking than others. Nevertheless, the message to the speaker is discomforting: "You are not important enough for me to attend exclusively to your needs." The crucial skill, then, is not only listening but also letting the other person feel heard.

Effective conversationalists will take turns speaking and listening as well.[6] Difficulty arises when people take more than their share of the talking time. This may happen when individuals feel others are not listening or when they suffer from lack of self-esteem.[7] When they let someone else speak, they fear they may not get another turn. Whatever the reason, regularly monopolizing a conversation is likely to alienate others. Of

Sometimes silence is confused with avoidance, especially when individuals are not given enough time to reflect and respond.

course, there are times when people have a need to be listened to rather than a need to converse.

At the opposite extreme is the individual who pouts and refuses to speak. People who have nothing to offer or are not sure they can control their emotions can instead say something like "That is an interesting issue," and then indicate whose turn is next:[8] "Inesa, what do you think of that?"

It has been decades since I consumed any alcohol, but I had an interesting experience as a seventeen-year-old in Chile. I attended a *ramada* to celebrate Chilean Independence Day. A worker from a neighboring vineyard approached me, staggering, with a glass of wine clutched in his hand and a singsong in his voice.

"*Patroncito, ¿se sirve una copita de tinto?*" (My young boss, would you like a cup of red wine?)

I politely declined.

"Ah!" the farm worker uttered. "One can tell you are not a *true* Chilean!"

His comments pierced me with anguish. "May I have that cup?" I demanded.

The worker gladly handed me the glass and said, "*¡Salud!*" (To your health!)

I gulped down its contents. If my original refusal had upset him, his facial expression now betrayed an even greater distress. After getting over the shock of being left with an empty glass, he proceeded to teach me a lesson in interpersonal relations.

"Here is what the *people* do," he began. "When someone offers you a glass, you accept, you hold it in your hand, you chat, and then you return the cup." After a pause he added, "Or you hold it in your hand, chat, take a sip, and then return it. But you don't *drink it all!*"

Perhaps this lesson can also apply to avoiding extremes in conversational turns. Keeping comments short and checking to make sure the other person is still interested are two essential dialoguing skills. In a mutually productive discussion, individuals normally share equally in speaking and listening.

Interpersonal Negotiation

Jack comes home from work, and after greeting his wife, he enthusiastically suggests:

"Sue. Hey, what would you think if we go to the river with the kids this Saturday?"

"Noooo, Jack," she responds in a complaining voice. "I don't want to."

Jack has suggested taking a trip to the river next Saturday, and Sue, his wife, has refused. This conversation, like a thousand others, could result in feelings of contention between the individuals—especially if Jack keeps insisting that they go to the river and Sue continues to resist the idea.

What are the options here? Sue and Jack seem pretty set in their ways. Perhaps they will shout, or stop talking to each other, or Sue will yield and go to the river but let Jack know how utterly miserable she is the whole time. Or maybe they will take turns going or not going and making each other miserable. Perhaps Jack will take the children and leave Sue behind, or go alone and leave the whole family behind. These solutions are likely to increase the feelings of contention between Sue and Jack.

Search for Interests

Some of the most powerful concepts are the simplest. One such principle was developed by the Harvard University negotiation team and is described in the book *Getting to Yes*.[9] People in disagreement, such as Jack and Sue, can benefit from focusing on their needs, fears, and interests rather than on their positions. Jack's stance is that he wants to go to the river. Sue's position is that she does not. By concentrating on *positions* we tend to underscore our disagreements. Roger Fisher and William Ury suggest that during a conflict, we attempt to satisfy the other person's needs as well as our own.

When Jack patiently attempts to determine what Sue's needs are—patiently, because Sue might not have considered her own needs very carefully—he begins to discover that, for his wife, a trip to the river normally means: (1) a long drive into town to purchase supplies for the picnic, (2) being left alone with the children for a couple of hours while Jack chats with the fishermen, (3) keeping her eyes constantly on the children because of the dangerous river currents, and (4) the responsibility of putting things away when they return home. In other words, the trip to the river is no picnic for Sue.

Jack has his own set of needs and fears. He wants to be away from the phone, because his boss sometimes calls him back to work and because he enjoys spending time with his family away from the distractions of the television.

Once Jack begins to understand his wife's concerns and the weight of responsibility Sue feels when they make the trip to the river, perhaps he can tentatively offer some suggestions.

While talking about our needs and fears may have been considered a selfish thing in traditional negotiation, in creative negotiation it is not selfish by definition, as it is not only our needs and fears that are being considered, but also those of the other party.

"Sue, I have to go into town a couple of times a week. Would it help if you gave me the shopping list and I brought those items home?"

Sue nods her head affirmatively, "Yes, that would really be nice."

"And you know me. I love chatting with the guys at the river. You always mention that you have no time to just read. How about if I take the kids with me while I go for a walk, and you take a good book to read?"

"I think I am liking this idea," Sue smiles.

"I realize I've been unfair to you when we get home and I just want to go to bed. What if we all pitch in, including the children, to leave things in some semblance of order when we get home?"

Would you be surprised to learn it was Sue who suggested they go to the river the next time? The additional work for Jack was minor. He ended up bonding with his children, who developed a love for their river walks with Dad.

Once we understand another person's needs and interests, we see that there are many solutions to challenges that seemed impossible.

In traditional negotiations we are inclined to focus exclusively on our own needs and assume it is the other party's responsibility to worry about having his or her needs met. Yet, by showing a sincere interest in the needs of others, we increase the chances of having our needs met. While talking about our expectations and fears may have been considered selfish in traditional negotiation, creative negotiation entails the consideration of not only our needs and fears but also those of the other individual.

When the light goes on, we realize it is not a zero-sum game in which one person must lose for the other to win. Nor is it necessary to resolve disagreements with an ineffectual compromise. Instead, both parties can be winners. Individuals can learn how to keep communication lines open and overcome challenges when things go wrong.

Interest-based negotiation, then, is built upon the principle of meeting the needs of all the individuals or stakeholders. "Deep conflict requires a tremendous exertion of psychological and physical energy," argues Jay Rothman. "Such conflict may be creatively transformed when adversaries come to learn, ironically perhaps, that they may fulfill their deepest needs and aspirations only with the cooperation of those who most vigorously oppose them."[10]

Seek to Understand

Steven Covey reinforced an important notion in his book *Seven Habits of Highly Effective People*: "Seek first to understand, then to be understood."[11] If we encourage others to explain their side first, they will be more apt to listen to ours.

In the process of conducting organizational interviews, one day I came across an executive who was less than enthusiastic about my study. It was clear from his words and tone that I would not be interviewing anyone at his operation, so I switched my focus to listening. The manager shared concerns about a number of troublesome issues, and we parted amiably. As I began to walk away, the executive cried out to me, "Go ahead!" I turned around and inquired, "Go ahead and what?" To my surprise he responded, "Go ahead and interview my employees." The principle was at work.

Problems are likely to increase, however, if we put all our needs aside to focus on another person's perspective. The other party may think we have no needs and be taken aback when we introduce them all of a sudden, almost as an afterthought. In order to avoid such unproductive shocks, I like the idea of establishing a psychological contract with the other person in the conversation.

Successful negotiators are more likely to label their intentions, such as a desire to ask a difficult question or provide a suggestion, and yet are less prone to label disagreements as people tend to become defensive.[12] Therefore, in order to make my intentions clear, but at the same time allow the other individual to speak first, I say something along these lines: "While I want to share my needs and views with you later, let me first focus on your thoughts, needs, and observations." At this point, I attempt to put my own needs aside and truly listen. I might say: "So, help me understand your concerns regarding . . ."

That is the easy part. The difficulty comes in fulfilling the resolution to listen—to resist the tendency to interrupt with objections, no matter how unfounded the comments we hear may be. Instead of telling someone that we understand, just so the person can finish and give us a turn to present our perspective, we can be much more effective by revealing exactly what it is that we understand.

All along we must resist, as we listen, the temptation to bring up our viewpoints and concerns. In trying to comprehend, we may need to express our understanding in the form of a tentative question and avoid being judgmental.

We can refine our statement until the other party feels understood. Only then can we begin to explain our perspective and expect to receive the other party's complete attention. Once everyone's concerns have been laid out, we can both focus on a creative solution.

If we have no history with someone, or if the relationship has been a troubled one, we need to use more caution when disagreeing. The potential for a disagreement to be sidetracked into contention is always there, so it helps if we have made goodwill deposits over time. Otherwise, differences can lead to defensiveness.

Control Emotions

Our emotions regularly get in the way of effective negotiations. Nothing kills creativity quicker than anger, pride, embarrassment, envy, greed, jealousy, or other strong negative emotions. Anger is often an expression of fear or lack of confidence in our ability to get what we think we want. Emotional outbursts tend to escalate rather than resolve a conflict.

If we can improve our ability to manage our emotions and respond without getting defensive, we have gone a long way towards creative negotiation. Kamran Alavi, a friend, once wisely said, "When we permit negative emotions, such as anger, to take control of us, this is a sure sign we are about to step into a trap."

It is extremely difficult to hide our emotions, especially when we feel there is much in the balance. Our body language, particularly our facial gestures and voice qualities, often give us away. We are not emotionless robots. However, it is better to describe negative emotions (e.g., a feeling of disappointment) than to display them.

When it comes to managing emotions, I recommend the chapter "Master My Stories" in the book *Crucial Conversations*. The authors contend that negative emotion is *always* preceded by *telling ourselves a story*. This may happen in milliseconds. The more critical the situation, or the more important our relationship with an individual, the more likely it is that we are vulnerable to such storytelling.[13] When we presume to understand another's feelings or intentions, we may come up with the worst possible scenario in terms of future consequences.

Some years ago, I was asked to address a group of young adults at church. I noticed that as I spoke, a young man would lean toward the young lady beside him and whisper in her ear. I found this to be very distracting and annoying. I feel very strongly that only one person should speak at a time, so every time he began to talk, I stopped. When I stopped, he stopped, and so it went. I later learned he was interpreting for a visitor from Japan. The story I had constructed, however, was that this individual was flirting with the young lady and was being rude.

Have you ever gone into a difficult situation with intentions of putting forth your best behavior, only to fail partway through the experience? After attending a *Crucial Conversations* seminar, I came to understand that this happens to us because we permitted the negative story to prevail. In other words, it is difficult to control our negative emotions as long as we give preeminence to our unproductive stories.

As we give people the benefit of the doubt and consider alternative narratives that avoid the presumption of evil, allowing for more honorable or even noble motives, we will succeed in managing our emotions.

Our emotions regularly get in the way of effective negotiations.

Avoid the Presumption of Evil

One individual tended to think, anytime he saw two people conversing, that they were talking about him. This is called *negative attribution*. It is all too easy to incorrectly interpret another person's innocent behavior and assume the worst.

An effective practice, when we do not know how to interpret something, is to very *briefly* describe a situation, behavior, or apparent fault without offering an interpretation—and then permit the other person to explain. Such a description should avoid inferences as to why someone did something. We will often find out there was a good reason for what took place or at least give others the opportunity to explain their perspective.

Break down Bigger Issues into Smaller Ones

An effective negotiator is constantly looking for ways to break down challenges into smaller, more easily solvable issues. For instance, if a supervisor is resisting the introduction of new technology to track employee performance, it helps to talk it over and find out specific concerns. There may be some apprehension about (1) the reliability of the system, (2) setup time, or even (3) staying on top of production data. Each of these concerns can be addressed separately.

Move away from Blame

It is unfortunate that people often feed on fault-finding. If individuals are sufficiently introspective, they will often acknowledge that they had some blame in the matter. As long as the contest is about blame, peace will flee.

At one time, I was responsible for a large group of teenagers. A man arrived in the middle of an activity and demanded to take two sisters home. He seemed very agitated. I was aware that at one time he had been a close friend of the girls' mother, but he was not the legal guardian of these two young women. He became increasingly anxious when I would not let him take the girls without first ascertaining the mother's wishes. Unfortunately, the mother was not answering her phone. I was not about to let him depart with the two young women, but he kept insisting. In desperation, I asked, "Who are you?" (as if to say "What makes you think you can take these girls?") To say he was offended would be an understatement. I made arrangements to have two of the adult leaders take the sisters home. They were met by a panicked mother who was waiting for her daughters to arrive so they could leave town. A relative had been in a serious accident.

While no one would question the wisdom of refusing to let the young women go with this man, I blame myself for having offended him. Many individuals have, with great fervor, told me it was not my fault. They have either focused on the responsibility held by the man or by the mother.

In discounting my fault in the matter, they are making the mistake of thinking that the difficulty of the situation excuses my failings. Yet, if I were to hold others culpable but not myself, I could not have grown from this experience. I have often reflected on alternative approaches I could have taken, which would have permitted me to keep the young women safe *and* avoid being rude.

Focus on the Problem, Not the Solution

The suggestion of concentrating on the problem rather than the solution may sound counterintuitive. Yet, for a number of reasons, it is one of the keys to effective negotiation. The more complex the situation, the greater the importance of this principle. When someone comes with *the solution*, even when that solution is a good one, it gives the other party the feeling of not having any control. Research has shown[14] that people often prefer an outcome that is not as beneficial, as long as they have some control over the results.

Even when parties have gone out of their way to find a fair solution for all involved, when one person presents the solution as firm, it tends to put the other individual on the defensive. A family business partner who was presented with a firm solution felt coerced to do all the compromising. She was not able to see the concessions being made because of the poor manner in which the other party negotiated.

The timing and approach must be right. An individual with an excellent idea needs to wait until the predicament has been rigorously discussed and the needs of all concerned understood. Only then can the solution be presented, and this needs to be done in a tentative fashion. "Would such and such an idea meet your needs, or can we play with the concept and twist it a bit so it does?"

In an emotionally charged atmosphere, or when there is much riding on the outcome in terms of consequences for individual parties, this approach may make the difference between success and failure. An effective negotiating technique, then, is to come to

As long as the contest is about blame, peace will flee.

the bargaining table with the idea of studying the problem and individual needs, rather than imposing a solution.

Coming right out with a solution, and doing away with all the bargaining, is known to most of us as the "take-it-or-leave-it" tactic. In collective bargaining, one variation of this tactic is called *Boulwarism*, after former General Electric vice-president Lemuel R. Boulware. Under his leadership, the company's management would propose a final offer to the trade union up front. The members of the management team went out of their way to study all the facts that could pertain to the contract and to make it fair for all involved, "trying to do right voluntarily." They refused to budge from their position, however, unless any "new facts" of sufficient strength were presented. Such an approach was highly resented by the union representatives, who felt undermined. Two "new facts" played key roles in defeating Boulwarism: (1) the practice was found, to some degree, to constitute bad-faith bargaining by the National Labor Relations Board and the courts, and (2) the union made a very strong point against the tactic through a successful labor strike.[15, 16]

When we are the ones being presented with a possible solution, it is good to be slow to find fault. If someone's proposal is quickly followed by our counterproposal, the other party is likely to feel slighted. There are two key reasons for avoiding quick counterproposals: (1) individuals are least receptive to hearing another proposal after setting theirs on the table, and (2) such counteroffers are often perceived as disagreement, or an affront to "face."[17]

At the very least, efforts should be made to let others feel their proposals are being taken seriously and have been understood. If a counterproposal builds on the other party's proposal, and credit is so given, then the chances for negative feelings are further curtailed.

Reject Weak Solutions

As negotiators, it helps to learn about other people's preferences and to make our own clear. One manager explained that it was hard enough to understand his own needs and preferences, let alone be able to concentrate on someone else's. And perhaps that is one of the reasons we do not see interest-based negotiation used as frequently. It does take a certain amount of exertion, especially at first. With time, it can begin to feel more natural.

In traditional negotiation, as soon as individuals get close enough to the desired solution, they are prone to accept another person's yielding. While some people's motives may be selfish, others believe that their solutions will best serve all involved.

Sometimes a person will yield or pretend to yield—asserting, out of frustration, "That's fine; do it your way." By accepting another's yielding, individuals reduce their future negotiating power.

Instead, negotiators obtain better solutions when they first ensure the other person is completely satisfied with the solution. They gain the trust of the other party and can thus increase their negotiating strength.

Emotion may indicate strength of conviction in another person. The very opposite may mean the individual is giving in rather than agreeing. Either way, parties may want to step back and consider together what unmet needs still need to be addressed.

Yasuo and Akemi Matsuda were making some joint family plans. They came to an agreement, but Yasuo noticed that his wife had done so hesitantly. Rather than just accepting Akemi's agreement and moving on with his own plans, Yasuo said, "I notice you're not totally pleased with our decision. It's really important to me that you're as happy with this decision as I am."

Akemi said she felt comfortable with the decision, but Yasuo still sensed otherwise. Yasuo might have been justified in moving forward and doing things his way, but he hesitated: "I still sense there's something you're feeling, perhaps difficult to put into words, that's causing you some uncertainty."

"Actually, you may be right," Akemi responded. She agreed to think over the matter. That night, they had another chance to converse at length, and Akemi was able to articulate her fear. As a result, she and Yasuo were able to make some small yet important adjustments. Moreover, Akemi was able to further build her trust in her husband. He had honored her feelings, thoughts, and opinions.

Conversely, it is important to be clear regarding our own needs. In the 1980s, when non-smoking policies had not yet been implemented in Chile, I was teaching a three-month graduate course on human resource management at the University of Chile. Perhaps as many as 80 percent of the class participants smoked. I did not want to be impolite, yet I knew the cigarette smoke would give me an unbearable headache. After introducing myself, I told the students: "I want all to know that you can smoke anytime you desire. However, I would request that you do so outside of the classroom." The comment was taken in a positive manner.

Look for Creative Solutions

A needs-based approach to negotiation frequently calls for creative thinking that goes beyond the poorly devised compromise—such as those arrived at when there is a rush to solve before an effort is made to comprehend. We frequently fail to explore beyond the obvious solution.

The following six-step process has been suggested to get the creative juices flowing: (1) define the problem, (2) actively consider alternatives, (3) internalize the data, and (4) set the challenge aside and wait. Wait for what? For (5) a sudden flash of inspiration, which needs to be (6) carefully tested.[18] The first four steps may need to be repeated several times until that inspiration comes.

Consider the Worst Alternative

Sometimes people are afraid to act for fear that speaking out will have detrimental consequences. Even not agreeing to negotiate is a form of negotiation. If we cannot come to an agreement, what is the worst possible outcome? In thinking of the worst alternative, it is useful to consider *both* how the other party and how we will be affected.

Negotiation can suffer when we think the other person is the only one who will undergo negative consequences or when we think we are the only ones who will lose.

A man would not listen to his wife, who had asked for some changes, as he never imagined she would leave him. At work, a supervisor never confronted an employee with his shortcomings for fear the employee would leave. Often, the worst alternative is not talking things through in a calm manner.

Maintain Integrity

At a time when many decisions were made on a handshake, my parents—grape growers in Chile's central valley—invited their children to a family conference.

"Earlier this year, we came to an agreement with the winery for a price," they explained. "Since then, many vineyards were affected by a terrible freeze—one that has meant a huge decline in supply. Had we waited a few more months, we could have gotten a much better deal."

My parents asked each of their five children for his or her opinion. The answer was a unanimous decision to honor the oral agreement. At the time, I was impressed that my parents would ask for our input. Since then, I have come to the conclusion that they knew the answer all along but wanted to teach us an important lesson about integrity.

Trustworthiness plays a huge role in successful negotiation. Dependability, honesty, and consistency are all part of trustworthiness. I often hear individuals involved in negotiations say, "I don't trust that person."

It has also been said, "It is more important to be trusted than to be loved." When we lose trust for people, we begin to think of them as undependable or dishonest.

Understand Time Pressures

Deadlines are often self-imposed. How often do we feel obligated to respond right away when facing a difficult situation? Why not solicit a little more time to study a matter or to accomplish a task? Do not be afraid to explain, "This is a tough one. It is now 8:15 and I'm tied up for the next two hours. If I call you between 11:00 and 11:30 this morning, will that work for you?" This type of detail takes only a few minutes longer to negotiate.

If we can build a little cushion for the unexpected, that is helpful. Most people do not mind waiting longer if they know what the real situation is. If a deadline seems hard to meet, ask to renegotiate an extension *before* the due date. An effective negotiator will ask the other party to suggest, or take a role in establishing, a deadline rather than arbitrarily impose one.

"I will call you back as soon as I can" or "I will call you right back," on the other hand, can leave much to be desired. The recipient of that message will wonder whether a call will come in the next half hour, two hours, or week. "Can I go to lunch," the person may question, "or do I need to sit here and wait?"

Lack of clarity can also come across as an avoidance tactic. To be credible, we need to be specific about time and about the nature of the task to be accomplished.

To do what we say we will do, in a timely fashion, builds trust. People who can be counted to follow through with what they say they will do are considered invaluable.

The suggestion of first concentrating on the problem rather than the solution may sound counterintuitive.

Admit Error and Apologize

If the foundation is wrong, we may have to undo all our work and begin from scratch. Depending on how far into a project we are, this can be quite painful and expensive. We must first recognize that we have been wrong before we can make things right.

If we notice that the concrete foundation for the structure we are building is faulty, we can close our eyes and continue work at our own peril. As painful as it may seem, the sooner we recognize our mistake and make the necessary expenditures to break up and remove the concrete so we can start over, the better off we will be.

Sometimes, we become overinvested in an idea. It may be as hard to admit we are wrong as it is to break up that concrete. People who are willing to admit their mistakes are more likely to be considered trustworthy.

A proper apology is extremely convincing. So is sharing a new interpersonal skills goal. If we have been critical in the past, it helps to let people know we will be working to eliminate that negative trait.

To be genuine, an apology must not come across as a justification for what we have done wrong. A true apology is also accompanied, when possible, by an offer to make restitution. Furthermore, a sincere apology implies a willingness to make the appropriate changes commensurate with the wrong that has been done. When it is warranted, I like the idea of asking the person who has been offended, "Will you accept my apology?"

When someone expresses regret yet makes little effort to change, it is hardly an apology. As powerful as an apology can be, when an individual rescinds it by word or deed, it would have been better if no regrets had been offered. For example, in cases of domestic violence (physical or verbal) it is not uncommon for the aggressor to be contrite after beating his wife. By the next day, he may have begun to minimize the damage, start to blame her, and not long thereafter begin striking her again. Domestic violence is a very serious matter that requires professional help.

But returning to the general topic of apologies, a person who is willing to accept an apology and forgive another is, likewise, in a better position than one who is not. It is difficult to trust a person who will not acknowledge a sincere apology accompanied by behavioral change. An individual who has truly forgiven another does not continually remind the other of that fact. Some comments and deeds are so hurtful, however, that it may take time before a person can truly feel free of the associated pain.

Value Others and Oneself

Everyone brings *inputs* (or "contributions," such as a person's job, education, skills, or efforts) into a relationship. People put a value on each other's inputs. The best way of preserving the value of our own contributions is by valuing the contributions of others. The value placed on a person's *time* is a good proxy for power, which helps explain why quality time spent with people can be so meaningful.[19]

Conflict may arise when other people's assets are not valued. One young woman, a college graduate, may look at her formal education as an asset. A more seasoned individual might look at her life experiences. Neither may value the other's assets. Both may compete for privileges or status based on their perceived contributions. Instead, they would be better off by acknowledging each other's strengths.

For some people, it is very hard to say something kind about another. "I shouldn't have to say it," they reason, "because my actions should show my positive feelings." Others have trouble accepting the sincerity of affirming comments.

Part of healthy interpersonal relationships is being able to both offer and accept positive comments: "Thanks. I appreciate your kind words. They made my day."

Use Humor Effectively

Humor, when properly directed, can help break up tension and make us more effective negotiators.[20] It helps if the humor is clever; it makes light of the situation or ourselves, but never the

Trustworthiness plays a huge role in successful negotiation. Dependability, honesty, and consistency are all part of trustworthiness.

other party; it does not involve potentially offensive ideas or language; and the timing is right. Some of the most effective humor is subtle, and we often arrive at it by accident. Humor may involve telling about life events that were embarrassing at the time but that show we are human. Effective humor communicates to others that we are willing to take ourselves lightly. Humor, of course, can do more harm than good when it is not used appropriately. Sometimes people think they are quite funny when they are not.

Be Flexible in terms of a Negotiation Approach

Not everyone finds the interest-based concept easy to swallow. A little caution, if not cynicism, may well be necessary. While we can attempt to model effective negotiation strategies when dealing with others, at times we may have to resort to a more traditional approach. Research has demonstrated that those who prefer mutually productive tactics are considered more credible negotiators when it is known that they are willing to stand firm, if necessary.

For instance, Daniela, a relatively new executive, had heard of the obstinate reputation developed by John, one of the assistants—although she had never encountered any difficulties with him. Daniela approached John one day and found him sitting with his feet up on a table, reading a magazine. She apologized for disturbing him, assuming that perhaps this might have been his break period.

"John, when you have time, could you please pick up some supplies for me?" Daniela asked politely.

John answered rather curtly, "Right now?"

Daniela, refusing to be intimidated, responded, "Well . . . Wow! That would work great for me. Thanks!" John continued to show difficult behaviors with other individuals but never again showed Daniela any discourtesy. I am not suggesting that Daniela took the best approach available, but it served her well on that occasion.

Show Patience

Effective negotiation frequently calls for a great amount of patience. Logic is not the only thing that prevails in bargaining efforts. Allowing other people, as well as ourselves, the time to work out problems is vital.

Avoiding the appearance of wanting something too much is related to patience. When we become overly narrow as to the result we will accept, we put ourselves at a negotiating disadvantage.

So it was when my wife and I bought our first home. We were so openly delighted with it that we lost an opportunity to bargain much over price. Of course, there is a balance between being desperate and playing hard to get, neither of which is very helpful.

Separate Problems from Self-Worth

Without a doubt, it is a mistake to permit an issue to become intermixed with our self-worth. It is ineffective and manipulative, for instance, to imply that disagreement with our ideas is equivalent to a vote of no confidence in us. Such an approach will sooner or later make us feel rejected.

While we often have a great need to share feelings with those who can be supportive, we ought to choose such confidants with care. People who tend to see matters from our perspective may not be doing us any favors.

Individuals who feel validated elsewhere sometimes put less effort into improving failing relationships. A healthy relationship is one in which the listener can help identify when the speaker may have contributed to the problem. We all need people who can help us discern our blind spots.

Prepare Carefully

When a person is willing to spend a little time comparison shopping, often the same product or service can be found for vastly different prices. Also, it helps to gather factual information that can be shared in a spirit of discovery, rather than one of superiority. Parties can even seek out the facts together.

Preparation entails understanding the situation and the personalities involved as much as possible. An effective way to prepare for difficult or emotionally charged encounters is to role-play ahead of time. Taking the role of the party with the perspective opposite the one we hold can be particularly enlightening.

Avoid Threats and Manipulative Tactics

Threats of consequences directed towards ourselves or others hamper our ability to negotiate. Any type of threat can greatly undermine our long-term negotiating ability. This is particularly so when the threat is not carried out. Furthermore, threats do not engender trust or liking.

Even inconsequential threats can be annoying. At a family game, one player repeatedly threatened to quit. After a half dozen threats, his mother told him, "The first time you threatened, I was concerned. By the last threat, I was just ready for you to quit and let the rest of us enjoy the game."

The greater the potential consequence of a threat, the larger the possible damage to the relationship. That is why threats to divorce or separate are so harmful to a marriage. The spouse who is threatened begins to disassociate psychologically from the other. The message given to the threatened spouse is that the marriage is not that important.

Some threats—as well as verbal or emotional abuse, intimidation, harassment, disruptive behavior, and bullying—may be considered part of workplace violence.[21]

Avoid Generalizations, Name Calling, and Labels

Vague or broad statements, generalizations, insults, or labels—such as selfish, inconsiderate, overbearing, and racist, to name a few—do nothing to facilitate mutual understanding. All of these expressions have a certain sense of fatality, almost like saying a person is tall or short—not something that can be changed. In contrast, talking about specific events behind these generalizations and labels opens the door to improving communication and solving challenges. A wife's complaint that her husband is lazy is likely to place him on the defensive. A more specific request for him to help the children with their homework, in contrast, is likely to be received in a more positive light and to promote dialogue.

Calling someone by a label, even when the person identifies with it (e.g., a person's nationality), can be offensive, depending on the tone and context. A more subtle—but still ineffective—way of labeling is describing our own perspective as belonging to a desirable category (e.g., a particularly cherished philosophy, principle, belief, or status group) while assigning another person's perspective to a less desirable category.

Parties also look for ways to enlist even theoretical supporters of their views. They may attempt to inflate the importance of their opinions with such statements as, "*Everyone* else agrees with me when I say . . ." Or they may attribute their words to a higher source of authority, such as a boss, an author, or another respected person. Individuals sometimes discount the opinion of others by the way they refer to their own experience: "In my twenty years with this organization, I have never encountered any problems with . . ." Once again, the tone and context of a conversation may make some of these statements appropriate in one circumstance and not in another. People may resort to dysfunctional tactics when the force of their arguments does not stand on its own merits.

Avoid Distorted Mirroring

People involved in highly charged conflicts frequently try to ridicule their contenders by distorting or exaggerating what has been said. I call this *distorted mirroring*. For instance, a person may inaccurately mirror a comment by saying, "So you are telling me that you *never* want me to go fishing again"; "I get it—you're the *only* one who does any work around here"; or "It seems that you are *always* upset these days." Likewise, it can be quite hurtful to say, "You used to be [something positive], but now you're [something negative]."

CONFRONTING PEOPLE AND SITUATIONS

People may avoid acting for fear of failure. Those who have overcome difficult obstacles in the past often gain the confidence to try to resolve new challenges. Both failure and success can transform into either a vicious or a positive cycle. Modern theories suggest that self-esteem is strengthened when people face rather than avoid challenges.[22] The following steps can be adapted to a particular situation in order to confront differences (these points summarize much of what has been said):

1. *Make psychological contact.* By speaking about an *unrelated* subject that is of interest to both, a positive psychological connection is built in which mutual validation takes place. It is important, before tackling a challenging issue, to remember what things we have in common with one another. I suggest that we do this until we can relax enough to step back a

To be genuine, an apology must not come across as a justification for what we have done wrong.

little from the negative feelings we may be experiencing. In some cases, this may take a long time. In effect, we want to both see the other person as human and be seen as human.

2. *Introduce the idea that there is an important subject you wish to discuss.* Say something like "Changing subjects a bit, there is something I have been meaning to discuss with you for a while."

3. *Let the other person know something you value about him or her.* "Before getting right into the topic, I want to tell you how much I admire your ability to know each of the employees in the whole department by name." Hopefully, goodwill deposits have been made all along. Make sure the trait you choose to mention (as something you value in the other individual) is *not* related to the troubling issue you will bring up. What you are doing here is separating the issue at hand, as well as the potential negativity of the challenge, from the personalities.

4. *Briefly introduce the topic, but let the other individual speak first.* The key here is *brevity*. Let the other person know you wish to hear from him or her first and that later on you will share your feelings. You may also wish to bring up the topic in a way that makes it clear you are both fighting together against the challenge, rather than against each other: "We've both agreed that our finances are tight. So, I am concerned about purchasing a car right now." You can slow your speech pattern, inviting the other individual to interrupt you before you finish the sentence. At this point, the focus needs to be on listening and, if needed, taking notes. Encourage the other person to speak. Some of what the other person has to say may sound somewhat abrasive or hurtful at first. Make every effort to avoid becoming defensive. Try to make out the needs and fears behind the other person's position.

5. *Attempt to show understanding.* Without being cynical, pouting, or using other dysfunctional conversational techniques, tentatively let the other individual know what you think you have understood.

6. *Present your interests and fears.* After you have made it clear that you understand the challenges as presented by the other individual, make your interests and fears clear.

7. *Look for sustainable solutions.* Look for solutions that will be good for both of you in the long run. Do not permit yourself to take the position of either victim or aggressor. Keep insisting on a

solution that will meet the needs of both of you, else you might be revisiting the challenge sooner than you expected.

Involving a Third Party

Differences in power, personality, or self-esteem among the participants in a disagreement may require the participation of a mediator. For instance, one volunteer leader had resorted to bullying and implied threats to get his way. "I would have gladly tried to find a way to help this leader achieve his goals," another volunteer explained through her tears. "But now I'm so sensitized, I'm afraid of talking to him."

Telling people to work out their troubles on their own, grow up, or shake hands and get along may work occasionally, but most of the time the conflict will be sent underground only to resurface later in more destructive ways. One option is to allow individuals to meet with a third party, or mediator, to assist them in resolving their differences.

Choosing a Mediator

All things being equal, an outside third party has a greater chance of succeeding than a family member, friend, co-worker, or other insider. Such persons may be part of the problem, or they may be perceived as favoring one of the disputants. Individuals may be hesitant to share confidential information with insiders.

If the third party is in a position of power, such as a supervisor or a parent, the mediator's role becomes more thorny. People who hold power often tend to become overly directive, taking more of an arbiter's role and forcing a decision upon the disputants.

A mediator should treat issues with confidentiality, with some exceptions (e.g., sexual harassment in the workplace). All parties should be informed of exceptions to the confidentiality rule ahead of time. Any sharing of information based on the exceptions needs to be done on a need-to-know basis to minimize potential harm to one or both of the parties.

Many conflicts involve personal issues that may be embarrassing. People are less hesitant to speak out when assured

Labels do little to facilitate mutual understanding. They have a certain sense of fatality, almost like saying that a person is tall or short—not something that can be changed.

of confidentiality. For this reason, mediators of organizational conflicts should permit the parties to decide exactly what it is that they will share with management. I do not believe that mediators should submit reports or summaries to the organizations that engage them.

Researchers have found that, in some instances, mediation works best when the third party is able to change roles and, in the event mediation fails, become an arbiter. On the plus side, parties may put their best feet forward and try hard to resolve issues. Unfortunately, while some mediators may be able to play both roles without manipulating the situation, the road is left wide open for abuse of power. People may feel coerced and refuse to trust a mediator when what is said in confidence might be used against them later. More importantly, such a strategy discounts the third party's efforts to explain that the role of the mediator is to *facilitate conversation*, not to decide who is right.

The conflict management process is more apt to succeed if individuals have respect for the mediator's integrity, impartiality, and ability. Esteem for the mediator is important, so parties will be on their *best behavior*, a key element in successful negotiation. Although not always the case, over-familiarity with an inside mediator may also negate this "best behavior" effect.

Mediation Styles

A mediation style's efficacy depends on the situation and the personalities and preferences of the parties involved. One variable is the degree to which the mediator controls the process. While some mediators are capable of using multiple approaches, let us discuss some of the extremes.

Mediator-Directed Approach

At one extreme, we find mediators who will listen to the interested parties and help them find a solution. Generally, in order to avoid giving the impression of favoritism, these mediators will meet with both parties at once in a joint session.

The mediator asks one of the parties to explain his or her perspective while the other individual listens, and then the roles are reversed, with the other person doing the talking while the first one listens. The parties face the mediator rather than each other.

Some of these mediators are especially talented in perceiving solutions the parties themselves have not seen. Such an approach is suited to situations in which (1) resolutions to specific challenges are more important than the ongoing relationship between the parties and (2) the parties do not interact on a regular basis. The disputants' emotional investment is generally less intense. One disadvantage is that the mediator can favor one person over another, despite the suggestion that mediators are neutral parties. Another disadvantage is that conflicts that on the surface appear to be about substantive matters, often have large interpersonal components.

Party-Directed Mediation

At the opposite extreme, we have Party-Directed Mediation, an approach that seeks to empower individuals by offering contenders negotiating skills that will help them manage the present contention, as well as improve their ability to deal with future conflict. The two most important elements of Party-Directed Mediation are (1) a separate meeting between the mediator and each of the parties *prior* to the joint session (in what is called a pre-caucus or pre-mediation) and (2) a joint session in which parties face and speak directly to each other rather than through the mediator.

During the pre-caucus, the third party mostly listens empathically. But there is also time for the mediator to help parties prepare to become more effective negotiators and to determine if it is psychologically safe to bring contenders together in a joint session.

More harm than good can take place when contenders who are not ready for the joint session use it as safe ground on which to insult each other. In some instances, the pre-caucuses may be so effective that parties go on to resolve their conflict without further assistance from the mediator.

During the joint session, the disputants sit directly across from each other and address each other with very little interference from the third party. In fact, the mediator sits at a substantial distance from the parties to underscore the fact that the conversation belongs to the disputants.

Issues of mediator neutrality become a little less relevant, because the contenders control how challenges are overcome. In Party-Directed Mediation, the whole process underscores the fact that the mediator is there to promote effective conversation, negotiation, and mutual understanding—not to come up with the solution.

Party-Directed Mediation requires more up-front preparation and in the short run is often more time consuming than a more traditional style. The concept behind Party-Directed Mediation, then, is that, to the degree that the case lends itself to it and the individuals wish to spend the time to acquire the skills to become more effective negotiators, they can be empowered to do so. When the conflict involves deep-seated antagonisms, and when the participants will continue to live or work together, interacting on a regular basis, Party-Directed Mediation can be especially effective.

SUMMARY

We negotiate our way through life. While there are no easy answers that will fit every occasion for negotiation, there are some important principles that will help us become more effective. Negotiation calls for a careful understanding of the issues involved, the ability to break down big issues into smaller ones, caring about the needs of others as well as our own, and focusing first on the problem rather than the solution, to name but a few.

Interpersonal communication skills affect our success with people and can help us avoid or defuse conflict. Strokes tend to validate a person's sense of worth. Most people expect a stroking exchange, or ritual, before getting down to business. Being able to hold a conversation—a key interpersonal relationship skill—is based on the participants' ability to give and take.

Everyone brings a set of inputs or assets to a job or relationship. Little trouble may occur as long as there is agreement about the value of these assets. Individuals who want to preserve the benefits of their contributions, whether personal or organizational, need to value the assets held by others.

Creative negotiation differs enough from the way we may have reacted to challenges in the past that it is not a matter of simply reading a book in order to successfully incorporate the needed skills into our lives. It will be necessary to make a proactive effort to improve in these areas over time.

I keep these thoughts alive from day to day by reading good books, listening to programs, and attending seminars related to this topic. There are many excellent books on interpersonal negotiation, listening skills, conflict management, interpersonal communications, and so on. Your local library may offer some real treasures. You may wish to keep notes on what you read, as

One way of being tentative is slowing down our speech pattern, inviting the other to interrupt us before we even finish the sentence.

well as your day-to-day observations about your own interactions and those occurring around you.

At the core of creative negotiation is the idea that it is possible for all parties to get more of what they need by working together.

The foundation of effective problem solving is understanding the challenge. Otherwise, it is all too easy to build solutions on a false foundation. After understanding is achieved, creative negotiation involves looking for the hidden opportunities presented by challenges.

There are two contrasting third-party styles: mediator-directed negotiation and Party-Directed Mediation. The latter is particularly well suited for the resolution of deep-seated interpersonal conflict when individuals will continue to live or work together after the mediator leaves.

As I grow older, *doing* right has become more important to me than *being* right (in the sense of winning). There is a great amount of satisfaction in giving a *soft answer*.[23] This is a journey. One embarks on it knowing the challenge is so difficult that one can never truly say, "I have arrived."

As we practice creative negotiation, faith in our ability to turn challenges into opportunities will increase. This self-confidence will help us focus on problem solving and reduce the chances of falling back on contentious, unproductive negotiation.

CHAPTER 4—REFERENCES

1. The story is attributed to Mary Parker Follett by D. M. Kolb (1995). In The love for three oranges, or: What did we miss about Ms. Follett in the library? *Negotiation Journal*, 11, 339.
2. Berne, E. (1964). *Games people play: The psychology of human relationships*. New York: Grove Press.
3. Yupanqui, A. (Performer) (2000). Bagualas y Caminos. In *Colección aniversario feria del disco 44 años folclore argentino: Versiones originales*. (CD Recording No. 2–499505). Santiago, Chile: Sony Music Entertainment Chile.
4. Berne (1964) discusses stroke intensity, cultural differences, and dysfunctional communication patterns in *Games people play: The psychology of human relationships*. New York: Grove Press.
5. Nichols, M. P. (1995). *The lost art of listening: How learning to listen can improve relationships* (p. 14). New York: Guilford Press.
6. Elgin, S. Haden (1983). *More on the gentle art of verbal self-defense*. Englewood Cliffs, NJ: Prentice Hall.
7. Dobson, M. (1991, July). *How to solve communication problems*. Fred Pryor Seminar, Stockton, CA.
8. Elgin, S. Haden (1983). *More on the gentle art of verbal self-defense*. Englewood Cliffs, NJ: Prentice Hall.
9. Fisher, R., & Ury, W. (1981). *Getting to yes: Negotiating agreement without giving in*. New York: Penguin.
10. Rothman, J. (1997). *Resolving identity-based conflict in nations, organizations, and communities* (pp. xii–xiii). San Francisco: Jossey-Bass.
11. Covey, S. (1989). *Seven habits of highly effective people*. New York: Simon & Schuster. This quote is often attributed to St. Francis of Assisi.
12. Rackham, N. (1999). The behavior of successful negotiators. In R. J. Lewicki, D. M. Saunders, & J. W. Minton (Eds.), *Negotiation: Readings, exercises, and cases* (3rd ed.) (p. 348). Burr Ridge, IL: Irwin.
13. Patterson, K., Grenny, J., McMillan, R., & Switzler, A. (2002). *Crucial conversations: Tools for talking when stakes are high*. New York: McGraw-Hill.

14. Swann, W. B., Jr. (1996). *Self-traps: The elusive quest for higher self-esteem* (p. 47). New York: W. H. Freeman.
15. Sloane, A. A., & Witney, F. (1981). *Labor relations* (4th ed.) (pp. 205–206). Englewood Cliffs, NJ: Prentice Hall.
16. Peterson, W. H. (1991, April). Boulwarism: Ideas have consequences [Electronic version]. *The freeman: Ideas on liberty*, 4. Retrieved July 31, 2008, from http://www.fee.org/Publications/the-Freeman/ article.asp?aid=798
17. Rackham, N. (1999). The behavior of successful negotiators. In R. J. Lewicki, D. M. Saunders, & J. W. Minton (Eds.), *Negotiation: Readings, exercises, and cases* (3rd ed.) (p. 347). Burr Ridge, IL: Irwin.
18. Sperber, B. (1983). Fail-safe business negotiating: Strategies and tactics for success. In R. J. Lewicki, D. M. Saunders, & J. W. Minton (Eds.). (1993). *Negotiation: Readings, exercises, and cases* (2nd ed.) (p. 173). Burr Ridge, IL: Irwin.
19. Brown, R. (1986). *Social psychology: The second edition*. New York: Free Press.
20. Forester, J. (2003). Critical moments in negotiations: On humor, recognition, and hope, or, "Writing's easy," Gene Fowler said, "All you do is stare at a blank sheet of paper until drops of blood form on your forehead." Retrieved July 31, 2008, from CU People, Cornell University website: http://people.cornell.edu/pages/jff1/Pon.htm
21. See USDA (http://www.usda.gov/news/pubs/violence/wpv.htm), FBI (http://www.fbi.gov/publications/violence.pdf), and OSHA (http://www.osha.gov/OshDoc/data_General_Facts/factsheet-workplace-violence.pdf) factsheets. 29 September 2008.
22. Bednar, R. L., Wells, M. G., & Peterson, S. R. (1989). *Self-esteem: Paradoxes and innovations in clinical theory and practice*. Washington, DC: American Psychological Association.
23. Proverbs 15:1 KJV, "A soft answer turneth away wrath."

Part III – Joint Session

5
Mediating the Joint Session

The mediator has now listened to and coached the parties and has determined they are ready for the joint session. No matter how well disputants have been prepared through the pre-caucus, they are likely to be anxious at the idea of confronting their adversary. Along the way, each contender has had to traverse a thorny path—and deal with feelings of discouragement, fear, and frustration.

The joint session should take place in a location that is neutral and private, without phones or other interruptions. A comfortable setting will also help reduce tensions. Furthermore, it is vital to allow sufficient time for the parties to fully engage in dialogue.

We will examine matters related to:
- Seating arrangement
- Opening the mediation
- Getting the dialogue started
- Agreements

SEATING ARRANGEMENT

A mechanical aspect that is extremely influential in Party-Directed Mediation is the seating arrangement: the two parties sit facing each other in a position that promotes good *eye contact*.

Eye contact tends to increase aggression among disputants. Yet, once parties have begun the trajectory towards reconciliation through the process of pre-caucusing, eye contact can help soften feelings of aversion. This is powerful medicine for mutual understanding.

Eye contact serves to remind parties of the positive affect they may have felt for each other at one time, though they have now relegated such feelings to their subconscious. They are ready to begin to see each other as real people.

One option is to seat the parties at a table. This allows for a personal safety zone with the additional comfort of a physical barrier between the contenders. The ideal is a long rectangular table. The contenders sit across from each other at one end of the table while the third party sits at the other end, far away from them (Figure 5–1, and Chapter 5 opening photo).

Another alternative is to use a set of comfortable armchairs and do without the table. The chairs should be placed at a distance that permits sufficient personal space between the disputants. I usually place the chairs somewhat farther apart than is probably required. Parties often choose to move closer on their own. The neutral party may, at times, be surprised by the proximity chosen by the disputants.

In Party-Directed Mediation, the mediator sits far enough away that the contenders must turn their heads if they wish to make eye contact with him or her. This way, it is not easy for the parties to check whether they have "scored points" or to enlist the mediator's support for an argument. If parties do turn towards the mediator, the intermediary can encourage them to address each other instead. This seating arrangement—in which parties face each other rather than the mediator—underscores the message that parties are there to *talk to each other*. It constitutes the second pillar of the Party-Directed Mediation approach (the pre-caucus being the first).

In more traditional mediation settings, disputants sit facing the third party rather than each other (photo p. ix). The not-so-subtle message is that the third party will resolve their disagreements.

It will not hurt to mention the seating mechanics before participants arrive at the joint session, as some parties are accustomed to facing the mediator.

The day of the joint session, one of the parties will likely arrive before the other. The mediator may invite individuals to sit down and make themselves comfortable, but remains standing until both contenders have arrived. This detail sends a clear message to the party who is last to arrive—that the joint session has not started without him or her.[1]

FIGURE 5–1

Seating arrangement during the joint session. The mediator sits at the far end of the table.

Effective Party-Directed Mediation requires a belief in the inherent goodness of people as well as confidence in the process itself.

OPENING THE MEDIATION

If permission to do so has been obtained, the mediator may wish to share the positive aspects raised about each contender by the other party during the pre-caucuses. Taking time to do so helps break the ice and reminds the disputants that there is hope.

This is *not* the time, however, to ask the individuals to share these positive comments about each other. Parties are seldom psychologically ready to begin with affirmations. During the joint session, the mediator may underscore transformative comments that come up naturally but generally does not ask contenders to share such validating comments. Doing so weakens the value of transformative discourse. It may appear as if the mediator is (1) manipulating contenders to say something nice about each other or (2) discounting the many unresolved issues that have brought the parties into the dispute. Instead, parties will make their own validating comments when they are ready and without any prompting.

The mediator may wish to remind individuals that they can take breaks, ask to caucus with the mediator, or take time to call a stakeholder at any time. My experience is that pre-caucusing greatly reduces the need for such interruptions.

GETTING THE DIALOGUE STARTED

After any additional introductory comments from the mediator, the time has come to turn over the reins to the contenders. Mediators can explain that they will bring up topics—from the lists developed during the pre-caucuses—and ask one party or the other to expand on the subjects and thus begin a dialogue.

Although the mediator may pick the first topic, one option is to permit the parties to continue the conversation from there. When disputants are allowed to bring up their own topics, the mediator ensures all issues are exhausted before the joint session is over. The mediator will easily note when parties move evasively from one subject to another as a defensive or offensive tactic.

When the parties are doing a good job of managing their own topics and coming up with sustainable resolutions, mediators have little to contribute other than the comfort of their presence. Mediators also note any agreements or concerns that might need to be revisited, such as patterns of troubling interaction between the parties.

Generally, I prefer to begin with topics that appear simpler and more substantive, rather than complicated emotive or affective issues.

At times, an individual will have expressed a great desire to apologize to the other contender about some matter, and this also may be a good starting place. What is essential is to give the parties a balanced opportunity to speak and address issues of importance to them.

Successfully dealing with any issue under contention (e.g., the offering and accepting of an apology or reaching an agreement on how to deal with a future difficulty) can be very energizing and give the participants the confidence they need to face other challenges.

The mediator does not present or summarize the difficulty itself, but only triggers a memory: "Mei, could you please explain to Hua the matter of the letter you found?"

Mei shares with Hua her concerns about the letter and gives Hua the opportunity to react. When both have finished the conversation on this matter, the mediator may invite Hua to tell Mei about a specific worry brought up in her pre-caucus.

While the ideal in Party-Directed Mediation is for the contenders to speak to each other with as little interruption as possible, there are times when the mediator must intervene and help parties overcome dysfunctional communication styles. Or deal with power imbalances.

The seriousness of communication infractions, as well as differences in mediators' styles, will dictate the frequency and degree of mediator intervention. Time spent role-playing and developing negotiating skills in the pre-caucus will result in a smoother joint session.

Parties will share positive, validating comments about the other contender when they are ready and without any prompting.

At times, it may be tempting, during a joint session, to ignore an area of concern brought up during a pre-caucus. Shortly after the first edition of this book was published, I was conducting a seminar. One of the participants raised his hand and mentioned that there happened to be two individuals attending the workshop who were involved in a long-term contentious relationship at work. Class participants requested that we incorporate the case into the seminar. The contenders, Keith and James, agreed to have the workshop participants play the role of the mediator with my help.

James was sent out of the conference room while the seminar participants and I listened to Keith. Once the pre-caucus was concluded, we reversed the process.

During his pre-caucus, Keith explained that James had cheated his employer by adding two hours of overtime to his timecard. Keith, as a way of showing what an honorable person he was, told us he had never mentioned any of this overtime mischief to his boss.

The joint session proceeded very well, with both contenders speaking to each other and solving the difficulties that had been raised. The parties were about ready to finish, so I had to decide whether to have them discuss the honesty issue. Inspired by Robert Baruch Bush and Joseph Folger's *transformative* approach to helping contenders apologize or share feelings of regard for each other and the authors' belief that it is more important to have parties come to a better understanding of each other than merely find short-lived agreement,[2] I ventured to bring up the subject.

I was taking a huge risk. James explained to Keith that he had worked the two extra hours at a different location before Keith arrived. Had they not cleared up this issue of integrity, it is doubtful their newfound harmony would have endured.

It is good to talk about the past. It can help unravel patterns of conflict and provide transformative opportunities. Without understanding the past, it is hard to prepare for the future. At some point, however, the focus must turn to dealing with future behaviors rather than nursing past injuries. Party-Directed Mediation normally permits disputants to naturally transition from speaking about past behaviors to discussing mutual understanding and required changes for the future.

Agreements

An essential aspect of becoming a good negotiator is to truly understand the challenge being faced. The mediator needs to be especially sensitive to signs that one or both parties are capitulating just to move on. Or out of the mistaken idea that they are pleasing the mediator. Such behaviors can often be noted in the tone of voice and body language of the contenders, but not always. Mediators may ask parties some pointed questions about their agreements, encourage specificity, and question agreements

The mediator needs to be especially sensitive to signs that one or both parties are capitulating just to move on.

that seem weak and unlikely to endure. When dealing with more difficult challenges, part of the role of the mediator is to keep the parties from becoming overly discouraged. This can be be done, at times, by talking about the progress that has already been achieved.

In Chapter 4, we referred to the Harvard negotiation approach introduced by Roger Fisher and William Ury in their seminal work, *Getting to Yes*.[3] They suggested that by concentrating on their *positions* (i.e., proposed solutions) parties accentuate their disagreements. When, instead, people focus on the *needs* and *fears* behind their stated positions, they are more likely to find mutually acceptable solutions that address the needs of all involved. Resolutions based on this approach are not only more acceptable to the parties, but they are also more likely to be long-lasting. When the light goes on, disputants realize that it is not a

The interpersonal negotiation skills gained are exactly those that will help individuals deal with future conflicts without the aid of a mediator.

zero-sum game in which one person must lose for the other to win.

Mediators should not rush to move participants from (1) their position statements and explanations of their fears and needs to (2) problem resolution. It is vital to first truly understand the nature of the difficulty being faced. I find that allowing parties to temporarily maintain their initial positions permits each to feel understood and to retain a sense of control and ownership of the process. At some point, it helps to have each party explain, to the best of his or her ability, the position of the other.

Contenders often discount each other by refusing to acknowledge that the other party has a position worth considering. Years ago, I conducted a communication seminar hosted by a large enterprise. Without realizing it, I selected two individuals to play roles in a hypothetical conflict that turned out to be all too real. The mediation scenario used a more traditional approach without any pre-caucusing.

The head cook was asked to recognize, in his own words, that the field foreman needed meals to arrive in a timely fashion. Yet the cook could not focus away from the fact that meals were being wasted each day.

"You see, it's his fault because . . ."

"We are not talking about faults at this time. Instead, we just want you to state the perspective of the field foreman," I interrupted.

"Well, you see, he thinks he can get away with . . ."

The cook had to be repeatedly stopped. It was difficult for him to even state (and thus validate) the other party's position.

Once he stopped evading the process and described the position of the foreman, and the foreman did the same for the cook, they quickly came to a clever solution that benefited everyone and saved the corporation money.

An intermediate step—one that might have helped smooth the transition between a solely internal focus and stating the other party's position—would have been to encourage the parties to ask nonjudgmental, fact-finding questions of each other.[4] An agreement was made that the field foreman would call the cook with an exact meal count for the day. Because the cook had an exact count, he had fewer meals to cook and thus could produce them faster.

A structured way to clarify positions versus needs is outlined in Sidebar 5–1.

Sometimes, negotiation is attempted, but people's needs are incompatible. This may be especially so when no distinction can be made between needs and positions. When negotiation has failed—for whatever reasons—mandate may require the dispute to be resolved through arbitration or the courts. Bush and Folger

Sidebar 5–1

Positions vs. Needs in Conflict Management

1. Parties divide a paper, chalkboard, or wipe board into four sections as shown below.
2. Parties seek to understand and record each other's *position* (i.e., stance).
3. Parties are free to restate, modify, or further clarify their own positions at any time.
4. Parties then seek to understand and record each other's *needs*. Taking the time to ask effective questions of each other is an important part of reaching such understanding.
5. Parties brainstorm ways of fulfilling the needs of both contenders. In some cases, solutions may not be obvious at once, and disputants may want to sleep on it. For brainstorming to be effective, possible solutions should not be evaluated at the time, and even outlandish and extreme solutions need to be entertained. Only later, in Steps 6 and 7, are these solutions examined for positive and negative factors.
6. Parties are asked to resist devising resolutions in which they no longer are required to interact with each other. To avoid each other takes little creativity and is seldom the best solution. Instead, participants need to seek creative, synergetic solutions.
7. Tentative co-authored agreements are evaluated and refined in light of potential obstacles.
8. Agreements—including a possible co-authored position—are recorded.
9. Parties consent to evaluate results at predetermined intervals.
10. Agreements are fine-tuned as needed and other challenges are addressed together.

Position A	Position B
• Need A-1 • Need A-2	• Need B-1 • Need B-2 • Need B-3
• Fear A-1 • Fear A-2	• Fear B-1

suggest, however, that if a door is left open for continued conversation, and if individual empowerment and mutual recognition have taken place, then mediation was not a failure. Much more of a failure, they convincingly argue, is for a mediator to be so focused on having parties come to an agreement that the resolution is forced, reducing the chances that it will be long-lasting.[5]

John Forester suggests that even when there are deep value differences, and basic needs are incompatible, parties may come to an understanding on peripheral issues. People may agree to disagree while recognizing some common goals.[6] For instance, each spouse may have profound religious convictions that are incompatible with those of the other (e.g., values they wish to instill in their children) yet come to an accord on how to live with such variances in such a way as to minimize harm to their offspring.

Summary

Party-Directed Mediation requires a certain belief in the inherent goodness of people, as well as confidence in the process itself. In this chapter, we considered the importance of the seating layout for the joint session, one wherein parties can focus on each other rather than on the third party. The seating arrangement underscores the contenders' responsibility for finding a viable solution.

Disputants can put to use the negotiation skills they acquired during the pre-caucus. In the joint session, the mediator or the parties may introduce topics of conversation. The key is that all the topics are discussed, even sensitive ones. If the pre-caucuses have been effective, the mediator's interruptions may be minimal, with parties taking responsibility for dealing with the past as well as making decisions about future behaviors. The skills gained through the process will help individuals deal with future conflicts without the aid of a mediator.

Finally, we considered one way to implement Fisher and Ury's negotiation approach, in which individuals separate their positions from their needs.

Chapter 5—References

1. Dana, D. (2000). *Conflict resolution* (p. 69). New York: McGraw-Hill.
2. Bush, R. A. Baruch & Folger, J. P. (1994). *The promise of mediation: Responding to conflict through empowerment and recognition.* San Francisco: Jossey-Bass.
3. Fisher, R., & Ury, W. (1981). *Getting to yes: Negotiating agreement without giving in.* New York: Penguin.
4. Bodine, N. (2001, July). Founder and member of board of directors of the Workplace Institute (now Center for Collaborative Solutions), personal communication.
5. Bush, R. A. Baruch, & Folger, J. P. (1994). *The promise of mediation: Responding to conflict through empowerment and recognition.* San Francisco: Jossey-Bass.
6. Forester, J. (1999). Dealing with deep value differences: How can consensus building make a difference? In L. Susskind, S. McKearnan, & J. Thomas-Larmer (Eds.), *The consensus building handbook.* Thousand Oaks, CA: Sage.

Part IV – Mediation Case Study

6

Introducing Nora and Rebecca

Nora

Rebecca

Nora, a microbiologist, and Rebecca, a chemist, have had a long-standing conflict. Both are degreed professionals employed by a medium-sized analytical laboratory near the California coastline. They occasionally need to work together on a project. Nora and Rebecca are co-workers supervised by Ken Matsushita, the laboratory manager. It was Matsushita who asked the author for help in resolving the conflict.

Over the years, the analytical lab has gained a reputation as an excellent employer. As a result, it has attracted some of the brightest in the field. A generally relaxed and collegial working atmosphere has prevailed at the lab. In recent years, with the downturn in the California economy, business has been sluggish. Some of the professional staff have been asked to pitch in with tasks formerly carried out by employees no longer working for the business.

Rebecca and Nora are extremely bright individuals who have become deeply invested in their conflict—one which has lasted more than twenty years. On a more personal note, both women are sports- and outdoor-oriented, which is what attracted them to this particular firm's location in the first place. Both have children of about the same age, and both have a passion for their chosen profession. They have much in common.

Rebecca is a people person. She is a close friend to all the other women in the lab, socializing with them outside of work hours. While Rebecca and Nora work at the same organizational level, Matsushita has given Rebecca the additional responsibility of collecting data from all the other lab professionals, including Nora, for a year-end report. Rebecca feels that no matter what approach she tries, Nora does not cooperate with her. She seems too wrapped up in her work to respond to Rebecca's requests. As a result, Rebecca has wasted much time trying to pry the information out of Nora.

On meeting Rebecca, we sense a person who is trying hard to keep emotion out of the interaction. Rebecca has been somewhat hurt by her past exchanges with Nora. She feels that Nora shouts at her. Rebecca points out that she is the only one Nora treats this way.

Nora is a task-oriented individual. She has been absorbed by her work and at first seems surprised at the mention of a dispute. Much of what Nora speaks of concerns how busy she is. Nora has so many ongoing projects that Matsushita has frequently assigned one or two people to assist her. Nora explains how the workload and the less-than-dependable help have made it difficult for her to respond to Rebecca's requests.

Like Rebecca, Nora has kept her emotions in check. There is a very light tone to most of her comments, and Nora speaks with a smile much of the time during her pre-caucuses. Only when Nora relates feeling left out of conversations among the other professional women in the lab does it become clear that she also has been hurt by her interactions with Rebecca. Nora has a deep need to avoid being at odds with others.

During their pre-caucuses, each woman explains that she wants to be treated with respect by the other, but that she is not looking for friendship.

The next five chapters include an annotated dialogue from Nora and Rebecca's mediation. Some of the facts surrounding their case have purposely been kept vague or altered to protect confidentiality. For the sake of brevity, conversations have been abridged, mostly by deleting repetitive comments.

The conference room utilized for the pre-caucuses, as well as the joint session, is quite comfortable and has no distractions other than some pleasing paintings of California's stunning coastline.

Although the text refers to only one mediator, in this case the third-party role was carried out by a mediation team that included the author. The intention here is not so much to analyze the effectiveness of the mediator interventions, but rather to invite readers to observe Party-Directed Mediation in action. Parties can do most of the talking and negotiating when they are allowed to do so.

It would be nice to rearrange the comments of the parties so they progress from one thought to another in a systematic way. But that would distort reality. Instead, the reader will often note that the discussion of a topic seems to be all but concluded when either Nora or Rebecca raises issues of concern again. One of the two might have finished describing her official stance on camera, but once the camera was turned off, she continued talking, sometimes really pouring her heart out. In a number of instances, the parties agreed to bring up an issue again, in front of the camera, so it could be properly captured.

As a third-party mediator, facilitator, or reader, you are likely to have varied reactions to Nora and Rebecca. These impressions probably will evolve as you join the pre-caucuses and then observe Rebecca and Nora during the joint session. Perhaps you will come to sympathize more with one than the other.

It is hoped that you will see the inherent good in both of these women as well as some of the challenges each has to face. Although we only allude to their background stories, each woman has had to overcome past abusive relationships.

Partly because of your own experiences, you may disagree with some of the analysis provided along with the dialogue. This last point deserves to be underscored: mediators *do* react to the individuals and *do* form impressions of them.

In traditional mediation, third parties wield much power, and their opinions and biases may greatly affect outcomes. What becomes clear through Party-Directed Mediation, however, is that when contenders have been adequately listened to by the mediator, they then become capable of dialoguing with reduced interference from the third party. And as a result, individuals build their own solutions and control the outcome.

7

Rebecca's First Pre-Caucus

The mediator begins by briefly explaining the philosophy and mechanics of Party-Directed Mediation.

MEDIATOR: Rebecca, it's a pleasure to have the opportunity to work with you. Last week, I mailed some reading materials for you to take a look at. I wanted to review just a couple of points and see if you have any questions. I'll meet with you first and listen with the idea of trying to understand the conflict from your perspective. [The mediator smiles frequently and speaks in a reassuring tone.]

REBECCA: OK. [Rebecca interjects several OKs as the mediator speaks and concludes each thought. The tone of her interjections express cooperation, understanding, and agreement.]

MEDIATOR: My first step is to understand you the way you wish to be understood. After listening to you, one of my jobs will be to prepare you to meet with Nora—when you feel ready. I want to stress that I'm not here to judge or decide who is right. I see my role as helping each of you by sharing tools and negotiation skills that will permit you to present your perspective in the best possible light, listen to each other, and hopefully solve this dispute. I'll be taking notes, so I can make sure I'm understanding you correctly. If you need to take a break at any time, just let me know. Do you have any questions?

REBECCA: Thanks for asking; not at the moment.

Searching for the Problem

MEDIATOR: OK, we're ready to begin. So, tell me, from your perspective . . . what has happened . . .

REBECCA: Obviously, I can only explain from my perspective. [Rebecca wants to appear cooperative, and shows insight. For every disagreement, there are at least two perspectives. This type of cooperation is elicited through the pre-caucus.]

MEDIATOR: Right. Exactly.

REBECCA: Do you want me to kind of outline the problem?

MEDIATOR: Right. Start there, and we can go into more detail as we need to.

REBECCA: Ken Matsushita, the analytical lab manager, delegated the completion of a year-end report to me. Each person in the team had to do his or her part, but it was my job to collect all that information and edit it into a coherent piece. [Rebecca seems calm and from time to time smiles and laughs a little as she goes into further detail. She seems to feel good about telling her side of the story.]

MEDIATOR: M-hm. [As Rebecca speaks, the mediator's positive minimal responses let her know he is listening.]

REBECCA: Nora had a lab tech working for her, to whom she delegated her portion of the writing. I hadn't received the report, so I spoke to her, left a couple of messages taped to her door, e-mailed her with a copy to Ken, and brought it up at staff conference. So, I felt I had given her ample notice that it needed to be done. We all have to do our part. I spent several days working on this and felt it was a reasonable request. So, that's the issue.

MEDIATOR: [The mediator finishes writing down some notes.] Still nothing has been done?

REBECCA:	No.
MEDIATOR:	OK.
REBECCA:	And this has been . . . easily a couple of months now.
MEDIATOR:	Is this an isolated instance, or are there others?
REBECCA:	There was another time when I needed her cooperation. I was helping Ken. When I spoke to her, she actually yelled at me and got very upset. And then I got upset. Don't shoot the messenger! I felt it was very unprofessional behavior that I didn't deserve. I just wanted to check it off my list. And so, that issue was turned over back for Ken to deal with. It's no one's highest priority, and maybe that's why it's not done. Ken has so much to do, and I just wanted to help. So he wouldn't have to worry about this also.

It takes about twelve minutes to come to some understanding of what was wrong, in very general terms, from Rebecca's perspective. When mediators let individuals get things off their chest, most parties can speak for a long time with very little prompting. Several factors might have contributed to Rebecca's reticence: the inhibiting presence of a camera; or a third party, who—despite his remarkable interpersonal skills—had limited exposure to the empathic listening approach.

But returning to the pre-caucus, a good way to test the waters and check if individuals have sufficiently unburdened their feelings is to ask people for the positive qualities of the other. Such a question is usually asked towards the end of the pre-caucus, after a person feels heard by the mediator. It seems an appropriate time to ask Rebecca, as she appears to be finished with her narrative.

Admirable Qualities of the Opposite Party

MEDIATOR:	So that we can look at the positive side as well—what are some positive things you admire in Nora?

REBECCA: [Her face shows some surprise.] I'm not sure what that has to do with an issue, or resolving an issue? We talked about a specific problem with a start, and hopefully, a finish at some time. I don't understand what positive or negative feelings towards Nora have to do with it.

Rebecca suggests that this is about *issues*, not about *feelings*. This might well be a clue to the mediator that despite Rebecca's calm narrative, she is far from being ready to meet with Nora.

MEDIATOR: In preparing to bring the two of you together—which is a goal of this process—we want this not to just be about the issues involved. Having mutual positive qualities brought out will help.
REBECCA: So, there's a technique that you're trying . . .
MEDIATOR: Yes. It may help to . . .
REBECCA: But, but from *my* position, I feel . . . I've done what I can to do my job. [Hopeless.] I've done what I can. I don't think there's going to be a response from Nora.
MEDIATOR: By having both of you meet together—not now, but when you're ready—some of these points may be brought up and discussed. Maybe we won't reach a solution. But maybe we will be able to. Considering positive attributes about each other may help us reach a positive resolution.

Rebecca listens intently. She seems absorbed in deep thought and unsure what to say. The mediator attempts to answer her concerns. Rather than assume Rebecca has nothing positive to say, the mediator feels that perhaps she has not given herself permission to see Nora in a positive light.

MEDIATOR: [Laughs gently.]
REBECCA: OK, this could happen. [Joyful tone matches the mediator's laughing.]
MEDIATOR: So, do you have any positive qualities you admire in Nora?

REBECCA: I don't really know Nora very well, personally. I know her as a colleague in the lab. So, I can't make any sort of comments on personal sort of things. I'm not really aware of them. Our work issues don't connect much, so I don't really interact with her on work issues. My only interactions with her are related to using the same equipment or sharing space and that sort of thing. I'm assuming that she does . . . just fine. She's been here for a long time and has a lot of experience and does a good job of helping her clients.

The mediator is now certain that Rebecca is not ready to allow positive feelings for Nora to surface. The first part of Rebecca's statement indicates her lack of personal knowledge about Nora. Later, we shall hear comments that show the opposite to be true. The second part of Rebecca's statement—"I'm assuming"—does not constitute a positive reflection about her contender. Her comments could do more harm than good in a joint session.

These kinds of responses tell the mediator there is a lot more to the story than what the first few minutes of the conversation have yielded. There surely must be other issues hidden behind the dispute narrative. Rebecca is not ready to validate anything about Nora.

The third party proceeds to elicit further comments from Rebecca about the conflict. He does so by reflecting on something Rebecca said earlier. The mediator's reflective comment serves to prime the pump and is picked up immediately by Rebecca.

REBECCA: Well, as I said, we've lost a lot of people . . . support staff . . . and now there are things around here that the professional staff have to take responsibility for, such as keeping lab areas clean, because we share . . . and that's an issue, if individuals don't see that as part of their responsibility. Just as important as other tasks.

Although the mediator encourages Rebecca to speak again about the conflict, her comments are few. At least for the moment, it seems there is nothing more to say. The lack of positive comments by Rebecca about her adversary should have been a warning. Thinking of a joint session is premature.

Preparing Parties for the Joint Session

MEDIATOR: OK, I'll be meeting with Nora individually, the goal being to bring the two of you together.

REBECCA: [Agreeing.] Yes.

MEDIATOR: The two of you will actually be sitting as you and I are now, where you can have eye contact. I'll be down towards the end of the table. Again, the objective is for the two of you to meet together and talk. It will be helpful, when you meet, if you will each use each other's names.

REBECCA: I don't have a problem with that.

MEDIATOR: Using each other's names, and having eye contact, will help keep this on a positive note. Sometimes, when there's a third party and there are differences of opinion, one or both individuals may start to look at the mediator for support—instead of at each other. Moving toward the goal of a joint session, one thing to keep in mind is trying to find positive qualities about each other. For you—to summarize—this is basically a simple issue: you want Nora to provide you with her part of the write-up, so you can turn in the report to Ken. The issue may be small to Nora—perhaps she doesn't want to be bothered with the write-up—or there may be other underlying issues. As she comes to the table, one thing to keep in mind is how she's going to respond—or feels she needs to respond. We spoke about helping someone save face. If Nora comes to the table feeling she just has to turn in her write-up and hasn't done it, she may feel that she has to come in and say, "I was wrong." This may seem simple, but for some people it may

	not be. As we examine all of this, we will keep in mind that it may not be the simple issue we, or you, feel it is.
REBECCA:	OK. [Throughout, Rebecca has been nodding and letting the mediator know she is understanding.]

The mediator is preparing Rebecca to discover that, for Nora, the issue may run deeper than it seems. Rebecca is being invited to keep an open mind—in the way of a very gentle challenge.

Postscript

After the camera was turned off, it became clear that other issues related to the dispute were deeply affecting Rebecca. The mediator listened to her for a considerable time. The fact that Rebecca hesitated to mention Nora's positive qualities confirmed that, despite the apparent simplicity of the conflict, Rebecca was not ready for a joint session with Nora. Issues of interpersonal relations were raised, in addition to the matter of unfinished reports.

When parties are ready for a joint session, they are able to talk freely about most—if not all—of the issues discussed in the pre-caucus.

Beginning with the next pre-caucus, the mediator elicits permission from Nora and Rebecca to "share some things." While elements of what is termed *shuttle* diplomacy may be taking place, there is a big difference between it and Party-Directed Mediation. In shuttle mediation, third parties attempt to help contenders solve a dispute without necessarily confronting each other. A proposal is taken from one party and discussed with the other, a counterproposal is prepared, and so on.

In Party-Directed Mediation, the objective in sharing issues ahead of time is to prepare the parties to dialogue. This is especially important when one or both parties' self-esteem is particularly low. Or when blind spots need addressing ahead of time. Either way, some of the element of surprise is removed. Mediators will have a sense as to when this technique will be useful.

Aspects of shuttle diplomacy may be incorporated into Party-Directed Mediation. The objective is to prepare contenders for dialogue by sharing issues—often emotional ones—ahead of time.

8

Nora's First Pre-Caucus

The third party gives Nora an introduction similar to the one provided to Rebecca in the previous chapter. Then, he invites Nora to tell him about the conflict. The mediator prompts Nora several times and asks questions to get her going.

Searching for the Problem

NORA: [Smiling.] OK, I'm sorry to appear a little bit clueless, but I'm not sure [Laughing as she speaks.] what the issue is.

MEDIATOR: Something about a write-up?

NORA: [Smiling, and nodding her head.] OK, the first time I was aware of this situation was when Ken Matsushita took us all out for pizza a month ago. Rebecca suggested that the data for my part of the report was due.

MEDIATOR: So, that was the first time you were aware that this was an issue?

NORA: [Still smiling.] That somehow there was an issue and that I was somehow involved in it.

MEDIATOR: Since then, have you gained a better understanding of what the issue was?

NORA: A little bit. I have an assistant who was preparing the write-up. I honestly don't know who prepared the write-up.

MEDIATOR: It was turned in?

NORA: I don't know if it's been turned in. I've been to the lab recently and saw some of the paperwork there. I can probably take care of it, if there's an expectation that this is something I was supposed to do . . . or even if there isn't an expectation that it's my responsibility.
MEDIATOR: Right.
NORA: But if I'm supposed to do it, then someone needs to tell me that I'm supposed to do it, because I really had no idea.

At this point in the narration, a traditionally oriented mediator might be saying, "Aha! You see. One of them is lying. If they were together, neither one would lie in front of the other." I happen to believe that each of the parties was telling the truth. But the issue of selective hearing has come into play.

Once, my oldest son and his wife left a few of their pets for my wife and me to take care of. When, during that same period, my wife left for a trip with one of our daughters, it fell on me to take care of the pets: two exotic Bengal cats and a killer fish. I was so worried about the instructions on how to care for the cats that when my wife told me I need not worry about changing the water in the fish tank during her short absence, my mind translated that as, "Don't worry about the fish." I didn't really hear her when she told me to feed the fish twice a day. Fortunately, after two days it dawned on me that the fish needed to be fed. The fish did not die, but I felt bad. Just because we transmit information does not mean someone else has the receiver turned on.

MEDIATOR: So, you are not clear . . .
NORA: Or why this even involves me. I haven't had time, and actually, I assigned one of my assistants, but had some pretty flaky help. I have more urgent things to do right now, such as dealing with samples that are in danger of spoiling. I really don't understand the dynamics of why, all of a sudden, this turned into a conflict.

MEDIATOR: So far we've focused on the write-up. Is there more to this issue, or some other underlying matter?

NORA: I . . . I'd have to suspect so, because the write-up is just one of a number of things that have become issues, not really for me, but I suppose it's more for other people. How can I say it? Sometimes it's really busy—you know, I have a lot going on—and at times it can appear untidy, because, uh, well, you know what the Bible says—that when you don't have any cows, you have clean barns.

MEDIATOR: [Laughs along with Nora.]

NORA: But, there are advantages to having cows. So, sometimes I have a lot of cows, and sometimes, when I have people working for me, I can't always control if they know they're not supposed to put something on a specific lab bench . . . But, then someone comes to me and says, "Your stuff is on that bench!" . . . OK, I'll go find them and tell them they're not allowed to put it on that bench. Even under the best of circumstances, we may have samples coming in faster than we can process them, and we may make a mess.

Here, Nora tells a story about her occasional dealings with Fred, another co-worker, and his spillovers into her space. She explains that there is usually an exchange of friendly banter with Fred, and in the end they arrive at solutions that do not involve escalation of negative feelings. Nora wants to present herself as a reasonable person, with a certain amount of patience for others, as well as a sense of humor.

NORA: I know that my stuff tends to crawl around a bit, like an octopus, and that it takes more space than it ought to. But if someone comes to me, we can try and find a solution. Likewise, with this issue regarding the write-up, making a big to-do about this strikes me as being a little excessive. [Nora is smiling again as she concludes the second half of these comments.]

MEDIATOR: A little excessive . . .
NORA: Yeah, a little excessive, especially since I had no clue that there were some expectations here. This was news to me, especially since, as soon I became aware of it, I told my assistant, "Hey, next time you're in the lab, take care of this." But the assistant flaked out and left me with this and a whole bunch of other things.
MEDIATOR: In addition to what you have . . .
NORA: In addition to the rest of my work, yes. [Long pause.] And . . . I guess . . . I guess I could also say that it really hasn't occupied a great deal of my thought processes . . . and it's not something I can deal with. And I can only deal with the things I can deal with and do something about. I recognize that someone else may be stewing about it . . . but unless they come to me, it won't make my priority list.
MEDIATOR: It won't make the list.
NORA: No, there are too many things that are not making the list that really are important.
MEDIATOR: Anything else?
NORA: [Long silence.] Uh . . . I don't think so. It's just, if something's an issue, you know, rather than freaking out over it, why can't we just talk about it?

The mediator summarizes what has been said so far and Nora lets him know that the summary is accurate. She also goes on to repeat some of what she has already said, before proceeding.

NORA: As far as I'm concerned, the work of others at the lab is just as important as mine. I really do believe that. Now, I can understand how some people might have a different perception, because . . . if I'm using part of the workspace that belongs to the community, then they can say, "She really doesn't care about my work because she's hogging the workspace." I don't feel that way, but we have to talk about it. Then we have to find a way to get everyone's stuff done, even

	though it may not be perfect for everybody, but we can find a way to do that.
MEDIATOR:	Find a way of working it out . . .
NORA:	It's not going to be perfect, but . . . [Once again, the mediator gives Nora a chance to expand and explain what she is thinking and feeling.]

The conversation seems over, and the mediator asks Nora for positive qualities about Rebecca.

Admirable Qualities of the Opposite Party

NORA:	Rebecca really cares about people. She has very good, uh, people skills. In terms of really caring about people and being empathetic and sympathetic . . . I remember the time when our whole staff was asked to fill out personality profiles. Almost every single person in the lab came out task-oriented, a get-the-job-done type personality of one permutation or another. She was the only person who scored way high in relational skills. I think her way of getting stuff done was to build partnerships and camaraderie. Everyone else was more likely to take logical steps and accomplish things.
MEDIATOR:	Get the job done.
NORA:	Get the job done. She was the only one who scored really high on "We are going to make relationships." And I think that's really neat! I think that's really important in this lab.

The conversation turns to other topics for a while, but Nora has some things she is still feeling.

NORA:	I guess one thing that people may find a positive thing, or somewhat annoying, . . . this whole thing about the write-up. I recognize that Rebecca might really be stewing about this stuff. Because I didn't meet an expectation. I have to admit that I really haven't thought about it. It's not that I don't care.

It's just that, uh, I guess one of the things I've learned in life is not to run away from conflict. It's not that I don't care about how other people feel, but I've learned not to let other people's problems, other people's feelings, other people's issues dictate whether I'm going to be functional and happy and make good decisions and good choices. I've had enough experience with really negative people in my life. Now, I have to make a decision. Am I going to let my good day and my good mood be trashed because a person comes in with negative baggage? No! I was in a good mood before you walked in the door, and I'm going to be in a good mood when you leave, because I have work to do and a life to live, and choose to be happy. It doesn't mean that I'm afraid of conflict, and it doesn't mean that I won't work with you, but if you're coming with a lot of emotional baggage and an expectation that I'm going to somehow . . . I don't know exactly how to say it . . . I'll work with you, but I'm not going to let somebody else's issues control my life. Does that make sense?

MEDIATOR: You're not going to let someone else's issues.

NORA: So, uh, that's just a choice I have to make for me. It may look like I don't care. It's not that I don't care. It's just that I have a lot that I have to get done. If I let myself go into a tailspin because someone else is ticked at me, I can't function. I'll put your issue on my list, and when I get to that point on my list, I'll do something about it. But I'm not going to let it affect dealing with all the other issues on my plate . . . I can't. I have to live.

MEDIATOR: Separating issues from emotions . . .

NORA: Yeah . . . but I'm not going to beat myself up . . . I have too many other things I could potentially beat myself up on. If I spend my life beating myself up for all my imperfections and all the expectations that other people have of me that I can't possibly meet,

I'll collapse. So, I want to be in control of what's on my list. Ultimately, I have to choose what's on my list and what I can get done in a day.

The conversation between Nora and the mediator continues in the same vein for a while. At one point, Nora tells of a specific life-changing event that taught her to be less defensive and, instead, focus more on her work. The mediator then coaches Nora on how to present her case effectively in the joint session. Just when the pre-caucus session seems over, Nora thinks of a particular situation that might have played a key role in the escalation of her conflict with Rebecca.

The Larry Incident

NORA: Let me bring up another issue from long ago. I think this is when my conflict with Rebecca really started to escalate.

Nora seems relaxed, but her smile is gone. She goes into a long and detailed explanation of how a former lab assistant, Larry, was assigned by Matsushita to work for Nora full-time. Unfortunately, both Rebecca and Nora thought they had requisitioned Larry's help. They both needed assistance in a critical way.

NORA: Rebecca came to me and said, "I had him signed up—you didn't—and I really need him." I told her, "It may be a moot point anyway, because I think Ken has assigned Larry to me full-time." I was *going* to say, "I really need him today, but because you have these things that have to get done, why don't we work it out so that maybe tomorrow—I had already blocked out the time—we can have Larry help you, even if he's been formally assigned to me." But before I could get the words out of my mouth, she wrote me off. You know, as soon as I said it was going to be a moot point anyway, because he was going to be working for me, she blew up, stormed out of the room, refused to speak to me the rest of the day—or the next two days. Larry and I tried to find her to tell her, "Hey, if you want some time, we'll get this done." But she wouldn't speak to me. She was so angry. She said, "The only person's work you care about is your own." I never had a chance, because she would never listen to me. I know her husband had to come and help her on Saturday, and it was a big fiasco. I would have helped her, but she left and wouldn't speak to me any more. Ever since then, she's just been on my case, as if I'm being a selfish person who only cares about my own work. Anyway, I think this incident really affected all those other incidents, and I'd really like to get it straightened out. It's really bothered me that I've never been able to, you know, set the record straight. I just have sensed she hasn't been, uh, as forgiving since then.

MEDIATOR: Uh-huh.

NORA: And I don't blame her, from her standpoint, but that's not the way I saw things, and I've never been able to set the record right.

MEDIATOR: It goes back to the issue of communication.

NORA: And not being able to finish my sentence on that one day.

MEDIATOR: Right.

NORA: We tried. [Smile appears again, as she lifts her hands.]

Time for a Joint Session?

After additional conversation between the mediator and Nora, we return to the question of the joint session.

MEDIATOR: We've met with both of you on an individual basis. The next step is to determine if it will be beneficial to bring both parties together. How do you feel about meeting with Rebecca? Are you ready for that?

Just because we transmit information does not mean someone else has the receiver turned on.

NORA: Mmm.
MEDIATOR: Or, are you at a point where we should still meet individually for another session?
NORA: Well, I really like having right relationships. [A smile briefly breaks upon her face.] And I admit that because of Rebecca's emotional response to me in the past . . . uh, it makes me nervous to actually sit down with Rebecca and try to be understood. I've just had such bad luck with that on a number of occasions [Smiles about this.] that it's really made me kind of leery. I've got lots of stress in my life, and this is one I really don't want to have to deal with, but it's much more important to me to have right relationships with Rebecca . . . and I'll do whatever it takes to make sure—as far as I can—that there can be peace and communication. I really like the idea of doing this in a controlled situation. All I can do is give it my best shot, I guess, even though for me it's a very uncomfortable thing, because I don't like other people's emotional stuff dumped on me. I've gotten pretty good at shedding it but it doesn't mean I don't care. You know what I mean?
MEDIATOR : M-hm.
NORA: You know . . . but my own feelings are not nearly as important as my desire to get it right.
MEDIATOR: OK. If we . . .
NORA: But . . . but . . . OK . . . OK, I'm going to introduce a caveat. I'm going to lean on your judgment because I don't have a clue as to where she's at. And I don't know how she's going to feel. I don't want to make things worse. I'm not really concerned about making things worse for me, because I will muddle through regardless of how bad it's for me. I don't want to make the situation worse. So, if you think she's in a place where she could hear my heart, I'd love to know it.

The mediator prepares Nora for the joint session by explaining the seating arrangement, the purpose of eye contact, and other issues, as he did when meeting with Rebecca. Nora is very attentive. With the mediator, she role plays bringing up the incident involving Larry. Although she is not asked to, Nora finishes her role-play explanation to Rebecca with an apology. The word *apology* triggers a strong emotional reaction from Nora.

Nora tells of the time she was collecting samples and returned to the lab somewhat dehydrated. She drank three sodas, full of sugar and caffeine, and subsequently exploded at the receptionist, who delivered a message about some trivial matter. Nora explains how out-of-character her behavior was and how shocked she and the receptionist were by her outburst. "It was the sugar," Nora insists.

If the situation with Larry were to take place again, Nora feels she would be just as unsure about how to handle it, despite the unfortunate consequences. Nora also speaks about how vulnerable she feels at this time in her life.

NORA: I guess what I was trying to say is that it's hard for me, uh, because I spent so much time—and this has nothing to do with Rebecca—being forced to apologize for situations I didn't create. And when I know I didn't do anything wrong. I've had to deal with a control freak who I couldn't ever please, and who subjected me to verbal abuse. So, I'm really sensitive about taking blame for something, taking ownership of a problem that really isn't mine. Just for my own mental health I have to be really careful to not be the cause of everybody else's problems. I have to retain who I am rather than what other people say I am. I guess I've built up some walls and defenses that are kind of fresh and new. I'm not really in a place where I'm willing to take a lot of ownership for blame I don't feel I deserve. But I'm willing to take the blame I do deserve, like the situation with the receptionist. Does this make sense?

The ability to offer and receive apologies is a critical interpersonal negotiation tool. Nora seems receptive to an example of an apology offered by the mediator—a situation in which he felt the need to apologize not for what he did or said, but for what happened as a result of a dispute. The mediator explains that it is possible to express regret for a situation without taking the blame for what happened.

NORA: And I'm very sorry about that. And I'm sorry for what it's led to. And I can do that. But to say that I caused all of that . . . I can't do that. Maybe in five years I can do that and it will be OK with me, but right now it's not OK with me.

NEXT STEPS

The mediator agrees to meet again with Rebecca and share some of the information gathered during Nora's pre-caucus. And to collect information to share back with Nora. In the weeks before the mediator is able to meet with Rebecca and Nora for an additional pre-caucus, the parties continue their soul-searching, which will do much to soften each of their stances.

9

Rebecca's Second Pre-Caucus

MEDIATOR: To start this session, I want to mention some things Nora wanted me to share with you. I haven't shared with her anything from our conversations.
REBECCA: And that's OK with her?
MEDIATOR: Yes, and she's hoping that maybe down the line, if you have something to share with her, that you'll do that. But don't worry about it right now. We'll just start with some of the things she wanted us to share. First off, I asked her the same question I asked you about positive qualities in the other person.

The mediator goes on to share with Rebecca the positive comments Nora made about her. Rebecca's expression to this point has been serious. She asks the mediator several questions about Nora's comments. She seems to be trying to decipher whether they were intended as compliments.

The mediator explains that, if there is a joint session, Nora wants to share her perspective of the incident that might have caused the conflict to flare. We pick up the conversation as Rebecca describes a few stressful encounters with Nora.

REBECCA: One time I asked her an innocent question—I certainly had no intentions of attacking her—and she began to yell at me. Again, the yelling, which I don't like. I had to tell her that it was inappropriate for her to be yelling. She doesn't do this with other people.

In another instance, I spoke to her, and again I got yelled at. There have been a number of these over the years. As a result, it makes me hesitant to approach her. I don't know what sort of reaction I'm going to get. It's never been a positive one . . . in the sense of getting some cooperation. Or, I know I've mentioned things to her. I needed some samples moved—she kind of leaves things around—and she goes into a lot of detail about her people not doing what they're supposed to do, but she won't take responsibility. Ultimately, it's her responsibility, not her people's. I could go on, but I think that's good enough.

The mediator recaps what he has heard.

REBECCA: So, yeah, it bothers me. It hurts . . . It hurts my feelings.

Having a party admit that something hurts is a positive step towards healing. The conversation continues, and the mediator picks up on something that was said earlier.

MEDIATOR: Can you describe how the conflict between the two of you, this tension, affects relationships in the lab?
REBECCA: [Drawing out the word.] OK. I can try to answer. I'm not sure I understand exactly. I could give more examples, but I don't think that's the point. A lot of the interactions that I've had with her are negative and are related to doing my job, such as helping Ken Matsushita with the year-end report. I have a certain responsibility to the other people in the lab, and to Ken, to make a little contribution—not twenty-four seven, but to the functioning of the lab as a whole, given that we're down in personnel since our downsizing. Lots of times, things get dumped on Ken's assistant, Mike Peck, and people will shout at him, "We don't have the supplies! We don't have the supplies!" I'm trying to give back a certain

Having a party admit that something hurts, or is a frustration, is a positive step towards healing.

percentage for the good of the order. And in the situation with Nora, the fact is that I get kind of blindsided with this yelling, and her behavior towards me is *sooo* defensive. I immediately feel this . . . wall going up. What I'd like her to realize is that this isn't personal. I'm not interested in the report, nor do I feel as if I own the lab and want it cleaned up. She has some obligations to clean up what she's messed up. I don't like her yelling, and since I'm not sure what I'm going to get, I don't go out of my way to engage her. If anything, I go out of my way to avoid contact. It's very uncomfortable, very defensive. There have also been some personal insults—because I do contribute to the overall good of the lab—implying, or rather, stating that essentially her job is so important and every second of her time is so critical that only people like me, that don't have a critical job like she does, waste time on these little things. And that's insulting. Her attitude towards me, word choices, posture, body language—she's in my face—and the yelling all add up to a situation that I'd rather avoid. So, there is no real social interaction. I don't ignore her and try and be rude. But I don't go out of my way to have any interaction with her. I guess that sums it up. I don't know how you would say all that concisely.

The mediator attempts to summarize, and Rebecca clarifies her feelings.

REBECCA: I don't like being a police officer. So, what do I do? Take it to Ken? He has enough on his plate. So, when things have to get done, I feel I'm removing part of his load. She doesn't see herself as a person who is a citizen of this lab who obeys its norms. It doesn't prevent me from doing my job. At this time, it doesn't have much of an effect on my mood, but it does bother me when these yelling episodes take place. I don't get upset just because I see her. It's not that way. So, what am I supposed to do when something isn't followed up on? Do I have to go back three or four times? Even when I do, it makes no difference. It never gets done. I'm not sure at this point how you handle a situation where there's no cooperation whatsoever. I haven't found any effective means to deal with her, obviously.
MEDIATOR: A negative situation for you.
REBECCA: Well, I imagine for her, as she gets upset.
MEDIATOR: Do you have any idea why she might be affected that way? Why Nora feels she has to yell or get in your face?

The mediator's gentle challenge comes at a time when Rebecca has been listened to extensively, for more than an hour. Rebecca repeats much of what she has already expressed, but then she comes back to the mediator's question.

REBECCA: Uh, it's obvious there's something that sets her off, and it may relate to something . . . an experience in the past she's had with me . . . so that when she sees me, the guards go up, the gates close, whatever. It's something I'm not aware of. I don't have an explanation for why this type of interaction occurs . . . but it's certainly uncomfortable for both of us.

This is a key moment in the pre-caucus. Rebecca is trying very hard to see things from Nora's perspective. After some conversation, the mediator eventually asks Rebecca if there is something from this conversation that he can share with Nora to help her better understand the situation.

REBECCA: I don't know the value of doing so. Everything we have spoken about is factual. *That* she can know, but if there's something . . . I get this really strong sense she doesn't care about anything I say or do, or how my feelings have anything to do with her, so I really don't see a point with it. Just based on our interaction, it's such a shutdown. I don't see what the benefit may be to her. Although you have indicated that she's willing to discuss things, so, uh, that obviously may not be the case. If you think . . . I don't know how it would help.

Rebecca is trying to cooperate with the mediator, but she has not given herself permission to think about Nora in human terms and thus keeps focusing on the *facts of the case* rather than on the *relationship* itself. Rebecca makes it clear that she does not have much confidence that the mediator can do any good by sharing information with Nora, but she is willing to let him try.

The mediator proposes four areas of concern that he would like to share with Nora, based on the pre-caucusing: (1) Rebecca has a year-end report due and needs Nora's cooperation to finish it, (2) Nora communicates through yelling and other dysfunctional approaches, (3) Rebecca feels that Nora treats her differently than others in the laboratory, and (4) Rebecca feels indignant because it has been implied that Nora's job is more important—that Rebecca is helping Ken Matsushita only because her own job is not that essential and she does not have enough to do. Rebecca agrees to allow the mediator to share these points with Nora.

Rebecca expands on each of these issues as the mediator speaks, correcting some of the wording and making it clear how burdensome this conflict has been. For instance, Rebecca explains that the year-end report is now seven months late and has increased her workload. Rebecca then says, "She should be ashamed. I'm angry. This is a wrong that needs to be addressed."

Expressing and exploring some of these frustrations is important. Before Rebecca can permit herself any validating thoughts about Nora, the mediator must listen intently. After expressing her frustrations and pain, Rebecca permits herself a moment of hope.

REBECCA: It would be interesting to approach her and have a normal interchange and have something resolved. It would be unbelievable. It would be inconceivable to me! I have no history of having it any other way. [Laughing.] If it makes her aware of her behavior . . . Maybe she does this with other people. I know that Nora isn't . . . Well, she is a good person, I believe, fundamentally. I have no doubt about that. I don't consider her a mean, vicious type of person, although some of the behaviors towards me are certainly that way. If she knew that, maybe she would see that it's not a kindness. I think she does have a belief system where she tries to treat people in a decent way, and maybe she'll see it's inappropriate, just wrong, to make such comments.

	You don't purposely try to put someone down. That's my belief system. I just can't understand it.
MEDIATOR:	Rebecca, is there anything else you would like to add?
REBECCA:	I think we've [Begins to laugh.] covered things pretty thoroughly. It's a value of mine: treat people the way you want to be treated yourself. This isn't something I try to do. It *is* me. It's a very basic part of my belief system that every person has value. I believe that caring about others is almost the most important thing on this planet. So, some of the things that have happened between the two of us have kind of violated that basic belief system of mine.

Disputants can begin to find hope and imagine what a positive interaction might look like.

A gentle challenge is most likely to have a positive effect when the disputant feels understood.

While at some points Rebecca seems distant and lost in thought, towards the end of this discussion she lightens up. At the beginning of the pre-caucus Rebecca hardly acknowledges the positive things Nora said about her. Now Rebecca accepts that these positive qualities are not artificial, but part of her core values. While Rebecca is still in a lot of pain, she allows herself to hear something positive from Nora about herself, and she also shares something positive about Nora. Perhaps, if their conflict had not been so protracted, all of this would have happened sooner.

MEDIATOR: You have mentioned a few positive attributes about Nora as we talked. Are there any more that come to mind?

REBECCA: I think she does a really good job in terms of her technical knowledge of lab equipment and computers, something I admire in her. We both use some of the same programs, but she's taken her understanding to a much higher plane. [Rebecca continues, going into some detail.]

The mediator talks about the goal of bringing Rebecca and Nora into a joint session.

REBECCA: Obviously the reason I'm here is that it's hopefully of value . . . I've said things that really are pretty nasty in some ways—you know, they're kind of negative—in relating experiences . . . in my interpretation. If we can improve the situation, heal the situation, or whatever words you want to use . . . I certainly think that's of value . . . I support that.

It seems as if the pre-caucus is over, but Rebecca brings up additional key information.

REBECCA: [Cheerfully.] I think people are a product of the interaction of their individual genetic makeup and their environment. [Seriously, but calm.] As a product of that interaction, there are certain responses that a person has to situations. They exist and do influence behavior and communication styles. And all I want to do is to point out, for example, in my case, I tend to be extremely . . . more sensitive than, maybe, is called for, but I do pick up on certain nonverbal cues, tones of voice, things like that, which kind of go through and synthesize how I interpret a situation or a person. In my case, the behaviors I elicit in Nora—the in-your-face kind of thing, yelling, negativity—the communication and interaction . . . I thought maybe bringing them out and making both aware of it . . . Maybe that cognizance is going to improve the ultimate results that we get here. And again, the objective for me would be to establish what I'd call a functional relationship, so the two of us can interact on a professional level at the lab and get done what needs to get done without all these negative overtones. It's certainly a poor pattern, a destructive pattern.

As Rebecca feels heard, she seems to consider that she might also have contributed to the negative interpersonal relationship. The mediator obtains permission to share Rebecca's additional insights with Nora.

REBECCA: I've been trying to explain my sensitivities, and then . . . recognizing the fact that she would also have her own . . . Maybe there's something that I do, unconsciously, that for some reason provokes a certain response in her. If that's the case, it would be something we would all need to be aware of—certainly me, so I can make sure not to do it.

SUMMARY

In her second pre-caucus, Rebecca feels heard and is willing to consider that there are *relationship* issues to deal with, not just *facts*. At first, Rebecca is concerned with the dysfunctional behaviors Nora brings to the relationship. Towards the end, Rebecca acknowledges she might also be contributing to the dispute. Rebecca has begun the transition to seeing Nora as a real person. Because of the protracted nature of this conflict, the mediator would have done well to engage the parties in a third set of pre-caucuses.

10

Nora's Second Pre-Caucus

The mediator opens with a general question about how things are going and then asks if Nora has any feelings about the mediation process in which she has been participating.

NORA: Things are fine . . . The process is fine. Uh, Rebecca was nice to me the other day. [Laughing.] I was floored. It was wonderful!
MEDIATOR: So, maybe there have been . . .
NORA: I think so.
MEDIATOR: . . . some changes . . . already.
NORA: I think so. Yeah.
MEDIATOR: That has been the goal, but we haven't brought you together, so hopefully . . . those steps can be taken . . .
NORA: Yeah. We've had some pleasant exchanges, and that's excellent.
MEDIATOR: Yes, well, good. If you don't have anything else, I just want to go back, because it's been a little over a month since we met, and review a few things with you.

The mediator summarizes Nora's comments from her first pre-caucus. Nora corrects a few notions but mostly agrees with the mediator's understanding of the situation. Nora thanks the mediator for the summary.

MEDIATOR:	And you want to right the relationship—improve the relationship—but your concern is the emotions that Rebecca exhibits.
NORA:	Yes.
MEDIATOR:	Which, it sounds, maybe are . . .
NORA:	Maybe things are simmering down.
MEDIATOR:	Right. And we shared with Rebecca the positive things you said about her. And asked her if there was anything we could share with you.
NORA:	OK.
MEDIATOR:	She also wanted to share the positive things. She brought these up before I had a chance to ask her.
NORA:	Oh, good!

The mediator shares the positive things Rebecca said about Nora: that she has a strong belief system, treats people well, and possesses an excellent understanding of lab equipment. The mediator goes on to explain some of Rebecca's concerns. These include the fact that Rebecca sometimes feels like "a cop" when she tries to get information from the staff for the year-end report. The mediator explains that Rebecca feels this way about her colleagues in general, not only her adversary. Nora acknowledges this might be so. We pick up the conversation as the mediator proceeds from the general comments to more specific ones.

MEDIATOR:	Now, this is something you have already alluded to. Rebecca gets the impression, at times, that you think your work is more important than hers.
NORA:	And I can understand how someone might feel like that, but that doesn't mean it's true. I'm just expecting others to tell me what their needs are, and we'll get it done.
MEDIATOR:	Talking things through with each other . . .
NORA:	Right. I told you there was a problem there.
MEDIATOR:	Finally, Rebecca feels you sometimes treat her differently than other people in the lab. She is not sure if it's something she's done or the way she responds. And the example Rebecca gave was that

Disputants often fail to recognize how tone of voice can give meaning to messages.

	she's heard you raise your voice at her but at no one else.
NORA:	[Nodding.] Uh . . . yeah . . . I . . .
MEDIATOR:	Those are the areas she wanted to share.
NORA:	OK. Can I give you my responses?
MEDIATOR:	Yes.
NORA:	OK. Repeat them one by one, and I'll respond to them.
MEDIATOR:	The cop issue.
NORA:	[Laughing.] I think I gave the example of the drill sergeant getting to be the crossing guard. I think she's mellowed out some on that. Some people can take their jobs a *liiiiiittle* bit too seriously. I don't know if I would share that with her.

Nora is able to express her feelings but realizes that the wording will have to be changed in order not to offend. This is a valuable aspect of the pre-caucus.

MEDIATOR: The responses you're giving me right now will get refined later.

NORA: [Laughing, followed by silence.] We'll decide on how we want to respond . . . the official response.

Individuals can express their feelings any way they wish during the pre-caucus, with the idea of later examining possible ways of presenting the material for better impact.

	Yes, I understand that she's got that task. People take on obligations, and I sometimes wonder why they take these on. Actually, the best boss I've ever had is our present boss, who has the job despite the fact that he didn't want it. Everybody I've ever worked for before who wanted that job has been a very difficult boss to have. There was a reason why they wanted to be the boss. While I understand that it's something that needs to be done, people take on different things because they have a reason, their own reason for needing to take those things on. I think she's getting better. If it's truly something that needs to get done, I'm as interested as the next person to make sure it's taken care of.
MEDIATOR:	Anything more about that?
NORA:	No. No. I am part of the team. We'll make it work, if it's really important.

During the joint session, we shall see this issue develop further. Nora admits there may be a need for change on her part. The mediator does not need to moralize.

MEDIATOR:	Rebecca was concerned that it was implied, as well as directly stated, that your work was more important than hers.
NORA:	Well, we'll have to get that straightened out.
MEDIATOR:	OK.
NORA:	We'll have to . . . I think I know how that came about, so let's get it fixed.
MEDIATOR:	Is that back to the Larry . . . ?
NORA:	Back to the Larry thing. And if that's not the issue, then let's find out what the issue is and get it fixed.
MEDIATOR:	Also, Rebecca actually heard it from others that you stated your work was more important than hers.
NORA:	[Nora, who has been quite cheerful until this moment, pauses, begins to shake her head, raises her eyebrows, and shrugs her shoulders as if searching. She then continues in a more serious tone of voice.]

	I don't know how to respond to that. I don't remember saying something like that . . . although maybe . . . maybe taken out of context . . . I don't know . . . But that's not how I feel, *sooo* we'll just have to get that fixed . . . get that straightened out . . . Sorry if . . . Now, she's saying that I said that to somebody else, and they said that to her?
MEDIATOR:	Yes.
NORA:	*Weeell*, I'll have to think if there is anything I've ever said that could have been misconstrued that way. I might have said at one point, when I had three people working for me, that I had more things going on than other people, but it doesn't mean my work was more important.

The mediator continues to listen. Nora expands a bit on what she has said. Her usual smile returns.

MEDIATOR:	The last issue is the fact that Rebecca feels she's sometimes treated differently than others in the lab. She wonders if she does something or has done something to cause that. She feels that you have raised your voice at her when you haven't necessarily at other people.
NORA:	[With a smile, nodding her head when she speaks.] OK, I have several responses to that.
MEDIATOR:	OK.
NORA:	I'll respond to the example first.
MEDIATOR:	OK.
NORA:	Uh, first of all, let's define "raising my voice." I can think of two incidents where I was irritated with her . . . where she interpreted it as "raising my voice." I wouldn't call what I did raising my voice. She said I was yelling at her? [Nora pauses, raises both of her hands, and, still smiling, continues.] Believe me, if I want to yell at somebody, *I'll yell at somebody*. It's not what I did. I don't do it to anyone who is not my child. But . . . that wasn't yelling at

her. Yes, there was some annoyance in my voice when after the third time . . .

Nora goes on to recount a situation in which there had been a miscommunication between the two women. She explains that Rebecca wanted to discard an old piece of lab equipment against her wishes. As Nora tells the story, she speaks quite a bit louder when she describes the incident in which she is accused of raising her voice.

NORA: Yeah, I guess I did raise my voice but that wasn't what I call yelling at her. I was annoyed and irritated.

Next, Nora explains how the same piece of lab equipment was needed by another lab employee a short while after Rebecca attempted to discard it. Nora speaks of another situation in which she became irritated, but she again claims she would not call what happened "raising her voice."

NORA: I would not say that I'm treating her differently, but I seldom have occasion to get annoyed at anybody else at the lab. We'll, no . . . Occasionally, I have gotten annoyed at people working for me when they've done something really stupid.
MEDIATOR: Yeah.
NORA: I'm not a yeller. But I am capable of being annoyed. So, I go around yelling at *her* and not at anybody else? That would be an odd thing to think.

Up to now, Nora has been trying to show a positive self-image for the mediator. As she speaks and is heard, she will be in a better position to recognize that even a moderate level of "raising her voice" can be a problem in her troubled relationship with Rebecca.

NORA: It sounds a little paranoid to me. Now, on the other hand, where I feel a little paranoid, I sense she treats me differently than the rest of the people in the lab.

> The specific example is that, besides me, there are five other professional women in the lab. [More serious, Nora continues.] And, somehow, they all seem to know what the others are doing on the weekend, and where they went, and who went hiking or to the beach, and who is seeing whom. If I walk up, and two people—say Rebecca and Adriana—are talking, not only do I not know what they are talking about, but no one includes me in the conversation. So, I don't know exactly how that all works. I don't think I've been unfriendly to anybody. I certainly don't think I've been in the loop.

Ostensibly, the conflict between Nora and Rebecca was about a year-end report, but this conversation demonstrates the importance of uncovering other underlying interpersonal issues.

NORA: When I try to bust into the loop, I don't feel particularly welcome, especially when Rebecca is part of the conversation. You know, I'm fine with everyone individually, but I get the impression that everybody else is doing things with other people, with each other, and I'm not. Which . . . since I tend to be busy it's not a huge thing. I'm not expecting people at the lab to be my friends [Begins to smile again.], but on the other hand . . . I do feel a little bit left out.

The mediator summarizes very briefly and asks if there is anything Nora wishes to add.

NORA: Mmm . . . I don't think so. I'm looking forward to things getting resolved . . . especially if there have been misunderstandings. I really want to get those taken care of. I may not be able to meet all the expectations, but we can be clear as to which ones I can meet and which ones I can't.

Time lapse between pre-caucuses can permit parties to begin the process of mutual validation while on their own.

MEDIATOR: That leads into the next question. Do you feel comfortable with the idea of a joint session next time we meet—bringing you and Rebecca together?

NORA: Sure, we can do that. We can do that. I'd like to know ahead of time the list of topics, whatever we're going to be discussing. Realizing, of course, that life does not always follow a list.

MEDIATOR: OK. Of course.

The time lapse between the pre-caucuses has permitted the parties to begin the process of mutual validation. The mediator now asks Nora to come up with two or three expectations for the joint session. Nora expresses her hopes in a sincere, touching way.

NORA: My personal goals would be, foremost, to communicate to Rebecca, somehow, that she's important to me; that her work is important to me; and that she, as a person, is important to me. And as an outpour of that, I want to have the air clear between us, so that the number one goal is not interfered with. Do you know what I mean? So there's no miscommunication. I want to have some sort of understanding that I'm not doing things to deliberately make her life difficult. Maybe then she will cut me some slack in terms of thinking the worst of my intentions. And I would like her to understand that if she has a need in her work, or otherwise, if somehow that can be communicated to me, then we can work it into the priority list.

MEDIATOR: You would like to be able to talk about work or what happens over the weekend. At this time, both of you are hesitant to speak to each other, not knowing how the other will react.

NORA: Right.

NEXT STEPS

Nora and Rebecca will have a chance to converse with each other directly and begin to resolve their differences. Much progress has been achieved already. For instance, each woman has recognized that she might be doing something to merit the other's negative reactions. Even though they have not met in a joint session, Rebecca and Nora are beginning to validate each other during their brief encounters at work.

Nora

Rebecca

11

The Joint Session at Last

As a horse trainer, I try to prepare a mount that has never been ridden so it will not buck or rear. I do not mind if the horse bucks a little, as long as the animal is moving forward and does not stop. It is when a horse stops moving forward that bucking or rearing can become dangerous. Only after mounting for the first time will I know if the horse has been sufficiently prepared.

Likewise, only after parties involved in a dispute are brought into a joint session can a mediator be sure that the preparation during the pre-caucuses has been adequate. The conversation between the disputants may at times heat up a little, but contenders should never cross the line so that psychological safety disappears.

In terms of mediator interference, referees provide a useful metaphor. People do not generally watch a soccer match—or any other type of competitive event—to observe the referee. They come to watch a game. Similarly, while making the necessary calls and taking all the necessary steps to keep everyone safe, a mediator should interfere judiciously.

As we shall observe, the joint session between Nora and Rebecca presents a number of difficulties. These include intense frustration, raised voices, and much tension, yet the contenders show a high amount of respect towards each other. Although they do not always succeed, one gets the feeling that the women are trying not to say anything hurtful to each other. Each attempts to communicate her own anguish and explain how she perceives the

The noninterference model can be pushed beyond its useful limits.

other, without being purposely unkind. Certainly, this was not one of the easy joint sessions described earlier in the book, in which the mediator only had to introduce the next topic and write down areas of agreement.

Our main objective is not, as was stated earlier, to analyze the mediator's behavior, but rather to point out how people who have been involved in a dispute can address each other and begin to resolve problems with minimal third-party intervention. Lack of intervention reflects the mediator's confidence in the disputants' willingness and ability to work out a solution on their own. Nevertheless, in this case, the noninterference model was pushed beyond its useful limits. Clearly, it was a risky approach in which the third party chanced a possible disaster—such as having one of the disputants leave the joint session.

The mediator would have done well to interfere sooner. This could have been done without necessarily taking much time. Also, the frequent changes in topics without resolving them certainly added tension to the dispute. In retrospect, perhaps a third set of pre-caucuses would have improved the disputants' preparedness.

Perhaps, for all these reasons, Nora and Rebecca's case illustrates how parties can control their own conversation despite trying circumstances. It should be clear that Party-Directed Mediation allows for differences in *levels of interference* during the joint session, taking into consideration the abilities of the disputants and the circumstances of the case as well as third-party preferences.

Several weeks have gone by since the last set of pre-caucuses. The time lapse has continued to help the disputants to soften their stances towards each other. The mediator checks in briefly with each individual before the joint session to determine if any new issues have developed. Nora and Rebecca seem anxious but are ready to speak to each other.

The conference room is set up so the parties can sit facing each other at one end of the table and the mediator can create distance by sitting at the other end (Figure 5–1).

MEDIATOR: Welcome, and thank you for being a part of this process. Thank you for the time that you've put in. It's taken a long time to coordinate everybody's schedule as well. I want to start by summarizing the positive aspects you have mentioned about each other.

After going through the lists of the women's positive traits, the mediator turns to Nora and asks her to share with Rebecca her perspective of the incident involving Larry, the lab assistant.

NORA: First of all, do you know what I'm talking about? Or do you have any clue? [Cheerfully.]

REBECCA: No, I don't. There's been a number, so tell me which one. [Cheerfully.]

The conversation continues in a more serious tone.

NORA: Well, the one that I really feel bad about is when both of us had signed up for the lab assistant, and Larry was making the transition from . . .

REBECCA: Oh.

NORA: . . . working for everybody to being assigned full-time to help me. And there was some sort of mix-up on the sign-up sheet.

REBECCA: Well, no . . . I signed up first. There wasn't a mix-up, but go ahead.

NORA: Well, I . . .

REBECCA: That was your point of view, but go ahead.

NORA: Well, I don't really remember exactly . . .

REBECCA: Actually, it's not a really big, gigantic thing for me.

NORA: Well . . .

REBECCA: It was an issue. Right?

NORA: It was an issue, and I felt really bad how it all came down. There was a lot of stuff that happened at that time. I felt what I was trying to do got really misinterpreted. I don't remember all the details of that day, and I suppose that if it was really important we could try and reconstruct them. But anyway, I thought I had signed up for Larry, but it also turned out that precisely that day, Ken Matsushita decided Larry was going to work full-time for me. What I had worked out with Larry was that, because you also needed him, he was going to help you. Just not that day. At another time. But we couldn't find you.

Larry looked for you, and I looked for you, but you were upset. We were going to get your work done, but at a different time, but we couldn't get ahold of you to let you know that. I was really trying to make sure that it got done, but you had already written me off. You assumed I didn't care about your position when I really did. I've never been able to communicate that to you, and there are a lot of other things that wind up being interpreted as if I don't care about you or your work. And that is not how I feel! That's really not how I feel!

Rebecca listens intently, sometimes making eye contact with Nora and sometimes staring at the table between them. Nora is combining several issues in her comments—not only the incident involving Larry but also Nora's sincere caring about Rebecca. The hurt Rebecca feels because of this long conflict, however, is simply too deep to permit her to accept the partial apology offered by Nora.

Nora's expression "you had already written me off" may also have contributed to Rebecca's rejection of the apology; it transferred much of the fault for the misunderstanding to Rebecca.

When someone has been hurt, the person frequently has a need to express that pain. Hearing about the pain we have caused another causes us discomfort. Yet, we need to acknowledge when we have hurt another.

REBECCA: Well, but in fact on several occasions, it's given me, and other people I've talked to, the impression that your work is the highest priority and that my work is not significant. These are things that have been alluded to, and basically said. Other people have heard, too, but I've gotten pretty much past that. You're just wrapped up in what you're doing, and you don't really know what I do . . . and that's that. I mean, you're entitled to your opinion.

NORA: But that's not my opinion.

REBECCA: Well, it's been expressed on several occasions, so I interpret it as your opinion. So . . .
NORA: Well, I mean . . . I'll do what I can to help you understand how I really feel and . . .
REBECCA: OK.
NORA: But . . . I mean, I can't make you believe something you don't want to believe.

In the pre-caucus, we heard Nora explain that at this period in her life, she does not want to apologize for things that are not her fault. Her comment about not being able to *force* Rebecca to believe what she does not want to believe is a defensive one. Because Nora is struggling with her own emotions, it is difficult to expect much more from her at this point in the interaction.

REBECCA: [Her voice begins to crack and show higher levels of stress.] It's not that I want to believe or not believe. I just know what I've heard . . . and there are not multiple ways to interpret it. So, it's just how I heard . . . but it's not what I would call a gigantic issue.
NORA: [Sighs.]
REBECCA: [More calmly.] The issue that I had—the latest thing that started all this—is getting you to turn in the stupid data I needed so I could complete the report, because it was just part of my job. And I was trying to do that job, not because it's my favorite thing to do, not because I don't have anything else to do, but because I'm trying to help Ken, who is really short-handed. I'm trying to support him. I just needed that thing done, so I could check it off my little sheet. I got yelled at a couple of times . . . and I didn't think that I deserved that. I was just doing a job. It wasn't even personal. It was basically your responsibility to do it . . . It was my responsibility to make sure it got checked off. [Rebecca laughs and with her hands makes a motion of checking off something from a list in the air.] And it took months . . . and that was the initial issue that brought us here—that ridiculous

report, which is unfortunate but has now been resolved. It's taking responsibility for following up after your own work. I don't even know why it was important, but I was told to take care of it, and that's what I was doing. [More calmly.] So, I didn't mean to . . . ride your case. It didn't seem unreasonable to me either. But I realize you have a lot of things to do, and details like that are just not the highest priority. I know that.

Rebecca's last comment about such *details not being the highest priority for Nora* could have caused a defensive reaction in Nora, but fortunately it did not.

NORA: Well, I had no clue . . . I had no clue . . . maybe somebody said it, and it went right over my head. Or I was in a fog . . . or . . .

REBECCA: Yeah, it did, because I said it three times, plus Susan said it.

NORA: Well, I don't remember being given the responsibility to turn in that data . . .

REBECCA: I ended up collecting most of it, except for the stuff that only you had . . . That was just a little piece. I did everything else, including getting some of the data from your assistants. I just needed for you to . . .

NORA: That never got communicated to me.

REBECCA: Well, I . . .

NORA: I had no idea . . .

REBECCA: Well, I personally communicated that to you several times, and to your assistant, and Susan did too. Let's face it, some things are mundane, they're not important, they're irritations, but they're part of being a team. Everybody is in this together, and we have to do our little parts to keep this thing running. That's the only point I wanted to make, really. I didn't appreciate getting yelled at. I didn't deserve that . . . because you're my colleague. You shouted

	at me before, when we were all cleaning up the lab together. I really didn't appreciate that. Because you're not my superior. You're just my colleague. I feel like I try to treat you with respect. [Rebecca's voice begins to break with stress.] I don't need any more yelling or dumping on in my life. I don't need it. [More calmly now.] I don't need it from anybody in this lab. I just don't see that it belongs in the workplace. Does that make any sense?
NORA:	[Sighs.] It makes sense from your perspective. I don't know how to, exactly, say all of this right. [Voice begins to break.]
REBECCA:	[Cheerfully.] Neither do I. We're just mucking through. [Both laugh.]

Both parties have gotten through some initial turbulence in the joint session. Both have shared some of their feelings. Each could have expressed her thoughts in a more effective way, but the mediator feels they are making progress on their own and does not interrupt.

NORA:	How it feels to me . . . And we all have blind places where we come across way different than how we really intend to . . .
REBECCA:	Absolutely!
NORA:	And I think I'm caught in one of those things right now. I think that 20 percent of what you say is what I did, and the rest of it I'm thinking, "*Whaaat?*"
REBECCA:	Well, you could ask the opinions of people that were in the lab that day when you lit into me, and you could see if it's 20 percent . . .
NORA:	And I . . . I . . . [Trying to interrupt.]
REBECCA:	And I'm making up 80 percent? You'd find out, talking to the individuals present, that that was not the case. I wasn't making a single thing up. I wasn't misinterpreting one single thing.
NORA:	[Softly.] Well, I guess then . . . You know . . . I guess . . .

REBECCA: So, if you were interested in finding out the specifics . . .
NORA: Then I have to go around to all the other people that you discussed it with?
REBECCA: No, not the people I discussed it with, people who were present at the time that it happened. Obviously, you think that 80 percent of what I'm saying is being colored . . . It's very unprofessional behavior, in my opinion. [Laughing.] We can lay into our kids sometimes, but it's really inappropriate to do that with a colleague, a professional colleague. Obviously, there can be an interpretation on my part, but it's absolutely what happened. Susan was there, Jim was there, Rodrigo was there, and I don't know

Party-Directed Mediation allows for differences in levels of mediator interference during the joint session.

	who all was there. [Now more tensely.] I'm not making up 80 percent of what I'm saying.
Nora:	I didn't say you were. But . . .
Rebecca:	I interpreted that's what you said.
Nora:	Well, I remember . . . [Sighs.] I'm feeling as if you're saying that the way you saw it, is, by golly, the way it was, and if I feel differently I'd better go and check it out with everybody else to find out that you were right and I was wrong.

After Nora and Rebecca converse for a while, Rebecca asks an important question based on something Nora said earlier.

Rebecca:	What do you envision by peace and reconciliation?
Nora:	My number one thing I want to express to you is that I really, honestly do care about you as a person, and I care about your work. That is genuinely how I feel, and I know that you don't believe that.
Rebecca:	[Sighs.]
Nora:	I've no idea how to get over how you feel about that, because that's not how you perceive me. I guess I could go through every incident and try and show . . .
Rebecca:	[Softly.] That the intentions were different.
Nora:	I don't think that would be very productive.
Rebecca:	No, I don't think it would be very productive. It would be a waste of time. I would like a professionally based, respectful relationship. Just because you're a human being, and I'm a human being. For that reason alone. If there could be some hearing on both sides . . . I like you as a person, and that's a fact. Maybe, if we can feel straight enough with each other, then we can talk about it instead of letting it build up. That's my vision. That was my hope coming into this. Discussing the specific issues would be a waste of time. That's where I would like to go. Does that make any sense?
Nora:	I . . . I . . .

REBECCA:	Or do you hear what I'm saying? Or is it difficult to . . .
NORA:	I . . . I hear what you're saying. I'm feeling [Sigh.] . . . I'm feeling judged. If you could hear my perspective on at least one of the old incidents . . .
REBECCA:	Please! I mean, feel free.
NORA:	You know, because I'm feeling [Sigh.] . . . There's no point for me to explain how I feel about something, because I'll be told that it wasn't true.
REBECCA:	Then, that would not meet my objective—to have a respectful, open relationship—if I wasn't going to listen to anything you said and try to interpret things from your point of view.
NORA:	Oh, good, then.
REBECCA:	I'm sorry if I'm coming across as judgmental. I have interpretations of how things went. My objective would be to clear up the clutter and start with this new sort of collegial relationship that we could have . . . without any undertones of anything else.
NORA:	That would be nice.
REBECCA:	Yeah, that's what I'm here for. So, even though you said it wouldn't be beneficial to go into any incidents in particular, well, feel free. If it helps me understand . . .

An Issue of Authority

Nora goes on to explain that the request for information for the year-end report was a surprise to her. Rebecca, in turn, recounts some of the many attempts to communicate with Nora on this issue. Nora gives the impression of someone who is trying hard to understand herself. She has indicated she resents the idea of Rebecca acting as her boss, a theme that will resurface later in the joint session.

REBECCA:	So, how do I reach you in the future? What would be effective?
NORA:	Uh, it's a little bit of a challenge for me when I don't know where something is coming from. If Ken

	comes to me and says, "Nora, I need this done," then it's OK. But if somebody else comes to me and says, "Here, you need to do this," then I go, "*Whaaat?*"
REBECCA:	[Sighs.] I'm not trying to come off [Sighs.] . . .
NORA:	I feel like I'm taking orders from you.
REBECCA:	Is that the problem? That you think I'm ordering you? Is that an issue?
NORA:	I . . . have to work that through. If it comes off like that to me, then I have to work through some stuff and say to myself, "OK, Nora, you can do this."
REBECCA:	So, you have . . . with everyone . . . or just with me?
NORA:	No, no, no! It's just . . . If anyone who isn't my boss comes with an assignment, I'm going to respond with an "Oh, really? Why?"
REBECCA:	Now, knowing me for all the years you've seen me operate, would I come up to you and say, "Do this," without any explanation? "Nora, get this done!" And walk out the door? I mean, I'm a talker. It takes me forty-five minutes to say what anybody can say in ten and a half seconds.
NORA:	Maybe that's how it got lost. I don't know. [Laughing.]
REBECCA:	It's either a resentful pseudo-authority thing, or I blabber so you miss the point. [Laughing.]
NORA:	Or how about "Can you come and let me show you something?"
REBECCA:	So, you'd like me to physically take you to the scene and hear it itemized point by point?
NORA:	It would help me feel that we're more of a team . . .
REBECCA:	OK. [Tone turns to one of frustration.] I'll try to make my explanations succinct, make the chain of responsibility clear—that it's not originating from me. I'll try to take you physically to the place . . . Do you want it in writing, too? Or is the writing ineffective?

NORA: Rebecca, Rebecca, no . . . What I'd like . . .
REBECCA: Yes?
NORA: . . . is to feel that I'm part of the team and not an underling . . . I've had a whole string of flakes working for me . . .
REBECCA: [Frustrated.] But now, Nora, the flakes are 100 percent your responsibility. I approach you on issues, and you say, "Flake Number One, Flake Number Two," but you're their supervisor. It's your job that they know the rules of the lab. Right? Ultimately, isn't the responsibility with you and not with them?
NORA: I'm feeling lectured, and I'm not feeling like it's a collegial thing.
REBECCA: Do you understand the point I'm making?
NORA: Of course I understand, but your tone . . .
REBECCA: I'm trying so hard . . . That's the problem [Rebecca closes her eyes and lifts her hands towards her face, as if she was making an immense effort.] . . . I'm trying to make an impact . . . because I feel like . . . it's just so difficult. OK. I apologize, if I was being . . . if I was lecturing.

The conversation continues in a very friendly manner for a considerable length of time. Rebecca acknowledges it would be frustrating to work with some of the assistants Nora has had in the past. Nora recognizes that, ultimately, those who assist her are her responsibility. The tone of the women's conversation is lighthearted, with some laughter and lots of give-and-take. Rebecca brings the conversation back to the issues surrounding the conflict.

REBECCA: I'm meddling? Is there something in my presentation that's irritating, basically?
NORA: I think the last statement is probably true. The first one isn't.
REBECCA: How I work with people is irritating?
NORA: I would have to say, yes.

Rebecca and Nora begin to negotiate how they want to approach future difficulties. Mutual understanding increases despite the lack of a clear path.

NORA: I feel like you come out with these mandates . . .
REBECCA: Excuse me! Mandates!?
NORA: Yeah! I'm going to use that word, because that's the way it comes across to me.
REBECCA: Like what's a mandate? What have I mandated you to do?
NORA: OK. I feel like you lecture me. You come across as "you shall" or "this is what I want you to do." I'm not saying that's what you're doing, but that's the way it comes across to me.
REBECCA: [Sighs, moves her head half way between a nod and a shake, a searching nod.] Fine line . . .
NORA: Hmm. OK.
REBECCA: [Nods.]
NORA: And then . . . OK . . . but . . . and then I feel there isn't any room for me to say, "Can we bring another perspective to this?"
REBECCA: So, you need me to approach you in a way that's nonthreatening, a nonmandating sort of way . . .
NORA: To where I feel I'm part of the team, and I'm not just being told what to do . . .
REBECCA: Like I think I'm your supervisor and have a right to tell you things?
NORA: Or to lecture me [Making her voice deeper.] "Thou shalt . . ."
REBECCA: Do I actually . . . ?
NORA: Maybe not in those words, but that's the way it comes across to me.
REBECCA: I think it's certainly not with those words, certainly not with that intention . . . I have a certain intensity to me . . .
NORA: As do I . . . which . . .
REBECCA: So, I'm coming across as a dictator . . .
NORA: Not as a colleague . . . As my mother . . .

REBECCA: [Sighs full of distress.] Ouch.
NORA: I feel like you try to parent me . . .
REBECCA: All right.
NORA: And as a colleague, I really resent that.
REBECCA: OK. Watch the tone of voice and the words?
NORA: Approach me as a colleague who is an equal.
REBECCA: Which is, by the way, what I've asked you for. [Begins seriously but ends cheerfully.] I make a point of always asking for things with a *please* and a *thank you*.
NORA: Just a *please* and *thank you* doesn't necessarily soften the . . .
REBECCA: So, I'm too direct in what I say?
NORA: Direct is not the word . . . Too parenting. You're the *only* person making an issue out of it.

When Nora says, "You're the *only* person . . ." the mood of the conversation takes a sudden, ominous turn. Rebecca seems hurt and irritated. After a long pause, Nora says she would like to bring up another subject. She assures Rebecca that, even though it does not seem related, everything will be connected in the end.

Spending Time to Know People Better

NORA: One thing I have learned from this process, where a light bulb really went off in my mind on how to relate to others in this lab—because I've always been one to dive into my work, so I get really involved in what I'm doing and minutes become really, really precious—is that I don't take any time to chit-chat.
REBECCA: Right.
NORA: But . . . the light bulb that came on in my mind, through all of this, is that chit-chat is really important . . . and that's never been my perspective before.
REBECCA: Mmm . . . OK.
NORA: Because one of the things that was brought up is that I feel there's a lot of women in the lab now, and

there's kind of a network, and I was starting to realize that everybody else knew what everybody was doing this weekend, and I didn't. You know? When I tried to join someone's conversation . . . when they were talking about so-and-so's backpacking trip, or surfing experience, I didn't feel welcome in that, because I really hadn't made an effort to be part of that little group. I'm realizing that it's in the context of people who are friends—not necessarily buddy-buddy, where we do everything together outside of work, but friends more than colleagues—that these kinds of things get resolved and don't ever become irritants. And then it isn't necessary to put notes in boxes, because . . . because . . .

REBECCA: You can just go and say it to them . . .

NORA: Yes. You can just go up and say, "Hey, let's figure out a better way to do this." And it doesn't become a note in a box, a mark on a record . . . It just becomes friends working together because we care about each other and we like each other . . . and . . .

REBECCA: That's where I've tried to come from.

NORA: But, I don't feel I've been a part of that little group. I don't feel those channels have been open . . . Like the whole thing with the lab cleanup, ideally, would have been, "Hey, guys, let's take twenty minutes at lunch today, and let's go and attack the lab and clean it up."

REBECCA: I spent two and a half hours cleaning it by myself.

NORA: But if I had known . . . in a different paradigm, then you wouldn't have had to spend the two and a half hours. We could have done it together, could have had a great time, and done it in an hour. That's what I want!

REBECCA: Boy . . . you're very difficult to approach like that . . .

NORA: I know! I've been . . .

REBECCA: It wouldn't occur to me to approach you like that, because that avenue has never been available.
NORA: Because a lot of times I'm really busy. I'm running from here to there. But I'd like for you to think of me as more than just a colleague . . . because that's how I feel about you. I really do.
REBECCA: I feel we have an excellent lab, and I enjoy every single person in this lab . . . and I think everybody has some wonderful gifts that they bring to this job . . . I certainly don't exclude you from that thinking in any way, shape, or form. But sometimes I do feel as if I'm talking to a wall.

Suddenly, Nora goes on the attack. She somewhat aggressively brings up issues raised by Rebecca early in the conversation, as if the two parties had not spoken at all during the past hour. Rebecca, for the first time, looks towards the mediator, as if to ask for help. Rebecca tries to tell Nora that some of her comments have been hurtful.

For the next few minutes, the conversation heats up considerably. Much of what was previously discussed is repeated or summarized. The dialogue, despite its more stressful and agitated nature, is a positive one. Both individuals are still exchanging information and trying to come to an understanding.

REBECCA: Am I that unreasonable? What have I ever done? I'm expressing some surprise here, because it's foreign that I would say, "It is time to clean up the lab! March!" Let me assure you, that's not me. I'm not that naive or ridiculous. My kids don't . . . My dog doesn't do what I tell her to do . . . [Laughs.]
NORA: [Laughs.]
REBECCA: [Agitatedly.] You know, people are people! I try and cut people slack, because I sure pray they're cutting *me* slack. You know . . . [Calmly.] I'm sorry. I don't know how you got that impression. It never was in my mind.
NORA: OK. I'll accept that.

This subject is dead for the moment. Despite Nora's assurance that she would "accept that," it is clear that Rebecca is hurt. There is silence.

Another Chance to Remedy Dysfunctional Communication

Having come to a stop in the conversation, the mediator suggests that both parties focus on how they come across to each other. The conversation continues with the calm and positive give-and-take seen earlier.

REBECCA: [Makes a facial expression like "Where has he been?"] I think we covered it, didn't we? Unless there's more [Points to Nora.], I'd like to hear what else . . .

MEDIATOR: We have done some of that, but . . .

REBECCA: Nora, are there . . . some other things? Because this is a good time. It's hard to get this kind of time to just chat in the lab, and with a facilitator . . . OK [Laughing.] and everything. So, if there are other things that I do . . .

NORA: Well, I feel you're always mad or frustrated with me.

REBECCA: What do I do that makes you think that?

NORA: [Nora sighs, lowers her head, and buries it into her hands, as if searching for words.] I know it's going to come across wrong, but I know what I'm saying. I connect with others in the lab in a positive way, even if it's just a wave. But with you, I wonder, "What mood is she going to be in? Is she going to respond?"

REBECCA: So you have some trepidation when you approach me?

NORA: Yeah, yeah.

REBECCA: That you don't know what . . . ?

NORA: Whether you're going to be friendly or not. I sometimes need those little reassurances that you're OK with me, and that . . .

REBECCA: Well, I don't feel very comfortable a lot of times with you.
NORA: Well, OK then . . .
REBECCA: You talk about me judging you. I feel that's a really big thing coming back my way.
NORA: And that's what I'd like to change . . . I'd like to know what it is that I'm doing to make you feel you wouldn't want that type of relationship with me . . . To where you could say, "Hi, how's it going?" I'm not saying I want to be your best friend.
REBECCA: You just don't seem open to it. You seem irritated or something . . . But certainly we've had great conversations during the years. We have a lot in common.
NORA: Sure.
REBECCA: I've always recognized that, by the way. But it's not comfortable for me a lot of times. I don't feel—probably because you're busy or something—that there's a real receptivity to that sort of thing. [At this point Rebecca begins to speak very quickly, at higher pitch, waving her arms, as if she was acting out a great sense of urgency.] And get to your job, and do your thing, and . . .
NORA: [Laughs.]
REBECCA: Da, da, da, da, da, da, da, you know, and "Don't talk to me!" [Returns to a normal calm conversational tone.] I try to respect the way you feel and everything, but that's the way you come across. So, I'm not just going to say: [Switching for a moment to an exaggeratedly sweet voice.] "Oh, *hi*!" It's not that I'm angry. I don't want to bother you. [Rebecca's voice becomes a little strained.] You basically don't have an interest, or a want . . . Do you know what I'm saying? In a way . . .
NORA: I know . . . I . . .
REBECCA: [Continues in a strained, intense voice.] In a way, it's out of respect to you, but it's coming across as

	rudeness or freezing you out or something when . . . I'm going along with the cues that you don't want to be bothered . . . You've kind of said things in here.
NORA:	Yeah, but . . .
REBECCA:	[Calmly.] And I'm kind of a flake that floats around. I don't want to inject myself into your life and be a negative thing.
NORA:	I understand that, but it's not how I feel. If I've got a deadline, I've got a deadline.
REBECCA:	[Kindly.] Don't we all!
NORA:	But, I guess I'm saying, I'd like to have a certain amount of warmth in our relationship.
REBECCA:	[Softly.] OK, so I'm misinterpreting some things.
NORA:	So, please don't feel that I want everybody to stay away from me. Of course, my time is really crunched—it is—but that doesn't mean that a certain amount of warmth has to take a huge amount of time.
REBECCA:	Certainly not. All right.
NORA:	And I think that would help with the other things.

Here, Nora begins to tie this conversation back to the earlier discussion of how Rebecca can obtain her cooperation. While Party-Directed Mediation is designed to allow the disputants to control the conversation, perhaps it's unfortunate that Nora changes the subject when this issue seems almost resolved. The mediator does not take the opportunity to stop and celebrate the small triumphs that had been achieved, underscore some of what has been said, and refine a few points by saying:

"Both of you have shared a little about the difficulties faced in the past, and even a certain amount of hurt that has arisen from this conflict. I have also heard each of you say some very positive things about the other person, as well as about the underlying message that you both care about each other and about the relationship."

A few examples of what was said could have been shared. Then, the mediator could have continued: "I also sense an agreement of sorts on how each of you will approach the other in the future, in terms of the interpersonal relationship. I'm not talking about being best friends, but friendship beyond just simply a collegial relationship."

While the parties have come to a better understanding of how each of them has contributed to the dysfunctional communication in the past, much of what has been accomplished can be overlooked without such a summary. We saw Nora jump from one topic to another earlier. She told us to trust her, that she would circle back, and now she has kept her promise.

Are You My Boss?

While taking a moment to celebrate the successes achieved at this point would not have eliminated the mounting stress, it would have reduced some of the tension and frustration the women experience next. Nora wishes for Rebecca to approach her with the *whole plan of work*, so she does not feel singled out. Rebecca has spent hours separating the portion of the project on which Nora needs to work, so as to avoid taking more of Nora's time.

REBECCA: [With frustration.] I made, on my own time, a separate sheet that includes only the issues that . . . so I didn't bother you with the part that corresponds to Tim, or . . .
NORA: And I understand that, but you see . . .
REBECCA: [With high frustration, raised voice, and a tone of supplication, as if saying, "Can't you understand?"] I made you . . . I separated the part of the report I needed from you—individual sheets for you personally. Just what you wanted!
NORA: But . . . but, Rebecca . . .
REBECCA: [With high tension.] I gave you just what you wanted! A list of things specifically related to you! I made you a separate document!
NORA: [Calmly.] OK. And I understand that in your mind you were doing me a wonderful favor but . . .
REBECCA: [Calming down.] Did you not ask me to do that? Give you specific . . . ?
NORA: No, no, no.

REBECCA: I'm sorry. I must have misinterpreted it.
NORA: I felt singled out . . . like . . . you were saying that I was the worst person in the lab. "You have a page and a half to yourself." If I had seen the whole five-page report and realized that my list was part of a larger report you had to do, that I wasn't the only one that had to do a report . . .
REBECCA: [With frustration.] Knowing you and your time . . . [With high frustration.] I didn't even consider that as an approach. It's a waste . . . [With frustration.] Did I specifically come to you and tell you, "Look! This is stuff you have to do because of all of your garbage." [With high frustration.] What? Do you think there might be some sensitivity on your part in interpreting some of this?
NORA: [In a louder voice than normal.] There certainly is! There certainly is! I feel kind of . . . Well, I can document it. I have, by far, the messiest space in this lab! [Smiling.]
REBECCA: [With frustration.] Who do you think is in the sharp running for number two?
NORA: Not you! [Laughing.]
REBECCA: Oh, it's me. And that's the way it is.
NORA: Anyway [Laughing.], I don't consider it a competition.

Eventually, Rebecca returns to the issue of the year-end report.

REBECCA: [Highly irritated.] Do you want Ken to deal with this? How can I possibly know that you need the whole report so you don't feel I'm pointing my finger at you? [These last words are pronounced while shaking her finger at Nora.] It was just a job given to me by Ken.
NORA: And you're going to turn around and give assignments to other people . . .
REBECCA: [With irritation.] That's correct, because that's the charge I was given. I think there's a certain

	sensitivity here that you've got to get past! [In utter frustration, Rebecca faces the mediator now.] Tell me what I'm missing.
NORA:	[Softly.] First of all, I'd like to say . . .
REBECCA:	[Highly irritated.] And how can I know? [She begins to repeat herself again.]
NORA:	[Softly.] Well, I guess I'm unreasonable.
REBECCA:	Nora, that's just a defensive comment! [Irritated.] How can I know that what you wanted is the big picture that takes up time you don't have?
MEDIATOR:	[Softly.] Rebecca, you need to permit Nora to respond. OK?
REBECCA:	[Addressing the mediator.] Oh, OK. [Irritated.] I'm trying to understand how to do something in a nonoffensive way, that doesn't put up barriers or show a lack of cooperation. [Softly, almost in tears.] That's my objective, so I'll be quiet.
NORA:	[Pauses, then softly.] I . . . I can't help but think, that if I spoke to you, the way you just spoke to me . . .
REBECCA:	[Softly sighs.]
NORA:	[Now almost in tears.] . . . you'd say I was yelling at you. [Pause, continues in teary voice.] And I wasn't acting collegially.
REBECCA:	[Irritated.] OK, I certainly apologize if that's the way I was coming across! There's a certain frustration level with . . . [Calmer.] I'm trying to see . . . [Softer, slowly, with measured comments.] I can't . . . envision the exact . . . perfect . . . approach for you. [Pauses, trying to find the words to continue.]
NORA:	Rebecca, I don't know if you heard what I said.
REBECCA:	You feel upset that I'm hammering on you.
NORA:	I'd like to take this opportunity . . . to ask for your understanding for me that when I get frustrated . . .
REBECCA:	[Intensely, still frustrated.] I'll certainly do that. [Calmly.] Except, can I say one thing? [Pauses.] When I went to talk to you in the lab, you said, "What gives you the right to come here and tell me

	what to do?" I consider that a little different from expressing frustration. Even though it was wrong . . . That's a little different from trying to . . .
NORA:	[Sighs.]
REBECCA:	[Intensely.] To me, it's different when someone says, "Who are you to come in here and tell me what to do?" That's a little more in-your-face type of challenging. I'm coming across as frustrated because I feel like I want to hit my head with a hammer because I'm not getting it. [Clenching her fists in frustration and moving them around.] I'm not getting how I can fix this thing.
NORA:	Ken gave you an assignment, so now you have the authority to tell everybody else what to do. That mechanism was never explained to me. I didn't know you were my boss in that context.
REBECCA:	[Softly.] Nora, I'm not your *boss*.
NORA:	But when you give me an assignment, and you tell me that Ken gave you this responsibility, then you're my boss in that context.
REBECCA:	Can't you just trust me that I wouldn't want to boss you around?
NORA:	In the absence of a warm relationship . . . that's hard for me . . .
REBECCA:	Why would I want . . .
NORA:	Well, don't ask a question if you don't want to hear the answer. [Laughing.]
REBECCA:	I do.
NORA:	There are lots of people in my life who . . .
REBECCA:	I want to know for me. Why would I . . .
NORA:	Why did all the other people in my life do it? [Raises her hands and laughs.]
REBECCA:	But me?
NORA:	I feel I'm being boxed in a corner that I don't want to be in. [Pause.] If I feel it's coming in a way that's dictatorial . . . that's hard for me.

REBECCA: Is it like an authority thing? Are you in a rebellion thing?
NORA: Even if Ken, or the owner of the lab, flew in, it somehow needs to fit in a day. I guess I have a really hard response with anybody who waltzes into my lab area . . .
REBECCA: *Waltzes*?
NORA: I'm not talking about you.
REBECCA: Oh.
NORA: With any relationship . . . Anybody who gives me a list of assignments or says, "You're going to do this," it doesn't matter who they are. Whoa! I can't . . . You can request to get things on the list, but please help me to understand how to fit it in to the rest of the . . . Rebecca, you've got to understand. It's not you. I want you to understand a picture of my life. Right now there's a lot of people mad at me, and I wish I could get them all in one room at the same time and have them work out what I should do first. Whose project is most important? Because when someone else walks in and throws something else at me, it's hard to fit it in, and I'm not going to welcome it with open arms.
REBECCA: [Looks down at the table.]
NORA: Do you know what I'm saying?
REBECCA: [Silence.]
NORA: Ken is very good about that. He lets me rant and rave for a few minutes, and then I add it to my list.
REBECCA: [Discouraged.] All right. I'm just trying to help Ken.
NORA: Then let me feel like I'm helping Ken rather than helping you. It's not that I don't want to help you.

Nora's last comment could be considered offensive, but Rebecca does not seem to take it that way. Rebecca has just about given up, however, and is exhausted. The third party understands that Rebecca is facing a very difficult situation. The mediator asks a tentative question.

MEDIATOR: Nora, you said that even if Ken, or the lab owner, asked for help, you might not be able to provide it, because you're so busy. Let me describe a scenario. Would you prefer, say, for Rebecca to finish what she can of the report, turn it in to Ken, and say, "Ken, here's the report. It's completed, except for Nora's portion. I tried to follow up, but couldn't get her part. If you want it, get it yourself." How would you feel if Rebecca took that approach?

NORA: If that's what needed to be, that's what needed to be.

MEDIATOR: Let me just respond, as an independent bystander, OK? I'm going to extrapolate a little bit, so please forgive me if I don't use the exact words. I hear Rebecca saying that she wants to do the job right. OK? But it's also taking an emotional toll, and though she didn't say it, it's taking too much of her time. Now, we started at the beginning with a comment made by Rebecca, that she felt your program was more important than her program. In effect, uh, even though the words are different, the context now makes me feel that you're telling Rebecca that your program *is* more important than hers, because unless Ken comes over and asks for something, you're not going to do it.

Nora listens quietly while the mediator speaks. Suddenly, she becomes extremely upset, throws up her hands, and pulls back her chair, and raises her voice.

NORA: You know what? No! I'm sorry, but I'm being painted wrongly. I did the stinking job . . . OK?

MEDIATOR: Nora . . .

NORA: What we are dealing with here . . . is a relational thing . . . [Calmly.] I thought we were talking about how to deal with things in the future, without relational difficulties. I thought that was what we were talking about.

MEDIATOR:	Uh-huh. All I'm saying is, in my corner—and I may be misunderstanding—I'm getting the feeling that you're saying that helping Rebecca do her job is not a sufficient reason . . . even though Ken delegated . . .
NORA:	[Waving her hand, agitatedly.] No, no . . .
MEDIATOR :	Oh, I'm sorry, I'm totally misunderstanding?
NORA:	You missed it completely.
MEDIATOR:	I'm getting the wrong message here, so why don't you explain it to Rebecca?
NORA:	[Facing Rebecca.] I understand you're helping Ken. You didn't have to separate my part and take the extra time . . .
REBECCA:	The real bottom-line issue here . . . There's something . . . I don't know how to extract it . . . What is the real issue here? Underneath that stuff?
NORA:	The real issue . . . The real issue is how you come across to me. And . . . or—maybe I should say it differently—how I perceive you coming across to me.
REBECCA:	[Calmly.] No, there's a resentment that I gave you a list of things to do in the capacity . . . It's a resentment . . .
NORA:	If you're going to be my boss in this area . . .
REBECCA:	[Sighs and speaks with a barely audibly and painful voice.] I'm . . .
NORA:	First of all, I need to be clear on that—in this context you're my boss.
REBECCA:	I'm not your *boss*! [Sighs.]
NORA:	[Intensely, moving about her arms.] Well, then, you're acting like my boss!

Nora goes on for a while using the word *boss* several times and insisting that Rebecca is her boss in these circumstances if the assignment came from Ken. Throughout the early part of the mediation—before Rebecca's frustration mounted so high—it was

Rebecca who was constantly trying to find a workable solution. A line seems to have been crossed after the first hour, however, when Rebecca's patience gave way.

REBECCA:	[Irritatedly.] What if the situation were reversed, and you had to come up with this report? Do you think you would be running around as everybody's boss?
NORA:	In that context . . .
REBECCA:	[Irritatedly.] Is that what you would actually be doing with the people in this lab, bossing them around? Being the big boss, writing this stuff . . . [Rebecca puffs her chest and draws with her hands.] Is that what you would think?
NORA:	[Intensely.] If it's to be done in that type of context . . . I don't understand . . .
MEDIATOR:	Let . . .
REBECCA:	[Sighs, then speaks softly.] I'm done. I'm finished.
NORA:	I don't understand.
REBECCA:	I don't either.
MEDIATOR:	I can see what Rebecca is saying. The word *boss* is a little bit strong—more than strong—because she is not your boss.
REBECCA:	It's a connotation . . .
MEDIATOR:	It's a little strong . . . to me.
NORA:	But I feel that what she's saying to me is pretty strong—that when she comes to me with something Ken has given her, it's not a request; it's a requirement.
MEDIATOR:	Can a requirement come from a colleague on behalf of somebody else, without . . . ?
NORA:	If it comes in the context of a colleague . . . [In a broken, teary voice.] My interpretation of *boss* is someone who gives you directives and may or may not have any consideration for how you're going to get them done.
REBECCA:	[Highly irritated, shouting.] Fine! OK! I've just had enough! It's not even something anybody cares

	about! I understand it's a stupid little job! I understand that! [Sighs.]
NORA:	Well . . . I . . .
REBECCA:	[Highly irritated, shouting, not at Nora, but in general.] And I'm so *sorry* that I provoke people by making a request in such a direct manner! I'll change! I'll work harder . . . put more time in figuring out how to get the job done in a more efficient manner, and I'll just figure out how everybody needs to be approached to do a *stupid* job that means extra time and that's of no benefit to me, or my job, or my paycheck . . . That frustrates me! Because it's stupid! [Pause.] I don't need it! Ken needs it. *He* needs it! [Raises her hand above her head.] He's up to *here*! Have you seen how the guy *looks*? He looks older. I mean, he's not even fun anymore. [Sighs. Then, intensely, but much more calmly.] But I can do a better job of communicating these issues. I sincerely say that I will, because it will get everything done more efficiently, and then I'll not have to deal with it. That's good . . . that's a good resolution.

Just when things are looking particularly difficult, Nora surprises us again.

NORA:	[Gently.] Well, Rebecca, can I help you with it?
REBECCA:	You want to take over the responsibility for the year-end report?
NORA:	No . . . no . . . no . . . no . . . no!
REBECCA:	[Calmly.] Yeah, you're not stupid. You're not going to do anything you're not getting any credit for doing.
NORA:	[Laughing.] Yeah, yeah . . . Is the fox going to guard the hen house? No . . . no . . . no. . . But I can see some ways that we can work together on it. Divide and conquer. I agree with you that Ken shouldn't

	have to do it all, but you shouldn't have to do it all, either. It's way too big of an assignment.
REBECCA:	This has turned into something a little more intense . . .
NORA:	This has turned into a monster and too much for one person to tackle. I'm saying, why don't we share it, so you're not stuck with the whole thing? Because you can't take the stress of it. Your job and your life is just as complicated as mine is.
REBECCA :	OK, I appreciate those comments. They're pretty reflective of how I feel.

Nora and Rebecca work out the details of a solution, so the burden can be shared, and Ken does not have to worry about the year-end report. The plan involves asking for the cooperation of all the lab professionals. Rebecca admits that other staff members have been almost as delinquent as Nora in responding to her requests for cooperation. Rebecca vents her frustration, and Nora tries to show understanding. At one point Rebecca, with great sincerity, says, "So, I'm glad you're on board." There is some joking and decompressing. The topic is concluded.

Next, the mediator asks Nora to expand on her desire to be a more integral part of the friendship among the female professionals in the lab. There has been no specific resolution to that issue.

REBECCA:	[Calmly.] OK. And can I say just one thing before we finish up the other topic? [Addressing the mediator.] Nora asked me to give her the big picture. Unfortunately, I gave the big picture in *very emphatic tones*. Nora got the big picture, and she put out the hand to help me. And I just learned a lot from that. [Looking at Nora.] I just wanted to say that I appreciate it . . . I get it.

Being Part of the Female Friendship Group

REBECCA:	Anyway, so, what was the question? About collegiality among the women?

Only after parties are brought into a joint session can the mediator be sure that the preparation during the pre-caucuses has been adequate.

MEDIATOR: I'd like Nora to explain the fact that she'd like to feel part of the friendship among the professional women in the lab. Go ahead, Nora.

NORA: And I alluded to that. That's something that I really . . . I didn't consider as important in the past as I do now, because I'm understanding . . .

REBECCA: [Whispering.] Oh, that's fantastic!

NORA: I'd like to feel, at least among the women, [With humor.] you can't just help some of the guys, [Looks at the mediator.] no offense . . .

REBECCA: No offense. [Also laughs and looks at the mediator.]

NORA: But I want to be part of the women's chit-chat a little bit.

REBECCA: Well Nora, what it takes is for you to have an interest in their lives—Vicky's surfing, Chiaki's backpacking trips, or something with their kids. It takes time to establish relationships.

NORA: Rebecca, I know that . . .

REBECCA: Oh, I'm being a little bit too simple.

NORA: Well, no . . .

REBECCA: So, jump in with twenty feet! Go for it!

NORA: I'm trying to, but I'm asking, if there are two or three people talking and I walk up, don't change the subject or walk away and ignore me, please. Recognize that I'm trying to make an effort.

REBECCA: Well, I was not aware . . . Do you think that happens?

NORA: Uh-huh.

REBECCA: And it's a conscious thing?

NORA: I don't know if it's conscious or not, but I sure feel it.

REBECCA: Well, then, that's a problem.

NORA: I'm *not* feeling terribly rejected. I'm just feeling frustrated.

REBECCA: Then, the only thing I can suggest is just what I said: making the time, seeking the people . . .

NORA: And I . . .

REBECCA: That's what I do. I like talking to women. It's a huge support in my life. Chiaki calls me if her car breaks down; Francisca, when her husband is out of town and she needs someone to get some medicine for her sick baby . . . It's a relationship. It nurtures me.
NORA: Well, I'm available for those things, too.
REBECCA: Then just come and be a natural part of it.
NORA: I'm trying to, but I'm feeling like . . .
REBECCA: Put those feelings aside, don't talk yourself out of this, don't . . .
NORA: Rebecca, let me finish my statement.
REBECCA: All right.
NORA: There have been times when I've tried to do that, and I've felt excluded. I'm asking, could you make an effort to include me? I'm not saying I'm not going to make an effort.
REBECCA: OK. [Drawn out.]
NORA: In fact, I've been making efforts, and I'm sure nobody noticed or nobody was aware . . . but when they were talking about somebody's backpacking trip, or somebody's something, and I walked up to join the conversation, the conversation stopped.
REBECCA: That would be extremely uncomfortable, to say the least.
NORA: And it doesn't make me think, "Oh, poor me," but I'm asking for you to help me, so that doesn't happen. Because I'm making an effort.
REBECCA: By saying that . . . do you think that somehow I'm responsible for the dynamics . . .
NORA: No, I'm not. I'm just asking . . .
REBECCA: OK, I'm just trying to straighten it out.
NORA: I'm just asking for your help. Since you're aware of what I'm trying to do, I'm asking for your assistance. I'm not saying you've done something wrong in the past. I'm not saying that at all.
REBECCA: But, I just get a sense of this racing, racing, running, running, and . . . What I'm saying is that I perceive

	you as being too busy for me to drop in and say, "I tried a strawberry jam recipe." I worry you might think, "What an idiot! Why does she think I care?"
NORA:	Why don't you try it?
REBECCA:	And I have.
NORA:	Sometimes I have a genuine deadline.
REBECCA:	Of course.
NORA:	Don't assume I'm not interested.
REBECCA:	That would be a disservice. OK. All right.
NORA:	So, I'm just . . .
REBECCA:	Fine! I think that's great! It's just that after twenty-something years [Laughing.] I haven't thought, like, there's a great deal, you know . . . I sometimes think people think I'm a frivolous type of person. I don't want to pass through here and not know anything about others. When you die, what are you going to look back at but the friendships you have made? Connections with people enrich our lives. We have more in common than not. We've been in this job for many years. We're more the same than different. But I don't feel comfortable . . . So you're saying it's OK to feel comfortable just dropping in once in a while to just say hello?
NORA:	Yeah! It always has been. Is it OK if I do that with you?
REBECCA:	Yeah! [Laughing.] Everybody else does. If that's something welcome with you . . . I never got that feeling from you.
NORA:	I'm sorry, because I've always felt like that. I've done a really poor job . . .
REBECCA:	Then, it's been a loss for both of us . . .
NORA:	I've done a really poor job . . .
REBECCA:	A loss for both of us . . . It's been a wrong assumption on both our parts, and we both lost out.
NORA:	And, yes, I'm very available to help people with whatever jams they may be in . . . and I often need help myself.

REBECCA: As the facilitator said when we started, I've always said and always known you have good intentions and a good heart. I know that. But sometimes you're a little brusque, and it's off-putting.
NORA: I'm sorry.
REBECCA: That's OK. I'm just telling you why . . . the approachability factor is a little less than comfortable. I don't want to feel like I'm barging . . .
NORA: I'll try not to make you feel . . .
REBECCA: We're not talking about a three-hour gab session every day.
NORA: No, we can't.
REBECCA: No, just stick your head in at lunch. I'd welcome it.
NORA: OK.
REBECCA: So . . . that would be a positive thing. If those sorts of positive interactions occur, then these other things won't be a problem.
NORA: That's why . . . That's one reason I really wanted to change my . . . I've always been a pretty nose-to-the-grindstone person here, and that's one reason why . . . in addition to the fact I really care about you guys . . . I do care about people.
REBECCA: I know that. I've always known that . . .
NORA: Sometimes I've isolated myself, because there were things going on in my life . . . and I didn't want to bleed all over everybody.
REBECCA: And it's a survival thing. But friends need to do that and take turns . . .
NORA: But you have to have those relationships established . . . and I didn't. I'm in a different place now.
REBECCA: That's a good thing. I'm a little too emotional, but decent.
NORA: Of course. That was on my list. And I've always admired how you always put people first. I've looked up to you. I really admire that.

This mutual validation goes on for some time, with beautiful sentiments shared between Nora and Rebecca. The parties freely exchange these positive aspects about each other without being prompted.

Postscript

I received the following note from Rebecca, a month after the mediation: "I just wanted to let you know how much you have helped Nora and me. We are now talking regularly, and I'm enjoying the contact thoroughly. All the negativity that had built up for so long is gone, and I feel like I've lost a hundred pounds! The process was tough, but the results were more than worth it."

Half a year later, I was able to catch up with Nora and Rebecca, who had cemented their friendship. They had recently gone out to the movies and their families were planning a joint camping trip to a nearby beach.

After the first edition of this book was published, I gave each of them a copy. Nora and Rebecca politely thanked me but independently explained how busy they were. I was quite surprised when they both showed up at my office, together, the very next day. Each had taken the book home and could not put it down. With huge smiles, and each pointing to the other, they said in unison, "You favored *her!*"

According to Nora and Rebecca, more than the mediation itself, reading this transcript of the dispute created a desire to change dysfunctional behaviors. One confessed, "I was afraid to walk out of my office and have people see me so naked, and then I realized that people around me have known all this time that I was naked. It was only I who did not know it."

Over four years have elapsed since the first edition of this book was published and the sending of this second edition to the printers. Nora and Rebecca continue to be good friends.

Specific research on conditions that favor sharing a transcript summary with the disputants might be an excellent addition to the body of knowledge about conflict management.

Part V – Preventive Mediation

12
Negotiated Performance Appraisal: Alternative and Preventive Mediation

After employee selection, performance appraisal is arguably the most important management tool in an organizational setting—yet it is greatly disliked and often avoided. In the traditional appraisal, the supervisor acts more as a judge than as a coach. Unfortunately, the focus is on blame rather than on helping the individual assume responsibility for improvement.

In contrast, the *Negotiated Performance Appraisal* promotes candid dialogue between supervisor and subordinate. It encourages the parties to speak about vital matters that are seldom addressed. For this reason, the model can also serve as a form of preventive mediation—before negative feelings mount.

The Negotiated Performance Appraisal also functions as an alternative mediation model—for dealing with disputes between supervisors and subordinates. It elegantly preserves the hierarchical power differences between them while at the same time allowing for a full dialogue about interpersonal issues that might be getting in the way of a positive relationship.

The process is carried out in the context of helping the subordinate thrive on the job, while it provides the superior the unique opportunity to examine his or her own blind spots. In one organization, an executive tried a traditional mediation with only partial success. At the conclusion of a Negotiated Performance Appraisal, he found this approach yielded the elusive beneficial results he had sought.

The Negotiated Performance Appraisal model leans heavily on Party-Directed Mediation in that it preserves the two pillars of the latter: the pre-caucus and the facilitation of a direct conversation between the affected parties through a joint session.

Individual Need for Feedback

Although people vary in their desire for improvement, generally they want to know how well they are performing. Some individuals imagine the worst possible scenario when organizational communication is weak or infrequent. Others tend to think that all is well despite the need for changes.

Subordinates will often be grateful for information on how to improve shortcomings when it is presented in a constructive fashion.

In general, leaders who tend to look for subordinates' positive behaviors—and do so in a sincere, nonmanipulative way—will have less difficulty giving constructive feedback or suggestions. Furthermore, in the negotiated approach, the burden for performance analysis does not fall on the supervisor alone but requires introspection on the part of the individual being evaluated.

People need encouraging feedback and validation on a regular basis. Few management actions can have as good an effect on individual performance as positive affirmation. Without these goodwill deposits, withdrawals cannot be made.

Next to the disciplinary process, performance appraisal interviews are probably the most dreaded management activity.

The subordinate often reacts with passive resistance or noticeable defensiveness. No wonder supervisors are often hesitant to deliver bad news to subordinates. It is easier to ignore the problem and hope it goes away.

Through the Negotiated Performance Appraisal, managers transfer a substantial amount of responsibility for improvement to those being evaluated.

A key manager went on to become an outstanding performer after concerns regarding his marketing responsibilities were clarified through the negotiated appraisal. During the pre-caucus, this same manager had voiced apprehensions that perhaps the organization did not need him anymore. Numerous enterprises have observed significant and encouraging transformations after going through the process.

While effective dialogue does not always constitute agreement, it permits both parties to make more informed decisions. The feedback I have received is that subordinates make huge strides in their job performance after the negotiated appraisal.

But not always. One subordinate decided to quit his job following what had appeared to be an excellent dialogue with the supervisor. The job expectations did not suit his needs. Better to discover this sooner than later.

At another organization, an executive and a key middle manager had a candid conversation about the need for the latter to become proficient in a second language. They had skirted the issue for years. After the negotiated approach, the middle manager discovered he was held in very high regard and was being groomed for a significant promotion. It happened that the new position required learning this language. The economic benefits offered by the promotion were considerable, yet the price required to learn another language is often hefty. Once again, the key is *having the conversation* that will clarify needs and expectations. While the Negotiated Performance Appraisal improves communication, it does not guarantee that subordinates will decide to make the necessary improvements. The open dialogue, nevertheless, along with the follow-up, will soon make

The Negotiated Performance Appraisal preserves the hierarchical power differences between a supervisor and a subordinate while at the same time allowing for a full conversation about interpersonal issues.

it clear to the corporation if it had found the right candidate for the position or needed to look elsewhere.

The best place to introduce the negotiated approach to performance appraisal is within the highest levels of the organization, where it is likely to make its most profound contributions. Middle managers, who in turn apply the approach with their subordinates, will have already participated in the Negotiated Performance Appraisal in their roles as subordinates and will therefore understand the value this tool can have.

Facilitator Role

Although the Negotiated Performance Appraisal can be carried out between supervisor and subordinate alone, the use of a third party can greatly facilitate the success of the approach. Certainly, it lends the process legitimacy and seriousness. The presence of a facilitator underscores the performance appraisal's value to the organization and ensures it is not seen as just another required form or procedure.

The role of the third party may be played by a facilitator, mediator, interpersonal relations consultant, or human resources manager. As in any mediation process, there are benefits to involving an outside party. This is vital when the Negotiated Performance Appraisal is used as a mediation tool.

During the pre-caucuses, the facilitator can help the parties learn how to present their thoughts in the best possible light and to focus on needed changes rather than on defending positions. The third party is also there to listen to the individuals, ask good questions, help brainstorm, examine the viability of solutions, and provide interpersonal negotiation training.

The third party's involvement in the pre-caucuses will vary depending on the skills of participants and the thoroughness of their preparation. Just as in Party-Directed Mediation, there will be times when additional pre-caucuses are required. It is the responsibility of the facilitator to gauge the safety of moving parties along to the joint session. Permitting a lapse of time between the pre-caucuses and the joint session may also allow individuals to work through complex feelings.

The role of the facilitator changes substantially during the joint session. Once again, depending on the effectiveness of the pre-caucusing, the skill of the parties, and facilitator style, the participation of the mediator can vary widely—from merely observing the discussion and recording agreements to actively making sure dysfunctional communication tactics are avoided.

Overview of the Process

Supervisors ask subordinates to bring three lists to the performance appraisal interview. That is, areas in which the subordinate (1) performs well, (2) has shown recent improvement, and (3) needs to improve.

Because the supervisor will also fill out the three lists, individuals are more likely to bring candid responses to the table. It helps for the subordinates to hear the supervisor say something like, "I will also fill out these three lists." The supervisor should then reiterate the purpose of each list by stating: "I will list (1) the areas in which you perform well and contribute to the organization, (2) the areas in which you have shown recent improvement, and (3) the areas in which you can improve."

It is a good practice for the supervisors to make eye contact with each of the subordinates while emphasizing each list. Eye contact transmits an important message to those present—that there are areas in which each of them excels and, just as important, areas in which improvement is needed.

It is human nature to dislike bringing up our own faults, but it is also human nature to prefer to point out our own shortcomings rather than to permit someone else to do it. This process allows subordinates to think in terms of their supervisor's perceived expectations as well as their own.

There is a *fourth* list to be filled out only by the subordinates—just as significant as the first three. Through the fourth list, the superior asks, "What can I do differently as your supervisor, so you can be more effective in your job?" One businessman replaced the words *be more effective* for the word *thrive*.

Note that the supervisor is not asking the subordinate, "Do you like me?" Rather, the focus is on what changes the supervisor can make to facilitate the improved performance of the subordinate.

If a supervisor is not genuinely willing to listen to what the subordinate has to say, the Negotiated Performance Appraisal should be avoided.

When several subordinates are scheduled to participate in a Negotiated Performance Appraisal over the course of a month or two, they can be brought together to hear an explanation of the procedure. This way, subordinates do not feel singled out, and the superior saves time by explaining the approach only once.

During the pre-caucuses, the facilitator can help the parties learn how to present their thoughts in the best possible light.

The facilitator meets separately with the superior and with the subordinate, during the pre-caucuses, to help each person brainstorm and fill out their respective lists with concrete examples in each category.

The subordinate fills out all four lists; the superior only the first three. Of the combined seven lists, three are particularly vital and often require additional time and thoroughness. For the *supervisor*, List I (what the subordinate does well) is the most demanding. For the *subordinate*, List III (what the subordinate can improve) and List IV (what the supervisor can change) are the most important.

It is appropriate to give subordinates enough time to think through these lists, perhaps two weeks or so to complete the assignment. Thorough instructions will save much time later on. The facilitator coaches the supervisor on how to fill out his or her lists as well as on how to introduce the program to the subordinates.

The Performance Appraisal Joint Meeting

When the time has arrived to sit and discuss the subordinate's performance, a relaxed, positive atmosphere should prevail. A location without distractions is essential. All phones need to be turned off and interruptions eliminated. Such measures give subordinates the message that they are the the recipients of the supervisor's undivided attention.

The supervisor and subordinate sit across from each other at one end of the table, while the third party sits at the other end, far away from both individuals, as we saw in Party-Directed Mediation (Figure 5–1). This is done to underscore that the conversation is between the two parties.

List I

The main purposes of the first list are (1) to recognize the subordinate's strong points and let the person know these positive qualities have not passed unobserved; (2) to increase the person's confidence and receptivity to constructive criticism (because individuals who are overly concerned about their self-esteem, or about being attacked, will naturally become defensive and less receptive to suggestions for improvement); and (3) to prevent coloring a subordinate's unconstructive behaviors with the same ink (i.e., to avoid labeling an individual as a difficult person rather than as someone who resorts to certain unproductive behaviors).

The subordinate is asked to read List I aloud. The superior listens intently and takes notes as needed. If the individual says something the supervisor finds strange, troubling, or unclear, the superior can ask the subordinate to amplify or explain the point. People seldom mind being interrupted when it means having the opportunity to offer clarification. Such inquiries ought not put individuals on the defensive, nor should they be comments disguised as questions.

The Negotiated Performance Appraisal model makes use of pre-caucusing and joint sessions. During the joint session, the facilitator sits away from the parties and permits them to mostly manage their own conversation.

Because subordinates read their list first, supervisors can add any missing praise to their own lists. This opportunity should not be taken lightly. At one firm, a superior focused on a person's early career contributions but missed the more recent ones. The subordinate was upset that the supervisor was not paying attention to her latest accomplishments.

These types of errors are more likely to occur in organizations in which performance appraisals are conducted on a regular basis and supervisors use notes from previous years. The supervisor needs to focus on more recent events without ignoring the past.

After the subordinate finishes reading the first list, the supervisor proceeds. The superior praises the subordinate's good points, even if the person has *already* mentioned them.

The first list is the vital foundation of the Negotiated Performance Appraisal. Time spent developing and discussing what subordinates do well is never wasted. In the rush of everyday activities, the supervisor often concentrates on what an individual is doing wrong. How often do we take time to give carefully considered praise? Frequently, a subordinate is visibly pleased when honestly complimented by a supervisor.

A subordinate's feelings of self-worth are strengthened by such validation. It can constitute the positive force, or momentum, that gives an individual the strength and determination to try harder in areas of weakness. As previously mentioned, sincere compliments are goodwill deposits without which withdrawals cannot be made.

Employees can quickly sense, however, when a compliment is not sincere. Also, when a supervisor is constantly critical and cannot find anything about a subordinate to compliment, the underrated person often has little desire to make needed changes.

Given the immense importance of the the first list, let us take a moment to consider what constitutes an effective compliment, one that is really *felt* by the recipient.

When someone does something that is appreciated, and we thank the individual, such appreciation is simply a matter of *good manners*. Feelings of resentment may otherwise surface.

If we return a few hours later, or the next day, and remind the person of the positive circumstances associated with the original compliment, the power of the praise is multiplied.

As a supervisor thinks about and prepares the first list—what the subordinate does well—positive labels such as responsible, dependable, observant, creative, efficient, hard-working, thorough, and self-initiating will come to mind.

Telling people that they are dependable, show creativity, or take initiative is equivalent to a three- or four-point accolade. The supervisor is not taking advantage of the opportunity to deliver a well thought-out compliment.

Consider the expression "takes initiative." Tell a subordinate that a person who takes initiative is one who (1) not only completes an assignment but does so in a timely manner, (2) informs the supervisor before the due date when additional time is needed to complete a task, (3) brings a problem outside his or her area of focus to the attention of the appropriate person, or (4) takes care of a matter without being asked—that *this* is to take initiative! When the supervisor adds a comment to the effect that the subordinate exhibits such a quality, instead of a three- or four-point accolade, it might be worth thirty or forty points.

The supervisor can increase the value of the recognition to sixty or eighty points by adding specific examples, also known as *critical incidents*. These critical incidents will often begin with a date, such as, "Three weeks ago . . . ," "Last month . . . ," or "Yesterday . . ."

For every positive category, the supervisor needs to explain what is so important about it and hopefully provide at least two examples of the evaluated behavior.

In the category of *observant*, for instance, a dairy herd manager might say: "Two weeks ago, when I was speaking with the veterinarian, you interrupted to tell us that the milk tank refrigeration was off. Your keen observation saved us thousands of dollars." An executive might say to an assistant, "At the last sales meeting with our French clients, when I was giving my talk, you noticed I had forgotten to bring the samples and managed to

The purpose of List I is to celebrate the accomplishments of the subordinate. This is done through talking about specific categories and sharing positive critical incidents.

make all the right phone calls to get those to me at the very moment in the presentation when I needed them. I still don't know how you noticed or what strings you had to pull to get those samples to me. Not only did it save me from embarrassment, but we ended up impressing our clients and securing a contract with them."

Have you ever said something nice to a person only to have the individual ask you what you just said? I have noticed that people often ask for repetition when hearing nice things about themselves that they appreciate but have not heard in general or have not heard from a particular individual.

The purpose of List I is to celebrate the accomplishments of the subordinate. On one occasion, a general manager being evaluated truly felt the sincerity and the power of the compliments she was hearing and joined the celebration by adding several examples of the positive behavior that was being discussed. One hundred points!

The word *celebrate* implies taking time to stop and dwell on what has been accomplished. Anything done to prolong the time spent on the first list will help the process of celebrating.

Imagine that you have just won an important match against another team. The players go out to dinner together after the game. An important part of the celebration is the repetition of exciting moments—a sort of *delayed verbal replay*. One player says, "Ah, that was so great when you were cornered and managed to pass the ball to me." The other answers, "Yes, and then you scored! Oh, that was beautiful." The coach adds something to the effect that the leg followed a perfect curve or a player wisely moved to an open spot.

Two measures that mark success in relation to List I, then, are (1) spending at least *twenty minutes* honoring what an individual does well and (2) having the subordinate join in the celebration by adding to what is being said.

One facilitator extended the time spent on the first list by asking the supervisor to read the whole list before going into the details. After the supervisor finishes with the details, this particular facilitator also reads her summary notes to the subordinate. The notes recap the supervisor's praise rather than the facilitator's opinions. An entrepreneur felt she could extend the celebration time and involve subordinates by asking them for details on how they succeeded in specific projects. As long as they are sincere, a number of approaches may be used to achieve these goals.

An executive once asked, "Besides pay, what tools do managers have at their disposal to help motivate people?" One clear answer is *individual validation*. I would dare say that few people ever receive the type of powerful praise we have been discussing. It is a scarce commodity. Precisely for this reason, these sincere and detailed accolades can have such a powerful effect.

In your youth, was there a favorite uncle or teacher who really believed in your potential? And as a result, when this person was around, did you try to give him or her your very best? Conversely, have there been people in your life who thought you would never amount to anything? People who did not inspire you to prove them wrong—at least not while they were present?

I do not recall where I heard about a leader who began each day with ten coins in one pocket. Every time he praised a subordinate, he moved a coin from one pocket to the other. His goal was to shift all ten coins every day. With time, he no longer needed the coins, as he became a person who looked for good in others. In the same way, the Negotiated Performance Appraisal's List I permits us to look for the good in others.

Managers who have implemented the Negotiated Performance Appraisal tell me it has changed their organizational climate for the better. A positive work environment has, in turn, noticeably improved productivity.

Interestingly, some of the reasons people do not compliment others include fear that subordinates (1) may ask for a raise, (2) reduce their efforts, or (3) think they have nothing to improve on. Each of these is a legitimate fear. Yet, the Negotiated Performance Appraisal permits supervisors to compliment freely, because each of these issues is in some way incorporated in the discussion. For instance, subordinates learn what they need to do in order to improve their chances of obtaining future pay raises or promotions. Because the Negotiated Performance Appraisal permits considerable focus on what people can improve, there is little worry about praising subordinates.

Even so, a significant number of individuals seem to experience a deeply felt fear of praising. They suggest that duty demands a certain performance level and that further commendation ought not be required. I have noticed a similar reaction to the idea of introducing a pay-for-performance compensation package. But the feelings of resentment toward commending or validating others tend to be especially emotional. "I shouldn't have to praise my employees!" or "I shouldn't have to tell my wife I love her—she should know it from my actions!"

Managers, then, often explain that they are not comfortable giving praise. Learning how to give powerful, earnest compliments is an investment that will pay off with dividends.

Electronic equipment, as the name implies, runs on electricity; to a great extent, people run on validation. Praise, of course, does not make up for a poorly designed compensation system. Most supervisors, when they finally understand the importance of sincere acclaim, go on to do an excellent job of commending subordinates during the joint sessions. In the end, however, it is up to the superior to make the best of this unusual learning and stretching opportunity or to let the moment pass.

During the performance appraisal, if the subordinate brings up, as one of his or her good points, a performance issue that the supervisor considers a weak point, the supervisor attempts to understand the subordinate's perspective and under no circumstances disagrees with the individual at this point.

It should be understood, also, that most positive traits, when taken to their extreme, can turn into weaknesses.[1] For instance, exaggerated perseverance may mean spending too much time on an assignment—refusing to move on to more critical matters.

While there may be disagreement between the manager and subordinate about whether something is a positive trait, this is not the time to discuss it. The opportunity will present itself when reviewing List III. Nor should a supervisor cloud the positive issues by telling the individual, at the same moment, that a certain point should be listed as a positive contribution as well as an item that needs improvement. Nonetheless, when discussing a subordinate's weak points later on, it can be very beneficial to reiterate positive traits.

List II

The function of the second list is to acknowledge efforts to improve. Of course, an individual's claim to have progressed in an area does not mean the problem has been conquered. Items from List II may also need to be addressed in List III as plans for expected improvement are refined. As before, the supervisor listens and asks for clarification without interrupting. After acknowledging the comments of the subordinate, the supervisor reads his or her own list. While the second list often takes relatively little time to discuss, compared to the first and third lists, it is valuable for subordinates to have the opportunity to speak about efforts they have been making to improve.

List III

The rationale of the third list is to help make good subordinates better at their jobs and to assist those who are performing poorly to progress to an acceptable level. Everyone can improve. Just as leaders may color individuals with negative strokes and not recognize the good in them, supervisors can also neglect to help outstanding employees or volunteers reach their full potential by failing to acknowledge strengths or by ignoring weaknesses, as insignificant as they may appear. In the process of sharing lists, misunderstandings can be cleared up. One subordinate, for instance, mistakenly thought her supervisor disapproved of her level of risk-taking.

A key role played by facilitators during the pre-caucuses is helping subordinates arrive at the joint session prepared with several viable solutions to problems in each of the spheres of weakness. At times, subordinates will struggle to think of areas in which they need to improve. The facilitator may help by asking, "What changes or improvements do you think your supervisor would like to see you make?"

Again, during the joint session, the supervisor allows the subordinate to go first. The subordinate is permitted to read the complete list, uninterrupted, except when clarification is needed. Ideally, the subordinate's self-report will be complete and accurate.

It is human nature not to want to bring up our faults; but it is also human nature to prefer to point out our own shortcomings rather than having someone else do it.

When a person speaks of something as being a problem or weakness, the supervisor should not jump right in and say, "I agree; I also think this is failing."

In fact, when it comes time for supervisors to read List III, there is *no need to repeat* what the subordinate has said. Or to mention that the issues described by the subordinate were also part of the supervisor's list.

Instead, the superior brings up *only* matters that have not been raised thus far. A key point is that once a subordinate acknowledges something as a weak point, the person has begun to take ownership of the problem.

Once the subordinate has acknowledged the need for improvement, the supervisor needs to be careful not to fall into a more traditional role: that of an expert pointing out faults. Instead, the supervisor can be an active listener, offering support to the subordinate who wishes to change unwanted behavior.

Once the third list is constructed (from the combined comments of the supervisor and the individual being evaluated), the superior can ask the subordinate to discuss specific items, as well as detailed plans for improvement.

A leader might say something like, "Yukiori, you say that you could improve on your organizational skills. Tell me what specific steps you'd like to take to strengthen them."

The supervisor need not discuss items on the subordinate's list in the order they were given, but rather, may opt to begin with an issue that appears to have a more straightforward solution. Or the supervisor may ask the person being evaluated to choose a listed item to start the conversation.

A subordinate may provide an overly vague or simplistic solution to a problem, such as, "I'll try harder." Good intentions may not yield positive results, however, unless plans for exactly what will be done differently are established. Nor does it help when an individual sets unrealistically high goals that have no reasonable chance of being carried out.

As solutions are examined, the manager may be asking, "How will we know in three days, three weeks, three months, or a year that the goal is being met?"

Despite what has been said about allowing people to solve their own problems, sometimes it helps for the supervisor or facilitator to offer a few alternatives. The subordinate needs to feel empowered to accept, modify, or reject the suggestions. This is why it is vital, then, for the facilitator to help the subordinate come to the joint session with not only a list of areas to improve but also precise plans to do so.

Depending on the extent and importance of the challenge involved, thinking through a particular work process and all the likely places where obstacles may be introduced may help both parties to better understand the difficulty. The effectiveness of brainstorming sessions might depend on the willingness of participants to think outside traditional solutions.

Concrete solutions have a greater potential for success. An employee in charge of a shop came to an agreement with his supervisor on how to make tools accessible and, at the same time, make sure they were returned. Another person agreed to give colleagues a little advance notice that he would need their assistance rather than demanding instant help, unless, of course, the situation was an emergency.

By the time the subordinate and the supervisor are reviewing the third list, both individuals may be emotionally drained. They may be tempted to solve a difficulty with haste. Also, the subordinate might begin to get defensive, negating the good already accomplished.

The role of the facilitator is to watch for viable agreements and be sensitive to the participants' emotions. Superficial agreements, so parties can move beyond uncomfortable topics, need to be avoided. The facilitator might ask, "Javiera, how do you feel about this agreement?"

The worst thing that can occur is for the parties to simply plow through without concern for each other's feelings or the viability of agreements. This is not to say that in the natural course of conversation—in the joint session—there will not be a number of tense moments. Periodically, the supervisor may want to remind the subordinate of something discussed in List I (what the person does well).

The role of the facilitator is to watch for viable agreements and be sensitive to participant emotions.

Take, for instance, a situation in which the subordinate and the supervisor have been discussing an individual's tendency to be a little self-righteous and discount other people's opinions. The manager senses that the subordinate is beginning to feel somewhat deflated. The superior may say something like, "You know, Kenny, I realize that it's *because* you care so much about this operation, *because* you take pride in your work, *because* you want things done just right, that you wish to express your opinions. We certainly want to keep hearing them. The challenge, as I see it, is to encourage others to feel that their views are important—especially those who are shy about speaking up."

There may come a point when more good would come from continuing the appraisal at a different time. Supervisor and subordinate may want to set a date to meet again—say, in two or four weeks—in order to brainstorm potential solutions. When the parties are well prepared through the pre-caucuses, only the exceptional case will require a second joint session.

All items raised in either the subordinate's or the supervisor's third list need to be discussed before moving to the next stage of the Negotiated Performance Appraisal. Sometimes a manager or a subordinate may leave an item out of the discussion. I generally prefer to err on the side of bringing issues up, even if it means having the parties tell me the topic has been sufficiently discussed. To do otherwise would be to risk neglecting important topics.

The supervisor is cautioned to avoid derogatory labels. Calling an individual lazy, stubborn, inconsiderate, or shiftless is likely to provoke a defensive reaction. It is fine to say something like, "I would prefer to see you suggest alternative solutions before bringing me a problem you're facing."

In providing feedback to a subordinate about substandard performance, it is all too easy to generalize or to fall back on more traditional performance appraisal approaches. Ones in which the supervisor assumes the position of an expert on the subordinate's performance. Instead, supervisors need to address separately the specific area of performance needing improvement or risk failing to communicate.

For instance, a subordinate may be demoralized by hearing she is a poor listener, especially when she has put much effort into improving her listening skills. Instead, the supervisor could have said that it appeared as though the employee tended to avoid conversations involving disagreement.

While an essential part of the Negotiated Performance Appraisal involves sharing positive critical incidents, the approach taken when dealing with negative issues is somewhat different.

In an earlier chapter, I spoke of using the smallest hammer possible when introducing negative feedback. Only if the subordinate seems lost is the hammer size slowly increased, first by introducing the general principle in more detail and then by adding a few examples of critical incidents if necessary.

After discussing List III or IV, it is useful to refocus and remind the subordinate of some of the positive contributions the person has made to the organization.

Before ending this portion of the joint session, it is good to review exactly what details remain pending and what agreements have been reached thus far. A copy of these points may be printed out and given to each party for further review and as a record of the meeting. Without specific goals and objectives, as well as timetables for their execution, the performance appraisal is of little use. Following through on the timely achievement of the established goals is just as vital. A valid alternative is to work on the detailed list of agreements after reviewing the fourth list.

List IV

The fourth list is based on the question asked by the superior: "What can I do differently as your supervisor, so you can be more effective in your job?"

When the question is sincere, and when subordinates are given time to prepare a thoughtful answer—especially after being put on notice that their own performance is being minutely evaluated—providing this opportunity for input can greatly improve the performance appraisal process. The subordinate is less likely to hold back suggestions at this point, especially if the supervisor's shortcomings stand in the way of the subordinate's expected achievements.

The wording is such that it elicits genuinely useful input. When the subordinate responds to the question, the supervisor needs to avoid the natural tendency to want to defend or explain past behaviors. During the pre-caucus, a facilitator coaches the supervisor on the importance of making an effort not only to understand but also to acknowledge the subordinate's perspective and to watch for feelings of defensiveness.

As soon as the subordinate realizes that the purpose of the discussion is to *solve problems* rather than *assign blame*, difficulties are more likely to be raised. This process presents an opportunity to correct mistakes and ensure tasks are carried out

Praise is a scarce commodity. Precisely for this reason, genuine and detailed accolades can have a powerful effect.

more effectively. Furthermore, when supervisors recognize—and act on—the need to make adjustments in their own behavior, it is easier for subordinates to do the same.

According to one employer's standard operating procedure, anyone ordering supplies had to check the prices being charged by three different vendors within a given time period. As a result of the Negotiated Performance Appraisal, a top manager suggested to his employer, "Since you keep the purchasing notebook in your office, when you're not here, I have to make three calls before I place an order. If I had access to that book, I could check to see if you had already made one or more of the required calls. If I ended up making any calls, the information in the book could be updated. It would save both of us time."

The most effective performance appraisals not only involve a discussion between supervisors and subordinates but also examine the relationships between subordinates and others with whom they come in contact. So, for instance, instead of asking for anonymous evaluations from a colleague with whom an employee works on a regular basis, each party can answer the question of how best to provide mutual help. The input is given in a collaborative, rather than competitive, spirit. The same process of mutual recommendations for improved collaboration can apply to business partners.

Performance Appraisal Follow-Up

A follow-up meeting is required a month or two after the initial performance appraisal, to discuss areas in which the individual has improved as well as areas that need special attention. At one operation, an employee had improved in a number of areas, but several other weaknesses soon surfaced—including some that were not discussed in the original joint session. These matters were dealt with in a successful follow-up.

When the Negotiated Performance Appraisal has been used to address an individual's substandard performance, the supervisor should be alert and offer praise for positive changes made by the subordinate. Managers often tend to forgive deficiencies, almost to a fault. But once these same supervisors decide that enough is

As soon as the subordinate realizes that the purpose of the discussion is to solve problems rather than assign blame, difficulties are more likely to be raised and shared.

enough, they can have trouble seeing and acknowledging individual progress.

In many ways, the follow-up is similar to the original joint session. The subordinate who was appraised should be given the opportunity to come prepared to discuss what has and has not worked thus far. The supervisor prepares the same way.

Focusing first on the positive is as critical to the success of the follow-up meeting as it was during the original. The idea is to prevent blaming and defensive behavior. The discussion during the follow-up joint session, then, is about specific obstacles preventing people from reaching their full potential.

Tying the Negotiated Performance Appraisal to a traditional appraisal process for making compensation decisions provides a built-in follow-up. It can act as additional encouragement for subordinates to put forth their best efforts. Individuals should be notified from the outset that a more traditional performance appraisal process will be used to make pay decisions and determine whether goals have been met. It is also useful to let individuals know, periodically, whether their performance, from management's perspective, meets the goals established through the negotiated approach.

Summary

The Negotiated Performance Appraisal, much like Party-Directed Mediation, is composed of both pre-caucuses and a joint session. While people in organizations often avoid sensitive topics in their day-to-day lives, the Negotiated Performance Appraisal encourages dialogue and improves communication. As a result, it is an excellent tool for avoiding conflicts or dealing with disagreement before the matter degenerates into a contentious battle. The Negotiated Performance Appraisal is also an effective alternate model for mediating disputes in which there are large differences in organizational power, such as those that exist between a supervisor and a subordinate. The model facilitates effective conversation through a combination of goodwill deposits and frank dialogue about needed improvement—a process that avoids focusing on blame and permits parties to save face. While the Negotiated Performance Approach cannot guarantee results, it does an excellent job of clarifying exactly what each party must do to achieve success.

Chapter 12—Reference

1. Oaks, D. H. (1992, November). Our strengths can become our downfall. *BYU Magazine*, 34(38), 42–43.

13
Negotiated Performance Appraisal Clips

Just as it was useful to "listen in" on a real mediation, we now have the opportunity to read clip highlights of several Negotiated Performance Appraisal transcripts. The identities of the individuals involved in the process have been obscured.

Special thanks go to the participants and facilitators who permitted the session recordings. Rodrigo López was the facilitator for Clip 2 and Clip 3, while the remaining eight clips were provided by Macarena Pons.

Pre-caucus: List I

The first list in the Negotiated Performance Appraisal is an attempt to underscore the positive contributions of the individual being evaluated.

Clip 1. Business Executive and Facilitator Discuss List I

In this clip, we join an executive who has given much thought to the positive qualities possessed by a subordinate manager. Rather than interrupting, the facilitator permits the executive to share his complete list before asking for examples of each positive characteristic being raised. Because an important purpose of List I is to celebrate the accomplishments of a subordinate, it is better to expand the number of categories rather than diminish them. It is not uncommon for individuals being interviewed to punctuate the end of what they have to say, as we see below.

[. . .]

FACILITATOR: Let us begin with List I, Aalim, regarding where you think that Kai's performance has been outstanding.

AALIM: All right! First of all, Kai has made an effort to organize the unit he's responsible for. He's attained the integration of the team, involving everyone in the work of everyone else, that is, being a support . . . creating a sort of synergy among those whom he's responsible for.

FACILITATOR: Uh-huh.

AALIM: He's also demonstrated a leadership quality. Let us say, he's been a leader for the team, and that can be seen in terms of the respect he has obtained from his work team. Let us say, they respect him as a boss, and basically—I believe this is one of those critical matters—that they recognize his knowledge and that he has contributed to the overall know-how. Mmm, do I continue?

FACILITATOR: Yes.

AALIM: He's adapted himself quickly to the workgroup. That is, he's not been with us for a long time yet he's quickly made himself a part of the enterprise—and that, without any problems of adaptation. He has a good handle on computer matters, which is key for us. Within a short time he

	had designed an information process . . . and has also known how to organize a work flow within the enterprise. That permitted us to reduce a series of risks and errors on the one hand, and on the other hand, organize the functions of each of the staff. For that very reason, he's been able to organize the internal administrative procedures of the enterprise, which in turn have permitted him to partially implement the new computer system, confidently moving forward with each module that has been incorporated. He has a good understanding of the computer software, which is an important thing, as one can begin to apply procedures as one understands them. He's been 100 percent involved in each step of this project, which gives me peace of mind. That is, let us say . . . the things he's implemented, he's done so taking personal responsibility for them . . . in terms of the development of the procedures.
FACILITATOR:	Uh-huh.
AALIM:	Another positive characteristic he possesses is his analytical thinking. Before making a change or implementing a strategy, he reviews it and puts it to a test. That is, he just does not jump in to do things which he later needs to undo. It's clear that he has a capacity for analysis and comprehension of procedures that need to be tested . . .
FACILITATOR:	Tested . . .
AALIM:	. . . tested before we begin to make changes, because there are individuals who are very good about making changes, but things end up not moving forward. Mmm . . . What other positive qualities does he have? Well, he has a good sense of humor—is likeable. He maintains a good work atmosphere, which is no small matter when one works with people, especially when one has to supervise people. Until now, I've not had

complaints that he's an annoying boss. On the contrary . . . he's been well received by his work team. His dedication, his commitment, his knowledge, and how he's responded to the challenges he's had to face during his short time . . . confirm that we were correct in selecting him. He's been with us only four months . . . or three . . . and to date we've seen progress, progress, and progress. That's it!

The facilitator begins to read over her notes and check her understanding of what the executive has said thus far. We pick up the conversation towards the end of that process.

AALIM:	I'm missing another quality, it seems. I don't know if I mentioned it—that he's clear in terms of teaching and transmitting his knowledge to those he supervises.
FACILITATOR:	Mmm . . . [Looks at her notes.]
AALIM:	. . . which has something to do with what has been said: the ability to engage his people. That is, besides being able to organize, he has the ability to educate. He's able to transmit his knowledge, which is no small matter, let us say. One thing is to know something and keep it to oneself, and another is being able to share it . . . and being able to get the most out of it. And that, let us say, is what's being accomplished.
[. . .]	

After completing the outline of positive issues to discuss, the next step is to plan a strategy to deliver them and drive the points home with force, including at least two examples of positive critical incidents. After doing so, the facilitator may ask the superior to role-play the discussion of one or more topics, as needed.

Clip 2. Front-End Supervisor and Facilitator Discuss List I

In this clip, the facilitator conducts a pre-caucus with a crew leader. The facilitator makes much use of his role as a coach, especially since the crew leader has little experience with any type of performance appraisal. This facilitator chooses to get examples after each type of positive attribution, rather than building a list first. The facilitator is carrying out this pre-caucus as a demonstration, in front of several managers, with some time constraints.

[. . .]

FACILITATOR: As we had mentioned earlier, we now want to begin the process of increasing our goodwill deposits. We want to do so with specific examples—not only say that he does something well, but ask such things as "When? Where? What?" so that when we speak with José, he will perceive that what you're saying is sincere, that it's something concrete that you've noticed and value in him. What will we do to to have him feel good about his accomplishments, in order to be able to address more difficult issues later and, as a result, come up with a plan of action? Remember that, in the end, I'll be a spectator, and it'll be your role to speak directly to your subordinate. We will also do some role-playing later. So, let us begin with some positive qualities you see in José.

RAMÓN: His positive attitude to do things. You just tell him what you want done, and he's willing to do it. He never puts on negative airs or complains. None of the "Hey, boss, why me?" sort of attitudes. That would be one of the first positive things.

FACILITATOR: Excellent. Now, let us obtain some details through examples, such as, "When I told you to do such a thing, you agreed," or some such thing.

RAMÓN: For example, sometimes a crew worker doesn't come on time . . .

FACILITATOR: Mmm.
RAMÓN: . . . and you tell him, "Hey, José, you need to take a co-worker's ladder out to the field, to the spot where your crew was switched." That's where this positive attitude shows up. Because there are people who say, "Hey, how is that my problem?"
FACILITATOR: He has a positive attitude, then, and we have a specific example of the ladder . . . Let us make it even more specific. What were you harvesting when this happened?
RAMÓN: Granny Smith.
FACILITATOR: Ah, then, let us add this detail to what you're going to say: "We were harvesting Granny Smith, and when a co-worker was late, I asked you to take out a ladder for him and you did it cheerfully."
RAMÓN: Yes, and what's more, the co-worker never showed up so it meant that José had to take the ladder all the way back to the shed at the end of the day!
FACILITATOR: Excellent! Now we're being very concrete. Here we have a perfect example. The idea is to try and have another example of how José's positive attitude shows at work. [The facilitator models for Ramón the complete example and how it could be delivered in the joint session.] We want José to say to himself, "Hey, Ramón really has noticed my efforts!" It is as if you were saying to José, "I'm giving you two concrete examples, and there are more, but you get the point, that I've noticed."
RAMÓN: There are different tasks that take place through the year, and I give instructions to the crew workers, and they go to different spots in the farm . . .
FACILITATOR: Uh-huh.
RAMÓN: Well, he has a positive attitude . . . he understands what I am saying to him. Does that make sense? Because I may tell him, "You have to do this specific job in such and such a place."

FACILITATOR: Let us be concrete. For example, "I sent him to prune" or . . .
RAMÓN: The example would be when he went out to train the plant and bend some limbs . . .
FACILITATOR: OK. Train . . . What happened?
RAMÓN: To be specific, it was in block seven . . .
FACILITATOR: Uh-huh.
RAMÓN: To bend some limbs in the Pink Lady variety.
FACILITATOR: Uh-huh.
RAMÓN: He immediately understood the idea, when we spoke in the shed, even though we were not even looking at the trees.
FACILITATOR: Uh-huh.
RAMÓN: That would be the positive characteristic.
FACILITATOR: Let me see. I'm understanding that . . . he's technically competent and able to understand instructions given at the shed, where instructions were given before the whole crew, and he understood. He thought of the Pink Lady, the training process . . . "I have to do such and such" . . . and he understood right away. I see that more as a technical skill, certainly an important one to add to the list, such as being able to give him instructions without having to repeat them as one might have to do with others.
RAMÓN: Precisely what I was trying to say.
FACILITATOR: We can consider that as another item in List I. [The facilitator thanks Ramón for the new item for List I, and asks for another example of José's positive attitude.]
RAMÓN: Another thing . . . It's very difficult to find him depressed.
FACILITATOR: He's always positive?
RAMÓN: Right.
FACILITATOR: He's an optimist . . .
RAMÓN: Yes.

FACILITATOR: . . . and cheerful. For example? Tell me about a situation when he was being optimistic or cheerful.
RAMÓN: . . . or cheerful . . . he suddenly will tell a joke.
FACILITATOR: To cheer up the crew? OK, try and give a specific example.
RAMÓN: When we began the Fuji pruning, he was willing to say, "Let us give the new piece rate approach a try," rather than being negative about it.
[. . .]

The pre-caucus continues in this vein, as the facilitator prepares Ramón to provide his comments from List I.

Clip 3. Role-Play List I

The facilitator explains, in this continuation of the pre-caucus, that Ramón will have only one chance to impress José during the joint session. That is why careful preparation is so critical. The facilitator suggests (1) showing enthusiasm with the tone of voice, (2) making sure to explain why each particular positive quality makes a difference for good in the enterprise, (3) giving the specific examples that accompany each positive area, (4) addressing the subordinate by name, and (5) speaking to him directly rather than to the facilitator. This pre-caucus, again, takes place in front of an audience.

[. . .]
RAMÓN: I'm not very expressive that way. It is hard for me, as I'm much more of a reserved type of a person. Furthermore, I'm not accustomed to this type of thing. It isn't me.
FACILITATOR: Uh-huh. Understood. We can certainly say to the difficult things in life, "That isn't me!" But it's also good to push ourselves, to push the envelope of what we think we can do. It can make such a huge difference in our roles as supervisors. José knows that you're not an effusive type of person, but he will notice your effort—that you're trying—and put a great value on your effort.

RAMÓN: True. The things we've been talking about are things I've not told him before.
FACILITATOR: Yes, you can even use that and say something like: "I have some things to say to you, that I have wanted to say but never have. This isn't easy for me." It is good to permit yourself to talk about your feelings. We want you to forget that I'm here, also, and truly talk to José.
RAMÓN: OK. "José, look, there are some work-related as well as personal matters that I admire in you. These are things I have never told you. You have a positive outlook on work, you worry about your co-workers, and you show concern for your family.
FACILITATOR: Yes, excellent! Now let us include the examples. Ramón, it's OK for you to read from your notes. Don't feel that you have to somehow memorize this whole thing and everything you want to say.
RAMÓN: OK. I'll make sure to add the examples, then.
FACILITATOR: Good. Let us practice that.
RAMÓN: Look, José, here we are. We've been looking at—evaluating—many of the positive things you bring to the enterprise. Both in terms of things at work as well as others that are more personal in nature. When it comes to work-related matters . . . uh . . . you've a great attitude . . . about fulfilling the assignments given to you—for instance, your willingness to go to other farm locations to work when needed. And in terms of items of a more personal nature, he does do well for his family.

The facilitator has been trying to encourage Ramón to visualize that he is addressing José, but occasionally Ramón reverts to addressing the facilitator instead. This time, he is not interrupted and naturally goes back to pretending that he is addressing José in this role play.

RAMÓN: And, when it comes to friendliness, you have a good way of showing friendliness to co-workers.

	You're capable of helping them and cheering them up when they have problems they bring to work. These things are those which you excel in. These are things I had never said to you, but this is an opportunity that has presented itself for me share these things with you.
FACILITATOR:	Excellent! This is really good. Now, we need to add the examples.
RAMÓN:	He's not going to read my notes?
Facilitator:	No. No, he will not. While it needs to be as natural as possible, don't hesitate to read from your list, along with the examples: "José, thinking about the positive things, here is what I wrote," and then just read it.

[...]

Little by little, this crew supervisor gets the idea of what is expected and has a productive conversation with the facilitator about how to speak of positive qualities. Also, he understands that it is fine to show affect when complimenting. Ramón goes through every item in his list, becoming more effective at his praise and needing fewer interruptions as he proceeds.

Clip 4. Subordinate and Facilitator Discuss List I

Here, we take a brief clip from a conversation between a facilitator and the subordinate she is preparing for a joint session with an executive. We join them as they come to the end of a discussion on List I.

	[. . .]
KEVIN :	And the last item from my list would be emotional intelligence . . .
FACILITATOR:	Uh-huh.
KEVIN :	. . . in day-to-day-circumstances. For example, conflict resolution, interpersonal relations, and reaching objectives.
FACILITATOR:	Could you share with me a specific case where you obtained a resolution to a conflict, one that

	your supervisor might recognize and say, "Oh, right, I remember that one"?
KEVIN:	Ah . . . Yes, I experienced one of these yesterday. [Laughs.]
FACILITATOR:	OK. Let us see. Tell me about it.
KEVIN:	One of our technicians wanted to quit right in the middle of a critical procedure. I had the opportunity to act as a quick mediator in the matter . . . talked to everyone involved. I was able to convince him to stay until the end of the day. I've set up several follow-up appointments for today, and I'm hoping we can arrive at a positive resolution.
FACILITATOR:	Perfect! Do you have another example?

[. . .]

PRE-CAUCUS LIST II

List II points out the areas in which the subordinate has improved.

Clip 5. Supervisor and Facilitator Discuss List II

In this brief clip, the subordinate explains how he has found it necessary to acquire knowledge outside of his area of expertise.

[. . .]

GORDON:	You see, my degree is in another field, so I've had a lot of catch-up work to do. That's what I mean.
FACILITATOR:	How have you accomplished it?
GORDON:	Well . . . uh . . . based on experience and reading a lot.
FACILITATOR:	Studying.
GORDON:	Studying the literature in the field as well as spending hours in on-the-job training.

[. . .]

Supervisors can (1) show enthusiasm with their tone of voice, (2) make sure to explain why each particular positive quality makes a difference for good in the enterprise, (3) give specific examples that accompany each positive area, (4) address the subordinate by name, and (5) speak to him or her directly rather than to the facilitator.

Clip 6. Subordinate Explains He Did Not Fill Out List II

It is important that the subordinate fill out all lists, perhaps with the exception of List II. Rather than insisting the subordinate move in an orderly fashion from one list to another, the facilitator has the flexibility of coming back to a list later.

[. . .]

PAT: Before we begin, I just want to tell you that, of the four lists, I only filled out three.
FACILITATOR: Mmm.
PAT: I filled out those things that I do well. I skipped the one where I've improved recently.
FACILITATOR: How come?
PAT: In my opinion, the amount of time I've spent with this firm is so short . . .
FACILITATOR: How long have . . .
PAT: August, September, October, November, December, January . . . Six months.
FACILITATOR: Mmm.
PAT: The "good list" and the "to improve list" get mixed up a bit . . .
FACILITATOR: . . . with . . .
PAT: . . . the "recently improved list."
FACILITATOR: Mmm.
PAT: That intermediate point, I believe, is somewhat difficult to define.
FACILITATOR: OK, we will see how it works out.
PAT: And the fourth list . . . I also filled that one out.
FACILITATOR: Perfect. Let us begin with List I, and when we get to List II, I can help you there.
PAT: Excellent!

The facilitator eventually brings the conversation back to List II and is able to help Pat gain a better perspective.

PAT: So . . . from here we move on to List III.
FACILITATOR: One moment. Let us take a look . . .
PAT: OK.
FACILITATOR: . . . at List II . . .
PAT: OK.
FACILITATOR: I understand that you've been here for a short time . . .
PAT: Uh-huh.
FACILITATOR: That . . . it's difficult for you . . .

PAT: Uh-huh.
FACILITATOR: But in five months—if you begin to analyze things by stages—your relationship with the rest of the firm (your supervisors as well as subordinates) has been the same since day one?
PAT: Uh. Let us see . . . Not really . . . We began with a slight sense of obvious distrust. Strictly speaking, there has been an improvement there. But I don't place it as an item on the list, because even before coming here . . . I consider myself an individual who doesn't have interpersonal problems with people . . . While it involved improvement, I knew it was not something that was going to be difficult for me.
FACILITATOR: It wasn't your problem . . . but rather, one related to the organizational change that had taken place . . .
PAT: Exactly.
FACILITATOR: . . . within the firm. Well, they had to have gone through an interview process . . . and asked for referrals, and all of that.
PAT: Uh-huh.
FACILITATOR: But do you think that the trust and credibility level placed on you has improved?
PAT: Yes. Yes, without a doubt.
FACILITATOR: OK. What would you say was responsible for that?
PAT: When it comes to my bosses, I have nothing but positive things to say . . .
FACILITATOR: Mmm.
PAT: They have always been very open with me, and I haven't had any problems in that regard. But, yes, in terms of those I supervise, the whole issue of communication, trust . . . the fact that one gives out signals at work . . .
FACILITATOR: But you . . . your communication . . . Has it improved or been constant?

PAT:	It did improve in relationship to the first few weeks, in terms of my subordinates. It was quite complicated . . .
FACILITATOR:	So, we could add it to the list.
PAT:	Yes . . . We could add it.
FACILITATOR:	We could add it.
PAT:	Yes . . . Yes.
FACILITATOR:	Communication with the . . . subordinates . . .
PAT:	Exactly . . . has improved since my arrival. [Writes on his list.] I wrote down [Laughs.]: "The ice is broken!"
FACILITATOR:	Excuse me?
PAT:	That the ice is broken. [Laughs.]
FACILITATOR:	Ah.
PAT:	At the beginning, it was much more complicated, without a doubt.
FACILITATOR:	A concrete example with someone . . . or . . .
PAT:	Yes . . . Well, I'm not going to name the individual by name.
FACILITATOR:	No, of course . . .
PAT:	At the beginning, the interpersonal relations with some of the supervisors who work for me was quite distant. They had taken a "wait-and-see" sort of attitude. We didn't have a good team relationship where this individual could count on me as a support. I wasn't getting results. I was just a person who was there. Now, I can be more pro-active . . .
FACILITATOR:	Perfect.
PAT:	. . . in terms of communication.
[. . .]	

Pre-caucus List III

List III involves consideration of areas in which the subordinate needs to improve.

Clip 7. Subordinate and Facilitator Discuss List III

Kai, the accountant in Clip 1, has carefully and methodically prepared each of the four lists. The facilitator has little need to participate, other than to let Kai know he is being listened to. The clip begins as Kai pauses at length and taps his notes against the table.

[. . .]

KAI: Uh . . . I separated this one from the last issue and have called it financial management.
FACILITATOR: Uh-huh.
KAI: Yes . . . I must improve on the financial management . . . That is, more or less, the explanation, despite the fact that we've advanced, and can *outline* the future of the cash flow . . . but we're not at the point where we can *draw* or *paint* it. For the moment, it's only an outline—something that isn't too clear. For example, there have been sufficient funds in the last two weeks to be able to execute some short-term, flash-type investments . . . to be able to get some interest. But we have not because of the lack of clarity as to the amounts we will need and when. If I had a clearer picture, I could have . . .
FACILITATOR: Right.
KAI: . . . invested in a mutual fund for the two-week period and recovered . . .
FACILITATOR: Perfect.
KAI: Another issue is that of sales . . .

[. . .]

It is not sufficient for the subordinate to expose areas of weakness. Before the pre-caucus is finished, the subordinate must be enabled to come to the joint session with a specific improvement plan. This preparation, for instance, may entail attending a seminar, reading a book, shadowing another manager, or agreeing to submit specific reports. Each proposal for

Each proposal for improvement should be something that can be measured in a follow-up interview.

improvement should be something that can be measured in follow-up interviews.

Pre-caucus List IV

List IV revolves around those areas in which the supervisor can make changes in order to facilitate the performance of a subordinate, as viewed from the subordinate's perspective.

Clip 8. Subordinate and Facilitator Discuss List IV

It is often difficult to get subordinates to suggest something their supervisor could improve. In this clip, a subordinate is ready with an example, and a facilitator attempts to see if additional items can be added to the list. It is important to have at least one substantial item on the fourth list. Sometimes, during the pre-caucus, subordinates incorporate additional items, once they see what will be expected of them.

[. . .]

FACILITATOR: Now the difficult . . .
CARLOS: The difficult.
FACILITATOR: Now to the difficult, the good . . . [Light tone.]
CARLOS: The easy . . .
FACILITATOR: That which will help . . .
CARLOS: Well. [More seriously.] In this area . . .
FACILITATOR: What changes can Isaac make, so you can improve your performance?
CARLOS: I defined it in one sentence, but . . .
FACILITATOR: Yes?
CARLOS: I consider it very important, and that is for him to participate in at least one meeting with the sales department . . .
FACILITATOR: Uh-huh.
CARLOS: . . . with the end of creating a relationship similar to that which exists with the production team. Let me explain myself. I'd like him to participate . . .

[. . .]

FACILITATOR: Anything else you'd like to see in your supervisor?
CARLOS: [Laughing.] That he doesn't change. That's all.
FACILITATOR: You had previously mentioned that you needed additional technical training. Is that something that he could support you in?
CARLOS: He's supported me, already.

[. . .]

JOINT SESSION

Finally, we examine two clips from the performance appraisal joint session. In Clip 10, the third party introduces the lists. An alternative is for the facilitator to prompt the supervisor to do so.

Clip 9. Joint Session: List I

This is an example of a successful celebration of what the employee is doing well, one in which the subordinate jumps in to help the supervisor underscore the positive. We have already met Pat, the subordinate in Clip 6, who had not completed all the requested lists. At the end of the conversation, both subordinate and supervisor are happily interrupting each other, underscoring what is positive.

[. . .]

CHRISTIAN: The dedication you've shown, your commitment, your knowledge, and how you've responded to the challenges we've placed in your way, confirm that we made the right decision when we hired you. I'm very, very happy. Very grateful. Another thing would be your sense of humor. It is a good thing.

PAT: [Spontaneous but reserved laugh.]

CHRISTIAN: You are a person who has brought humor to the workplace . . .

PAT: [Reserved and joyful laugh.]

CHRISTIAN: . . . and that has lifted up people's spirits. That is something you didn't know, because you didn't know how we were before.

PAT: [Laugh.]

CHRISTIAN: But the work environment has changed within the management team . . . a merit that is purely yours. This all has to do with being a leader, having knowledge, and having the capacity to extend knowledge . . . to teach. When people see that, it shows them how to do something and demonstrates it. [Taps three times on the table with the hand for emphasis.] This makes it so people become aware . . . and be at peace . . . that what they are doing, they are doing well. Another thing that is important, is that you're good at . . . I've heard it— that you motivate people through your expressions, you congratulate them, you say, "Well done!" That sort of thing is something they were not accustomed to . . . hearing that sort of thing from previous supervisors. They just felt pressured, besides the inherent pressure of the job. But with that characteristic of being on top of things and there to provide positive feedback, well, this has given them a confidence that I hadn't seen before. I see that people are now willing to take on challenges. That's something meritorious on your part. That's what I wanted to say.

The facilitator summarizes the key points of what has been said and thus continues the process of celebration. Both participants concur with her interpretation. She has afforded them the opportunity to continue celebrating before moving on to List II.

CHRISTIAN: I'm very pleased that Pat mentioned leadership. Sometimes one knows things but doesn't believe it.

FACILITATOR: Doesn't believe it . . . Or doesn't dare say it.

CHRISTIAN: Or doesn't dare say it. I think that is really important, Pat, that you had the confidence to say it. I believe you have the leadership capabilities that we need. That is good . . . good when you have a person next to you who is confident that what he's doing, he's doing well and that he can move forward with the people he's managing. That is a superb positive quality.

PAT: Yes. As you know, I've worked up through various jobs, so I feel confident in telling people, "This is this way," because it's that way! It isn't that I sort of believe something, but rather, there are facts that I know about . . . and so I have a bit of knowledge-based leadership, the experience in those things, perhaps something that might be considered routine, or small within the context of the whole

	enterprise, but . . . but that . . . gives me that level of leadership.
CHRISTIAN:	But leadership is more than that!
PAT:	Yes. It's much more than that, but with that . . .
CHRISTIAN:	Yes, of course.
PAT:	When someone makes a mistake . . .
CHRISTIAN:	A leader . . .
PAT:	However, from a technical perspective, then leadership . . .
CHRISTIAN:	Absolutely. Knowledge of the material is very important, but you have a leadership ability that goes beyond knowledge. You are also a person who transmits knowledge . . .
PAT:	Well, it's because I also like to explain things.
CHRISTIAN:	You see, then. The persons you work with are anxious to learn . . .
PAT:	Yes, of course.
CHRISTIAN:	. . . and every time they perceive . . . that they are being taught something . . .
PAT:	Uh-huh.
CHRISTIAN:	. . . they absorb it and they want it. Well, that is something very good—that you have people who want to learn and a supervisor who wants to teach.
PAT:	Yes.
CHRISTIAN:	In the past, we've had people who guarded what they knew and waited for people to fall down so they could correct them and come to the rescue . . .

[. . .]

Clip 10. Joint Session: Lists III and IV

Macarena Pons, the facilitator in this session, permits the parties to discuss both lists III and IV before asking them to narrow down the agreements. By doing so, all needs are assessed and everything is on the table.

Jason—the supervisor—gives few verbal signals, or positive minimal responses, that he is listening to Daniel. When Jason speaks, in contrast, Daniel makes sure his supervisor feels heard.

Jason was instructed not to agree with Daniel on items mentioned in List III. Jason can, however, show interest by taking copious notes.

In one instance, after we come to List IV, Daniel tells Jason that he is feeling "somewhat emboldened" by the conversation. If Jason expects certain improvements from Daniel, there are changes Jason can make to facilitate these—suggestions that would rarely be raised in a more traditional performance appraisal. Jason begins to reflect on the subject and realizes that he needs to work on being a better communicator himself, but not before becoming a bit defensive. Facilitators need to prepare superiors to deal with defensive feelings.

For the sake of brevity, the following transcript eliminates some of the specific examples provided by Jason.

[. . .]

DANIEL: I knew that I was correct regarding the data-entry procedure but mentioned it in a very unassertive manner. Waldo had a different opinion, and I didn't defend mine, so his approach was taken instead. After three weeks, I brought it up again, in a more assertive fashion . . . and that is what was done! Because of the way I framed the issues, well, we permitted three weeks to go by, whereas we could have done it correctly from the beginning. I should have been more assertive. At first, I wasn't capable of convincing you, Waldo, or anyone else. It was difficult for me to finally be more assertive. The next issue where I expect to improve is in taking less time in the execution stage. I was telling Macarena that I've noticed that this job entails a lot of putting out fires. One is under constant bombardment. Which I have liked, actually. In my previous jobs, there came times when, well, I frankly had nothing to do and had to get on the Web and try and find something to do. Not here. Every minute here is used more profitably, but what does happen, however, is this "putting out fires" syndrome. I've lost my capacity to act in a more strategic way. So, that is what I mean. By the time I notice something needs to be done and get it done, much water has flowed under the bridge.

I also believe I've been somewhat weak in my organizational skills. You know that this whole thing escaped my hands. I need to also increase my follow-up in terms of those whom I supervise. I prefer to give very thorough instructions and not leave until I'm sure people have understood me. Then, I can be at peace when I walk away. The challenge is that—because of the fires I'm putting out—I'm not checking people with the needed frequency. This is where I notice that, although I thought I had given clear instructions, my subordinates end up doing things very differently from what I thought I had instructed them to do. Some of the managers don't have this problem, but others certainly do. I need to improve on my follow up.

Another item: [Pauses and turns over a page.] I need to better manage myself, especially when it comes to time management. I need to be more proactive. I've failed to verify some critical issues. I need to set priorities, delegate, and act in more strategic ways. That is a little bit . . . where I'm coming up short. [Gestures to make it clear that he has finished his list.]

FACILITATOR: Jason, anything you have to add to Daniel's list?

Jason begins by giving an example of a difficult challenge that Daniel was able to deal with and expresses his confidence in Daniel's ability to handle the issues at hand.

DANIEL: Uh-huh.
JASON: I believe you can improve in the following matters: being responsible for a budget, as well as a monthly review process as to where we're at.

DANIEL: Uh-huh.
JASON: I believe you're capable of doing that at this point in your career. I'd like for you to keep better track of human resource costs through a computer spreadsheet. Nothing fancy. I'd like us to establish a more regular or formal communication, where I can be kept up to date with advances, costs, and so on. Maybe through that spreadsheet.
DANIEL: So we can show progress.
JASON: As indicators. I'd also like to see you come up with a timeline for each managerial team member. This way, each one of them will have clarity as to what they have to do and can carry out a self-appraisal as to how they are doing and know that they can proceed with confidence. And all of this needs to be tied to the budget, also. [Jason continues to add items to List III, with Daniel's encouragement and give-and-take between the two.]

[. . .]

FACILITATOR: Now, Daniel will read List IV.
JASON: [Smiling.] List IV?
DANIEL: [Laughs and pauses.] The truth is that I don't have much in the way of suggestions for you. Nothing but the truth. [Laughs.]
JASON: Nothing but the truth. [Laughs.]
DANIEL: But, there are two issues . . . and perhaps I'm feeling somewhat emboldened, but something from List III—the importance of organizing myself better—really depends to some degree on you. Despite the fact that I didn't come up with very specific cases . . . For example, often you've told me about important matters that were coming up with almost no notice. "Hey, such and such is on their way . . ." This sort of thing can add quite a bit of stress. Second, you've made some changes—excellent ones—but didn't notify me. So when I came back from my classes at the university, I

	found all of these changes and didn't know how to react to them. No one was able to explain what had happened until you arrived. This gave me a feeling of "What am I doing here?" These are the only things I could say about you . . . You are busy and just forget to tell me . . . That's all.
JASON:	What was item number one, again?

The facilitator reads the summary of what was said, and Daniel notes his agreement with her understanding.

JASON:	Yes . . . That's very much like me to do that. [Long pause.]
FACILITATOR:	Both issues revolve around communications.
DANIEL:	Yes.
JASON:	I don't quite agree with the communication—we actually communicate a lot.
DANIEL:	Uh-huh.
JASON:	Sometimes you're not here, and a decision has to be made . . .
DANIEL:	Yes.
JASON:	We communicate a lot. We just need a more formal communication process.
DANIEL:	Yes.
JASON:	Such as, "How are things going?"
DANIEL:	Yes, taking stock of where we are.
JASON:	I'd be upset if a change is taken the wrong way . . .
DANIEL:	Of course. Not at all.
JASON:	I think of myself as a good communicator . . . but now I'm beginning to question myself. [Laughs.]
FACILITATOR:	Am I that good of a communicator? [Laughs.]
DANIEL:	I believe you're a good communicator but that you sometimes forget. You have a thousand things going through your mind.
JASON:	Yes, this is important. We will have to be careful about this. [Laughs.]
DANIEL:	[Laughs.]
JASON:	I'll accept that . . . I'll accept it.

Daniel and Jason continue their jovial conversation for a while.

FACILITATOR: OK. Now we will develop a timetable of agreements by which these will be accomplished or evaluated.
DANIEL: Yeah.

The facilitator mentions the list of items on which the two men agree. Daniel notes his understanding or agreement by saying, "Yes," "Exactly," "Uh-huh," or the like. The facilitator then turns to Daniel.

FACILITATOR: So, speaking about the budget, what do you suggest?
DANIEL: We need a monthly budget review: a history of what we've accomplished and what we ought to have accomplished. So, the first thing we need to do is to give order to these things through a timetable that includes when specific tasks were accomplished as well as the allocated resources. I'd suggest, Jason, that I have a monthly meeting with you in which we can review the budget. This would include a review of what has been done as well as future events. All of these could be seen in the context of the allocated budget. Hmm . . .
JASON: I've something to say.
DANIEL: Uh-huh.
JASON: We have to turn in a yearly budget by the end of February.
DANIEL: Uh-huh.
JASON: I'd like it if you could work to turn this in by the 15th and give us time to review it.
DANIEL: And thus say, "This is what we've agreed upon."
JASON: This is what we've agreed upon. [Bangs desk with hand and makes a noise of explosion with his mouth.] Pshhhh!
DANIEL: This means I'll have to speak to the department heads, to each one of them.

JASON:	Yes.
DANIEL:	But I need an assurance that they will be committed.
JASON:	Absolutely.
DANIEL:	Yes, then we would have the commitment of the enterprise: mine, yours, and the department heads.
JASON:	But the bulk of the responsibility would fall upon you to coordinate all of this.
DANIEL:	I agree to have it done by February 15 so you can have time to review it.

Jason adds specific details of what the budget needs to contain.

DANIEL:	In order to accomplish that, I need for us to come to an agreement regarding some other matters ahead of time. What do I mean by that? For example, making a decision now about the investment plan . . .
JASON:	Exactly . . .
DANIEL:	Because what I intend to do this year, and I've conversed about this with Ulrich, and everyone . . .
JASON:	Perfect.
DANIEL:	. . . that we need an operations budget besides an investment budget.
JASON:	Yes.
DANIEL:	Then I'll need to know ahead of time our goals regarding . . . [Goes into detail on operational matters.]
JASON:	Yes . . . I commit myself to get answers for you on these items, but you agree to come up with the questions.
DANIEL:	Exactly. Perfect. I have a good handle on costs but not on revenues.
JASON:	Yes . . .
FACILITATOR:	OK, then . . . I hear an agreement, and I'll ask both of you to help me make it more detailed, so it

Jason and Daniel:	[In unison.] Yes, a yearly budget with monthly controls.
Jason:	And we could have the meeting the third Tuesday of each month.
Facilitator:	Next point: having a monthly meeting in order to formalize the communication process. Is that something you want to do at the same time?
Jason:	Well, we also meet every Monday of every week, so this Tuesday matter is more about the budget.
Facilitator:	About the budget . . .
Jason:	About the budget . . . Yes.
Facilitator:	OK. Planning surrounding the visits of the external consultants.
Daniel:	Exactly.
Facilitator:	How often do these external consultants come?
Daniel:	Look . . .
Jason:	Once a month . . . or . . .
Daniel:	This isn't a problem. This is very well planned. I'm completely clear on what I have to do there.
Jason:	Uh-huh.
Daniel:	As Jason says, I have to be clear on what was done, why was it done, or why was it not done, and be clear on what we will be asking from these individuals.

[. . .]

meets your needs. You will develop a yearly budget with monthly controls.

It is interesting to note that, beginning with the documentation of agreements, Jason provides a lot more support with affirming comments such as, "Yes," "Uh-huh," and the like. The conversation continues, with the individuals hammering out specific agreements. The role of the facilitator here is to make sure that all of these agreements are detailed and that everyone involved has the tools to accomplish the objectives. A follow-up meeting a few months later will be vital.

APPENDICES

Appendix I
Cultural Differences?

In 1993, I had my first opportunity to visit Russia as a representative of the University of California. I was there to provide assistance in the area of agricultural labor management. "Russians are a very polite people," I had been tutored before my arrival. One of my interpreters explained that, in Russia, a

Breaking through cultural, age, or status barriers can take time and effort. The amount of exertion will depend on many factors, including the skill of the individual reaching out and how alienated and disengaged from the mainstream the person being sought feels.

gentleman will pour the *limonad* (a type of juice) for the ladies and show other courtesies.

Towards the end of my three-week visit, I was invited out to dinner by my young Russian host and friend, Nicolai Vasilevich, and his lovely wife, Yulya. At the end of a wonderful meal, Yulya asked if I would like a banana. I politely declined, thanked her, and explained I was most *satisfied* with the meal. But the whole while, my mind was racing: "What should I do? Should I offer her a banana, even though they are as close to her as they are to me? What is the *polite* thing to do?"

"Would *you* like a banana?" I asked Yulya.

"Yes," she smiled but made no attempt to take any of the bananas in the fruit basket. "What now?" I thought.

"Which one would you like?" I fumbled.

"That one," she said, pointing at one of the bananas. All the while thinking about Russian politeness, I picked up the banana Yulya had selected. It was a matter of great anguish to me whether I should hand her the banana or peel it for her. What was the polite thing to do? At length, I decided to peel the banana halfway and hand it to her. Yulya's and Nicolai's kind smiles told me I had done the right thing. After this experience, I let the world know that in Russia, gentlemen, the polite thing is to *peel the bananas for the ladies*. Sometime during my third trip, I was politely disabused of my notion.

"Oh, no, Grigorii Davidovich," a Russian graciously corrected me. "In Russia, when a man peels a banana for a lady, it means he has a *romantic* interest in her." How embarrassed I felt. Here I had been proudly telling everyone this tidbit of cultural understanding.

David, my oldest son, had occasion to travel to the Ukraine for a brief student exchange a few years later. My family subsequently had the opportunity to host a number of Ukrainian youths and adult leaders in our home. Bananas were among the popular snacks. I noticed that our Ukrainian guests were peeling the bananas from the flower end rather than the stem end. I thought, "They have never eaten a banana before!" I felt an impulse to correct our guests, but fortunately I recovered my reason. I decided, instead, to peel my own banana from the flower end. It was easier than doing so from the stem end. The banana did not care, and it tasted just as good.

Certain lessons must be learned the hard way. Some well-intended articles and presentations on cultural differences have the potential to do more harm than good. They present, like my bananas, though perhaps less amusingly, too many generalizations or a distorted view.

Here is an attempt to sort out some of my thoughts on cultural differences. My perspective is that of a foreign-born-and-raised Hispanic male who has now lived for more than three decades in the United States and has had much opportunity for international travel and cultural exchange.

Besides being a native Chilean, I have met, taught, been taught by, roomed with, studied with, worked for, worked with, been supervised by, supervised, conducted research on, and been friends with Hispanics from every social class and almost every Spanish-speaking country in the world.

Frequent generalizations about the Hispanic culture include claims that Hispanics need less personal space, make less eye contact, touch each other more in conversation, and are less likely to participate during a meeting. Stereotypes are often dangerously wrong and can lead to contention. This is especially so when accompanied by recommendations such as: move closer when talking to Hispanics, make more physical contact, do not expect participation, and so on.

COMMONALITY OF HUMANKIND

Differences among the people of any given nation or culture are much greater than differences between groups. Education, social standing, religion, personality, belief structure, past experience, affection shown in the home, and countless other factors influence human behavior and culture.

Some have felt that by focusing on commonality, I am minimizing real distinctions among people. Certainly, there is a place for studies that focus on differences. Deborah Tannen, for instance, weighs in on the dissimilarities between the sexes: "Pretending that women and men are the same hurts women . . . It also hurts men who, with good intentions, speak to women as they would to men, and are nonplussed when their words don't work as they expected, or even spark resentment and anger." Furthermore, Tannen says, "The risk of ignoring differences is greater than the danger of naming them."[1]

CULTURAL DIFFERENCES? • 271

In Russia, women often walk arm-in-arm with their female friends. In Chile, women regularly greet both women and men with a kiss on the cheek. In some cultures, "yes" means "I hear you" more than "I agree."

I am an avid reader of Tannen's writings. I certainly would encourage continued studies about cultural and gender divergences. Published research on the latter currently seems to be more up-to-date.

In carrying out my own studies, I have come across a substantial number of individuals who explain how they conform to some of the stereotypes of their nationality, subculture, or gender, but not to others.

While there are real cultural variations to be found everywhere—there are organizational cultures, family cultures, religious cultures, big-city cultures, and sport cultures, just to name a few—there is a danger in acting on generalizations.

Surely there are differing approaches as to what is considered polite and appropriate behavior on and off the job, including:

- Length of pleasantries and greetings before getting down to business
- Level of tolerance for someone speaking a foreign language
- Loudness of conversations in restaurants or public places (i.e., appropriateness of attracting attention to oneself)
- Politeness, measured in terms of gallantry or etiquette (e.g., standing up for a woman who approaches a table, yielding a seat on a bus to an older person, etc.)
- Style of dress
- Method of food preparation
- Taste in music

In México, it is customary for the person who is *arriving* to greet others. Someone who walks into a group of people who are eating would say *provecho* (enjoy your meal). In Chile, women regularly greet both women and men with a kiss on the cheek. In Russia, women often walk arm-in-arm with their female friends. In some cultures, "yes" means "I hear you" more than "I agree."

Paying attention to customs and cultural differences can give someone outside a culture a better chance of assimilation or acceptance. Ignoring differences can get an unsuspecting person into trouble.

There *are* cultural and ideological differences, and it is good to have an understanding of a culture's customs and ways. However, acting on stereotypes about such matters as eye contact, personal space, touch, and interest in participation can have serious negative consequences.

While there are real cultural variations to be found everywhere, there is a danger in acting on generalizations about such matters as eye contact, personal space, touch, and interest in participation.

CROSS-CULTURAL AND STATUS BARRIERS

Sometimes, assertions about cultural differences are based on scientific observation. Argyle cites several studies on nonverbal communication that indicate Latin Americans make more eye contact, face each other more, and touch more when they speak.[2] Strong eye contact by Hispanics generally goes along with my

Differences among the people of any given nation or culture are much greater than differences between groups.

observations. If Hispanics face each other more, it is probably because of the desire for eye contact.

The eyes reflect so much of what a person is feeling. Eyes reveal both liking and genuine interest. While voice tonal qualities convey a large amount of information, the eyes provide key additional data.

Occasionally, I have found an individual who avoids eye contact, but this is the exception rather than the rule. Within some Hispanic subcultures, individuals tend to avoid eye contact when their personal space is violated, as when they are greeting another person. However, in other Hispanic subcultures, strong eye contact is maintained during similar circumstances.

Avoidance of eye contact is partly a factor of shyness; partly a measure of how safe a person feels around another; and partly an expression of power differential norms in certain subcultures.

This is not to say that one can count on any sort of uniformity. I am acquainted with a successful Mexican American attorney who was taught by her mother—through verbal instruction and example—to avoid eye contact with unfamiliar men as a matter of modesty. She grew up in humble circumstances within a religious family in a *rancho* in México. In contrast, I interviewed a Mexican woman, also from the *rancho*, who had not received this type of instruction nor heard of anyone who had.
   Reasons for reduced eye contact, then, may include (1) multitasking (e.g., reading or driving while carrying on a conversation), (2) shyness, (3) flirting, (4) modesty, (5) acknowledgment that body space has been violated (sometimes called *interpersonal overload*), (6) intimidation, (7) depression, (8) anxiety, (9) dislike, and (10) embarrassment.
   I have been married since 1976 to a Californian of northern European descent—and with a Canadian connection. My wife now realizes that I need to have eye contact while we converse. If she is reading, for example, she has learned that I stop speaking when she breaks eye contact with me. My children still give me a hard time about the year my mother came to visit and we drove to Yosemite National Park. They were all panicked because I kept looking at my mother as I drove. They felt I was not looking at the road enough and would drive off a cliff.
   Cross-cultural observations can easily be tainted by other factors. Perceived status differences can create barriers between cultures and even within organizations. Individuals encountering this status differential must show, by word and action, that they value the potential contributions of others.
   I do not believe that Hispanics touch more, with the exception of greetings. One of the studies described by Argyle showed that Latin Americans stand closer than North Americans (something that goes contrary to my observations) but that there are regional variations. Argyle asserts that there are few genuine cross-cultural studies of spatial behavior. Interestingly, yet another study showed that "middle-class Americans actually touched quite a lot" and that the U.S. is more of a contact culture than people think.[3]

Eyes reveal both liking and genuine interest. While voice tonal qualities convey a large amount of information, the eyes provide key additional data.

After moving to the U.S., for a long time I was also guilty of broad generalizations about those born in the States. While I have not conquered this disagreeable human inclination, I feel I am beginning to see the way. Often, observations on cultural differences are based on *our own weakness* and reflect our inability to connect with others.

As a young man, I found myself in an almost entirely Anglo-Saxon community in New Canaan, Connecticut. I remember that on several occasions I felt my personal space was being invaded and wondered how Anglo-Saxon men could tolerate being so close to each other. After all these years, I still feel uncomfortable sitting as close to other men as is often dictated by chair arrangements in the U.S. I am not the exception that proves the rule. Immigrants from México and Iran have mentioned feeling the same way.

Jill Heiken, an HRnet forum participant, explained her learning process this way: "I've taught ESL to many many different nationalities and lived in rooming situations with people from all nations and lived in Japan and Cambodia . . . It took me a long time not to generalize, and now when I hear others doing so . . . I know they are just beginning to 'wade in the river,' so to speak, of intercultural relations."

At times it may appear that some people, especially when there are social or ethnic differences, do not participate and interact as easily. This is not because they do not have ideas to contribute, but rather because they may need a little convincing that their ideas are valued. Once the floodgate is opened, the ideas will flow.

In some subcultures, once a person has given an opinion in a group setting, others are unlikely to contradict it. There are organizational boards whose members are asked for opinions in order of reverse seniority, thus increasing the chances that all members will speak freely. Certainly, setting up the discussion from the outset as one in which the opinions of all present are welcome can be very fruitful.

Historically, Americans have been welcome in most of the predominately Hispanic-populated countries in the Americas.

With a few exceptions, they are looked up to and treated deferentially. This polite treatment should not be mistaken for weakness, disinterest, or subservience. Studies conducted decades ago showed African American children preferred to play with dolls that had Caucasian features. This has been changing, as African Americans are less likely to discount their own contributions.[4]

I believe Hispanics, Asians, and other ethnic minorities are also valuing their contributions more than in the past, and so subservient behaviors are less likely to be observed. Only through equality of respect among ethnic groups, cultures, and nations can we reach positive international relations in this global economy—as well as peace at home. Cultural and ethnic stereotypes do little to foster equality.

Breaking through cultural, age, or status barriers can take time and effort. The amount of exertion will depend on many factors, including the skill of the individual reaching out and how alienated and disengaged from the mainstream the person being sought feels.

For example, in East Africa I observed a non-African manager speaking to his African accountant. The manager was quite arrogant, and the subordinate responded with submissive affirmations and little eye contact. When the same accountant communicated with his peers and subordinates, both African and non-African, he was full of ideas, and he made plenty of eye contact with those around.

In another example, an adult class of Spanish-speaking farm workers say nothing to their English-speaking instructor over a three-day period—even though they do not understand what is being taught. The same group of farm workers, when given a chance to be active participants in the learning process, become, in the words of a second English-speaking instructor at the same junior college, "the best class of students I have ever taught."

In yet another case, an Anglo-Saxon adult educator finds that Hispanics are apt to listen politely but not ask questions. He advises others not to expect much participation from Hispanics. Elsewhere, a Hispanic female wonders if the Hispanic farm

CULTURAL DIFFERENCES? • 279

Observations on cultural differences are often based on our own weakness and reflect our inability to connect with others.

workers she teaches decline to participate because she is a woman. The first instructor perceives that the lack of participation is inherent in the Hispanic population; the latter assumes that her gender is the cause.

Meanwhile, other Hispanic instructors—male and female—create so much enthusiasm and active participation by Hispanic audiences that those who walk by their conference rooms wonder what is going on. It is not just a cultural difference if someone can totally involve a group in a discussion within minutes, even when that group has had little experience with a more participatory method in the past.

Like ocean currents, also, cultural changes are always on the move. Tangible differences can often be observed from one year to the next.

INTERPERSONAL COMMUNICATION

There are important speech pattern variations, including the speed of speech, intonation, clues that indicate it is the other person's turn to speak, degree of enthusiasm, the use of questions to engage others in conversation, the value of silence, and the like. For instance, while one person might ask questions in an effort to keep a conversation going or as a way to show positive regard, another individual may interpret the questioning as an interrogation tactic. Discourse analysis scholars often speak of these types of interpersonal miscommunications as having a cultural or sex-based origin. I would particularly recommend the writings of Deborah Tannen, and those of Daniel N. Maltz and Ruth A. Borker on discourse analysis.[5]

Stella Ting-Toomey speaks much about distinctions among cultures. She suggests that we adopt a sort of *mindful stereotyping* when we approach situations by keeping in mind what we know about a culture. She cautions us to do so tentatively, while remaining receptive to data that may well contradict previously held notions and shatter the stereotype.[6]

Even better, John Winslade and Gerald Monk suggest a stance of *deliberate ignorance* (see chapter on empathic listening). They caution, "Never assume that [you] understand the meaning of an action, an event, or a word."[7] This is excellent advice for improved interpersonal communication skills.

CONCLUSIONS

Stereotyping can yield intense feelings of dislike and alienation. Faye Lee, a concerned Japanese American, wrote to me: "How anyone can try to make generalizations about an entire continent of people, plus all the Asian Americans, and the infinite permutations of people's differing experiences, is beyond me."

As we interact with others of a different culture or gender, there are no good substitutes for receptiveness to interpersonal feedback, good observation skills, effective questions, and some old-fashioned horse sense. There is much to be gained by observing how people of the same culture interact with each other. Do not be afraid to ask questions. Most people respond positively to inquiries about their culture. The key is to ask a variety of people, so you can get a balanced view.

Furthermore, it does not hurt to imitate—or at the very least be aware of—the interpersonal communication patterns we observe in others with whom we are communicating.

Making a genuine effort to find the historical, literary, and cultural contributions of a society; learning a few polite expressions in another person's language; and showing appreciation for the food and music of another culture can have especially positive effects.

My contention, then, is not that there are no cultural differences. Variances between cultures and peoples are real and can add richness—and humor—to the fabric of life. My assertion is that people everywhere have much in common, such as their need for affiliation and love, participation, and contribution. When the exterior is peeled off, there are not so many differences after all.

Appendix I—References

1. Tannen, D. (2006). Preface *and* "Put down that paper and talk to me!": Rapport-talk and report-talk. In L. Monaghan & J. E. Goodman (Eds.), *A cultural approach to interpersonal communication: Essential readings* (p. 180). Malden, MA: Blackwell. See other papers by Tannen (2001) in D. Schiffrin, D. Tannen, & H. E. Hamilton (Eds.), *The handbook of discourse analysis*. Malden, MA: Blackwell. Also see Tannen, D. (1986). *That's not what I meant! How conversational style makes or breaks relationships.* New York: Ballantine Books.
2. Argyle, M. (1988). *Bodily communication* (2nd ed.) (pp. 57–61). London: Methuen.
3. Argyle, M. (1988). *Bodily communication* (2nd ed.) (pp. 57–61). London: Methuen.
4. Brown, R. (1986). *Social psychology: The second edition.* New York: Free Press. Brown also includes an excellent discussion of interpersonal contributions.
5. Maltz, D. N., & Borker, R. A. (2007). A cultural approach to male-female miscommunication. In L. Monaghan & J. E. Goodman (Eds.), *A cultural approach to interpersonal communication: Essential readings* (p. 180). Malden, MA: Blackwell.
6. Ting-Toomey, S. (1999). *Communicating across cultures* (p. 163). New York: Guilford Press.
7. Winslade, J., & Monk, G. (2000). *Narrative mediation: A new approach to conflict resolution* (pp. 126–128). San Francisco: Jossey-Bass.

Appendix II
Contributions of Caucusing and Pre-Caucusing to Mediation

Wherever choices exist, there is potential for disagreement. Such differences, when handled properly, can result in richer, more effective, creative solutions. But, alas, it is difficult to consistently turn differences into opportunities. When disagreement is poorly dealt with, the outcome can be *contention*. Contention creates a sense of psychological distance between people, such as feelings of dislike, alienation, and disregard. Such feelings can get in the way of effective communication and resolution of even the most minute perceived differences (Billikopf 2000).

Deep-seated interpersonal conflict requires an enormous amount of skill to mediate, even when the best of present-day theory is put into practice by trained and skilled mediators. Yet others who may have little mediation training, such as facilitators, may at times find themselves in the role of mediator.

Despite years of experience as an admired and skillful facilitator, a colleague confessed that mediation required specialized skills. He described a recent intervention as a *third-party neutral*, one in which he felt thrown into a lion's den. The parties became involved in an ugly escalation right in front of him. As a mediator, he felt impotent to help and was even threatened by one irate party.

There are a number of subtle differences between what facilitators and mediators do. Although they both draw from a

---

© 2002 by International Association of Facilitators. Reprinted with permission of the International Association of Facilitators, from *Group Facilitation: A Research and Applications Journal*, 4, 3–11. Minor revisions, 2009.

subset of common tools, there are important distinctions. Generally speaking, facilitators tend to help groups through the process of problem solving and creative decision making. Mediators often deal with disputants who may be more openly antagonistic towards each other.

Facilitators, in many cases, work with situations in which people may not know the way but are excited about finding a common direction. Mediators, in contrast, often work with those who have lost faith in the other party as well as any hope of resolving the challenges in a mutually positive or amicable fashion. Having made such broad generalizations, it is important to note that individual mediators and facilitators vary enormously both in philosophy and approach.

There are times when interpersonal conflict may force a facilitator to concentrate on individual or group antagonisms. At times like this, the facilitator may benefit from additional mediation skills.

The focus of this paper is on the contributions of caucusing as a mediation tool and, more specifically, the use of pre-caucusing (or pre-mediation). In caucusing, the third-party neutral meets separately with each disputant, in the absence of the other contending party. In pre-caucusing, these separate meetings take place before the mediator brings the contenders into a joint session (Billikopf 1994; Billikopf 2000).

While countless factors are involved in successful mediation, some are so compelling that they may be called pillars of mediation. Pre-caucusing may well be such a pillar.

With notable exceptions, caucusing has received a somewhat uneven and often shallow treatment in the literature. Little is said explicitly about pre-caucusing. Certain value assumptions about mediation further complicate some of the controversy surrounding the topic. One of the most important of these values involves mediator choice between a *transformative* (Bush & Folger 1994) and a more traditional *directive* mediation.

The *directive* approach tends to focus on finding an acceptable agreement—one that may involve *settling* or *compromising*—between the contending parties. It is sometimes called directive because of the large amount of power and responsibility placed on the mediator. Some mediators may come close to acting as arbitrators, imposing a solution on the participants. Of course, mediators do not normally start out thinking that they will impose a solution. As situations become more difficult and emotional, however, it is increasingly likely that directive tactics will be utilized (Bush & Folger 1994; Folger, Marshall, & Stutman 1997; Lewicki et al., 1994).

Transformative mediation (1) allows parties to retain maximum control over the process; (2) creates an atmosphere in which disputants can begin to connect interpersonally (i.e., provide mutual recognition or support); (3) helps contenders become better negotiators and reduce dependence on neutrals; and (4) seeks solutions that are based on a careful understanding of the problem, rather than rushing into agreements that may be short-lived.

A study on self-esteem found that people prefer conflict management situations in which they have added control over the results, even when such control may mean making greater concessions (Swann 1996). My own preference towards transformative mediation affects how I see and utilize caucusing.

We shall first review what is said about pre-caucusing in the literature. The positive and negative attributes often associated with caucusing, and, particularly, the special contribution played by pre-caucusing, are mentioned next. Examples of pre-caucusing are drawn from my involvement as a researcher and mediation practitioner in organizational settings.

Pre-Caucusing in the Literature

Little is said in the literature about either pre-caucusing or the timing of caucusing in general. For instance, Moore suggests, "Mediators should take care not to schedule caucuses prematurely, when parties are still capable of working productively in joint session, nor too late, after unproductive hostile exchanges or actions have hardened positions" (1996, p. 320).

Bush and Folger are more explicit about the benefits of early caucusing: "Exploring delicate relational issues and laying further groundwork for recognition is sometimes easier in caucus, especially in the early stages of the process. Parties often find it difficult at first to give recognition directly to the other party, because it is difficult to give recognition to another person when feeling vulnerable oneself" (1994, p. 153). Having said that, however, they warn that breaking into caucus too early may interrupt the "transformative momentum" or positive conversation flow between disputants that may involve positive acts of mutual recognition (Bush & Folger 1994, p. 271).

There is one veiled reference to pre-caucusing, mentioned almost as an aside by Folger, Marshall, and Stutman. In a sidebar case, a mediator was using computer technology as an aid to conflict resolution. The mediator is reported to have met with the parties "separately prior to the session to help them clarify their needs and positions" (1997, p. 285).

Volkema comes close to suggesting a pre-caucus: "The first contact between the mediator and the contenders provides the first opportunity to establish public images. If this contact is between the mediator and one other person, only two identities need to be negotiated, although groundwork for others can be laid at the same time" (1988, p. 8).

Winslade and Monk (2000) are clear proponents of the pre-caucus, especially in cases involving entrenched disputes, although they studiously avoid the word *caucus*, given its negative associations:

> One of the first steps we prefer to take in a mediation is to meet with each of the parties separately . . . In our experience, it is in these separate meetings that a lot of the major work of the mediator is done . . . the separate meetings are a venue for significant developments in the mediation as a whole, not an optional adjunct to the process, to be used only when things are getting sticky. In our approach, they are central to what gets achieved. (2000, p. 137)

Despite Winslade and Monk's use of the pre-caucus, I found they failed to take advantage of all of the pre-caucus's transformative possibilities. In the joint session, parties tend to address the mediator rather than each other. In fairness to

Winslade and Monk, this happens even in the approach used by Bush and Folger (1994).

Positive Contributions of Caucusing

Positive attributes usually associated with caucusing include: deciding whether to bring the disputants together into a joint session (Moore 1987; Moore 1996); giving the opportunity for contenders to vent (Blades 1984; Emery & Jackson 1989; Hobbs 1999; Hohlt 1996; Moore 1987; Moore 1996; Pruitt et al. 1989; Welton, Pruitt, & McGillicuddy 1988); helping each party feel understood by the mediator (Emery & Jackson 1989; Hobbs 1999; Hohlt 1996; Moore 1987; Moore 1996; Pruitt et al. 1989; Volkema 1988; Welton, Pruitt, & McGillicuddy 1988); exploring positions and needs (Blades 1984; Castrey & Castrey 1987; Emery & Jackson 1989; Hobbs 1999; Hohlt 1996; Moore 1987; Moore 1996; Pruitt et al. 1989; Volkema 1988; Welton, Pruitt, & McGillicuddy 1988); reminding parties of the benefits of mediation (Moore 1987; Moore 1996; Volkema 1988); coaching parties on effective communication and negotiation techniques (Hobbs 1999; Moore 1987; Moore 1996; Volkema 1988); and appealing to parties' higher principles (Blades, 1984; Hobbs 1999; Hohlt 1996; Moore 1987; Moore 1996; Pruitt et al. 1989; Volkema 1988; Welton, Pruitt, & McGillicuddy 1988; Winslade & Monk 2000).

Each of the next several sections (1) presents a key decision or outcome of mediation, then (2) underscores the contributions of caucusing followed by (3) the additional benefits of pre-caucusing.

Deciding to Bring Parties Together

The ideal is to bring the disputants together so they can make a joint decision and retain maximum control over the situation. An important outcome of effective mediation is to enable contenders to handle future challenges without a mediator.

While the results of mediation can be markedly superior to those obtained through other third-party interventions (such as arbitration), this is not necessarily so with substandard mediation

(Castrey & Castrey 1987). When things go wrong in mediation, parties may take advantage of the sense of safety they feel in order to escalate the contention to even higher levels than before. It is possible that the mediator can do *more harm than good* by bringing the parties together.

Contributions of Caucusing

Moore suggests that a mediator may use caucusing to deal with relationship problems and that at times a neutral third party may want to "discourage or prevent the parties from returning to joint session . . . when extremely strong emotions [might] be a major stumbling block to further negotiations" (1987, p. 88).

Further Contributions of Pre-Caucusing

A central aim of the pre-caucus is for the mediator to assess the potential benefits and harm of bringing contenders together, before any damage is done. When contention is allowed to come into the mediation session, the opportunity for disputants to start with a clean slate is compromised. Emotional escalation, as Moore (1987) suggests, may also have a negative effect on reaching agreement.

In one of my early efforts as a mediator, a manager not only refused to look at his assistant in the joint session but turned his chair so as to present his back to her. After this experience I developed a litmus test to better help me gauge the likelihood that a joint session would be successful: asking a party for what he or she values in the other (Billikopf 2000). This question is telling because people involved in deep-seated conflict may have trouble finding anything positive to say about each other (Bush & Folger 1994). This is not a question to ask at the outset, as parties may be in too much pain to see very clearly. Nor should the mediator take the first negative expression as final. (For additional tests, see Lewicki et al. 1994, p. 360–361.)

In one difficult case, a top manager could not make a single positive remark about a subordinate, despite the positive things that had been said about him. I shared with the top manager my experience that there was little likelihood of mediation success when an individual could find nothing positive to say about another and suggested a short break. When we resumed our conversation, the recalcitrant manager was waiting for me with a list of sincere, positive feelings about the other party.

Opportunity to Vent

> Two couples sat on either side of the table, glaring hostilely at each other. At the head of the table, a schoolteacher in her thirties was explaining the service. "First you, Mr. and Mrs. A, will have a chance to tell your side of the story and Mr. and Mrs. Z will listen quietly. Then you, Mr. and Mrs. Z, will have the same opportunity. After that we will discuss the situation and try to find a way to resolve it." . . . While each side was telling its story, there were outbursts from the other of "that's not true" or "wait a minute," which the mediator strove to contain. (Pruitt et al. 1989, p. 202)

Mediators often struggle unsuccessfully to maintain control over conflict escalation. Early joint session phases—in which parties share their stories, come up with ground rules, or begin to interact—frequently lead to unconstructive exchanges. "After each parent has voiced concerns, the two parents are encouraged to discuss the issues freely. In the majority of cases, an argument ensues," say Emery & Jackson, who discuss child custody disputes. "The fight is almost always unproductive . . ." (1989, p. 6).

Kenneth Kressel explains that it is a "common theme in the mediation canon" (p. 25) to let each party tell his or her side of the story in front of the other. He then shares the destructive effect of this approach:

> Mrs. Smith would accept my invitation [to tell her side of the story] with relish, explaining that they were here because Mr. Smith was a worthless lout who cared nothing for his children or common decency and had been vilifying and humiliating her for years. For all she knew, he might also be an alcoholic and child abuser . . . She was in mediation by order of the court and was certainly willing to do her best to encourage Mr. Smith to "finally be a father" but was, shall we say, skeptical. Whatever the tonic benefits of this outburst for Mrs. Smith, for Mr. Smith and myself the results were clearly

unhappy: he would be provoked into an apoplectic rebuttal and I into a dismal contemplation of other lines of work. Yes, I exaggerate. But only a little. (1994, p. 26)

Some mediators feel that such loss of control is unavoidable, part of the process, or even necessary (Emery & Jackson 1989; Rothman 1997). I contend, however, that there is a better way; that parties have already experienced what does not work and remember it well. It is hardly necessary for them to re-experience it now in front of the mediator. Most third-party neutrals would probably welcome an approach in which such dysfunctional escalations were either greatly reduced or completely eliminated.

Some have suggested strategies for reducing such futile outbursts, including telling one party to remain silent or focus on listening (Hobbs 1999) while the other speaks. To make the point, the listening party may be given a notepad and asked to take notes (Emery & Jackson 1989). It has also been suggested that joint sessions be held in a public place to help contenders tone down their emotions (Folger, Marshall, & Stutman 1997). While the note-taking suggestion has some merits, in this context such artifacts may delay contentious outbursts rather than prevent them.

Contributions of Caucusing

Disputants may have some very poignant and deeply antagonistic feelings towards each other. When these can be vented in front of the mediator, the party often has less need to vent in a destructive manner in front of the opposing party. Defensiveness is reduced and creativity increased as the mediator protects parties from further mutual abuse.

There is little disagreement on this point: while involved in caucusing, disputants are less hostile than in joint sessions (Welton, Pruitt, & McGillicuddy 1988). When conflict escalates into contentiousness, as in these episodes, the mediator not only permits contenders to lose face, but just as importantly, she or he loses both control (Butler 1994) and face (Volkema 1988) in front of the parties.

Further Contributions of Pre-Caucusing

When dealing with acquaintances or strangers, individuals often go out of their way to make an effort to project their best possible behavior. This is especially true in what could be called a "courting period." This honeymoon period may last years, when parties view their relationship as fair and equitable. When the rules of proper interpersonal exchange are violated (Brown, 1986) and someone feels taken advantage of, the situation can change quickly.

Similarly, in a party's relationship with a mediator—assuming the mediator is a stranger and/or has the respect of the disputants—individuals often try extra hard to be on their best behavior (Folger, Marshall, & Stutman 1997), lest the mediator think that they are culpable. Parties are more likely to want to continue to make a good impression on the mediator after they have established themselves as reasonable people in the pre-caucus. Volkema suggests that "it is not unlikely that the parties will have established one image with each other and another image with the mediator" (1988, p. 11).

People also attempt to be consistent: "Consistency gives actors a desirable degree of predictability and trustworthiness, and it generates liking and respect" (Schlenker 1980, p. 232). Contenders are likely to feel a greater need to be seen as consistently reasonable by a mediator who has had sufficient time to meet with them individually. Effective listening is a very powerful tool, and people tend to respect those mediators who can listen with care and empathy.

Once the parties have exchanged insults in front of a third-party neutral in traditional mediation, on the other hand, much of the damage has been done. Disputants feel less motivated to show their best after exposing their worst behavior.

It is not that parties pretend to be people they are not. Because parties meeting with the mediator in the pre-caucus know they will be meeting with the other party in a joint session, it is my experience that they are likely to share their own shortcomings, rather than wait for the other party to bring these out. It is this new *facework* (in part, the practice of allowing another to save face) between contenders that the mediator wants to encourage in order to give parties an opportunity for a fresh start that is not based on blame.

Helping Each Party Feel Understood by the Mediator

It is difficult to expect disputants who have been involved in deep-seated conflict to put aside their own needs and listen to and focus on the needs of the other party (Bush & Folger, 1994). The natural tendency is for parties to want to express their own perspectives first. The more deep-seated and emotional the conflict, the greater this tendency.

At times, tension in deep-seated interpersonal conflict situations can reach almost unbearable levels. In mediating such conflicts within organizations, it is common for parties to strongly contemplate withdrawal from the enterprise. Psychological separation from the other party and possibly from the organization has already taken place. For instance, in child custody mediation, contenders have already separated physically and psychologically from each other, yet need to work together for the benefit of the children involved.

Contributions of Caucusing

Because parties have the opportunity to meet separately with the mediator, each gets the opportunity to explain his or her perspective first, before having to attend to the other participant. When the party feels understood, an enormous emotional burden is lifted, thus making him or her more receptive to listen to others (Covey 1989). It is true that disputants have a special need to be understood by the other party in the contention, but being understood by the mediator contributes much. Often, it is a necessary step in terms of a party gaining enough confidence to proceed further.

Some individuals tend to be more silent than others. Caucusing increases the chances that an individual will talk (Hohlt 1996) and express his or her feelings. It is hardly possible for the mediator to help individuals who refuse to speak about

Most criticisms associated with caucusing are really attacks on directive mediation rather than on caucusing itself.

"where it hurts." Mediators have the opportunity to show empathy to one party in a caucus situation without arousing jealousies in the other disputant.

Further Contributions of Pre-Caucusing

It is at the start of mediation that parties are perhaps most apprehensive as to what mediation may bring. Contenders often come to the table armed with and ready to deploy every defensive mechanism (such as sulking silence, angry outbursts, and combative body language). They may have trouble looking at the mediator, let alone the other party.

When a pre-caucus is used and the other contender is not present, this frustration and despair is re-directed in more positive ways. To have an empathic ear to listen to a party in such a nonjudgmental way is powerful medicine indeed. I have seen people who were supposed to be "silent types" open up and talk freely. Men and women have wept openly as they released tension. Such emotional releases are not available to disputants in more traditional mediation.

The Exploration of Needs and the Benefits of Mediation

The mediator attempts to understand individual items under dispute, as well as the general perspectives of parties, and helps disputants keep alive the benefits of mediation (in contrast to other alternatives, such as arbitration).

Contributions of Caucusing

An important benefit of caucusing is being able to explore beyond positional bargaining, into party interests and needs (Fisher, Ury, & Patton 1991). Parties can also be reminded that mediation confers tangible benefits over interventions in which they have less control. This is more likely to happen when individuals feel less vulnerable and defensive and are more willing to think aloud without feeling forced into making concessions. A mediator can increase her or his understanding of the situation through such exploration, but more important yet, the self-awareness of each party increases. For instance, it may become clear that a party desires an apology rather than some other remedy.

Further Contributions of Pre-Caucusing

When disputants enter the joint session with the benefit of a pre-caucus, the mediator can often take a less visible role. Each party comes to the joint session possessing enhanced clarity about the issues and self-confidence.

In one situation, after I listened to the contenders during a pre-caucus, they were able to go on and solve the problem on their own. Bad feelings had developed between them concerning how each introduced the other to visitors and the media. Not only did they solve this problem on their own; they also dealt with related underlying issues and even went on to discuss opportunities for future career growth and cooperation (Billikopf 2000).

As a neutral party, I sometimes do little more than introduce topics brought up during the pre-caucus. Allowing the parties to solve an easier problem early on may give them the needed boost to deal with more challenging issues later (Blades 1984; Emery & Jackson 1989). Furthermore, a mediator who understands the issues involved can make sure that significant matters are not ignored. Despite previous antagonisms, communication between disputants during joint sessions is sometimes so fast-paced that I have to scramble to understand and note their agreements. At times like these I feel like an unneeded observer. Setting up a situation in which parties address each other with little mediator interference takes transformative mediation to the next level. Although not all cases achieve this ultimate success, mediators can count on better communication flow and reduced contentiousness between parties.

Educate Parties on Effective Negotiation Skills

One measure of mediation success is when it equips contenders to handle future challenges on their own. While this may not necessarily happen after a single experience with mediation, the disputants can take with them increased self-awareness and conflict management skills.

Parties may be shown how they can present a perspective using neutral or nonprovocative language (Hobbs 1999) and without causing the other to lose face. An important part of conflict management is helping contenders recognize the need for the other party to build and save face (Ting-Toomey 1999; Volkema 1988; Blades 1984; Moore 1996). In the absence of these skills, people are likely to revert to a more dysfunctional and emotional approach to communication. Participants may also develop a better understanding of the nature of conflict—learning how to divide big issues into smaller ones and what constitutes a proper apology, for instance. Both parties gain negotiating power as they improve their ability to communicate in effective ways.

Contributions of Caucusing

Mediators have the opportunity to privately discuss participant behaviors that are working as well as those that are not. This avoids the appearance of favoritism associated with public compliments as well as the loss of face connected with open criticism.

Further Contributions of Pre-Caucusing

It is hard to expect the parties to have a positive mutual conversation when they lack even the most rudimentary notion of how their communication strategies affect the other disputants. Those who grasp new insights into the negotiation process early on are more likely to enter the joint session feeling confident and prepared, with some control over the results.

Among the potential positive outcomes of transformative mediation is giving parties the opportunity to apologize and to accept an apology (Bush & Folger 1994). One party had a history of vitriolic temper outbreaks when I first met with him. His anger often manifested itself in shouting and profanity. During the pre-caucus, it became increasingly clear that this party felt no regret about his temper tantrums. He was quick both to minimize the extent of his anger and to justify his bullying behavior. Had he defended such behavior in a joint session, his credibility would have been greatly damaged. Through a series of role-plays and conversations during the pre-caucus, he came to understand the importance of offering an apology for his profanity and anger. Furthermore, he suggested that the topic be brought up early in the joint session so he could have a chance to apologize. During the first role-play his words had sounded shallow at best. The actual apology offered during the joint session was moving and sincere.

Regular caucusing has one advantage over pre-caucusing here. While the mediator can observe and coach a party during a pre-caucus, some dysfunctional communication approaches manifest themselves only during the joint session. This is not a fatal flaw of pre-caucusing, because a regular caucus can be utilized later to deal with such issues.

Much of what has been said here also applies to the idea of appealing to a party's higher principles. Many transformative opportunities that could otherwise be lost present themselves during the pre-caucus. For instance, an owner-operator said something touchingly positive about one of his managers during the pre-caucus. I suggested that it would be magnificent if he could share that thought with the other party during the joint session. The owner explained that he would never do so. I challenged him to reconsider but left the ultimate decision up to him. The individual chose to share the affirming comment during the joint session, taking ownership for that decision, thus making it his own.

NEGATIVE CONNOTATIONS OF CAUCUSING

A number of challenges are associated with caucusing, including: lack of party truthfulness (Pruitt et al. 1989; Volkema 1988; Welton, Pruitt, & McGillicuddy 1988); mediator bias (Blades 1984; Engram & Markowitz 1985; Moore 1987, 1996; Pruitt et al. 1989; Volkema 1988; Welton, Pruitt, & McGillicuddy 1988); mediator control or abuse of power (Blades 1984; Folger, Marshall, & Stutman 1997; Keltner 1996; Moore 1987; Moore 1996; Pruitt et al. 1989; Volkema 1988); reduced likelihood that disputants will know how to handle future challenges (Pruitt et al. 1989); mediator violation of confidentiality (Blades 1984; Moore 1987; Moore 1996); interruption of positive movement (Moore 1996; Welton 1988); and free time for the other party to use in an effort to build his or her own case (Welton 1988).

Attacks on Directive Mediation

As we shall see, most criticisms associated with caucusing are really attacks on directive mediation, rather than on caucusing itself. When caucusing is instead used to increase party control through transformative mediation, most of these objections melt away.

As positive as mediator empathy towards a party may be, some fear that this may lead to party untruthfulness. They reason that the absence of the other contender during the caucus leaves the party free to exaggerate. Others argue that caucusing may lead to deals between the neutral party and one of the contenders. "Disputants often fear that clandestine deals or coalitions [may take place] between the other party and the mediator" (Moore 1996, p. 200).

Yet others suggest that caucusing simply gives the mediator too much control, lends itself to abuse of mediator power, and does little to equip contenders for future conflict in life. Instead, they argue, parties may become more dependent on mediation. "Caucuses . . . are explicit attempts to narrow issues, to push for compromise, and to synthesize arguments and positions" (Folger, Marshall, & Stutman 1997, p. 262). We even read that "caucuses provide mediators with the greatest opportunity to manipulate parties into agreement" (Moore 1996, p. 325). Volkema (1988) warns that mediators with a vested interest may promote one outcome over another. The assumption, in all these cases, is that agreement is reached during caucusing.

There is nothing inherent in caucusing itself, however, that leads to these difficulties. Quite the contrary, Engram and Markowitz suggest that "the judicious use of caucusing in . . . mediation can even enhance the perception of neutrality and will result in increased trust in the process of mediation"

(1985, p. 25). Likewise, when transformative mediation is used, caucusing may be seen as a tool to help disputants become better negotiators (Bush & Folger 1994).

In transformative mediation, *the parties solve their own disputes,* and there is little to be gained by attempts to influence the mediator. Contenders need not be concerned that the mediator will make a secret agreement with the other disputant. Caucusing is used to teach negotiation skills to parties rather than to circumvent individual empowerment.

Violation of Confidentiality

Another negative associated with caucusing is the potential for sharing confidential information obtained from one party, either purposely or through a slip. Certainly, mediators need to be careful not to divulge confidential information. Yet it should be clear that the purpose of caucusing is to help parties better understand their own needs and prepare to communicate these to the other party in the joint session—not to talk about issues a party wants to keep secret from the other participant. True, some subjects are originally brought up in a somewhat raw manner. These are translated into more effective messages that tend to reduce defensiveness. For instance, if a party feels the other is inconsiderate or selfish, the mediator helps the party better understand critical incidents that may have led to this evaluation. During the joint session, the incidents and behaviors are discussed without the labels.

As a mediator, I note all the issues that are important to disputants during the pre-caucus and give them a chance to expose these during the joint session: "A, could you share with B the story you told me about X?" Opportunities are balanced for both parties to bring up issues that are then jointly discussed.

Sometimes ethical issues require disclosure, such as when a spouse is hiding an asset from the other during a divorce settlement. In those situations, Blades (1984) suggests that the mediator make it clear to the pertinent party that the neutral's continued involvement in the mediation depends on the contender disclosing this information to the other party. Standards have been suggested for issues with and limits to confidentiality (Milne 1985; Moore 1987). Caucusing does not cause an inherently unethical situation to develop, however. It simply affords the mediator an opportunity to help correct an unfair situation. "Much of the controversy surrounding the issue of caucusing . . . stems from differences in training or orientation rather than from a real debate about ethics" (Engram & Markowitz 1985, pp. 24–25).

Interruption of Positive Movement

Caucusing may be called at any time, by contenders or by the mediator. Parties may even wish to caucus within their own team or with stakeholders, without the mediator. Alternatively, the mediator may need time alone and call for a "mediator caucus" (Castrey & Castrey 1987, p. 15). Any type of caucusing may interrupt the flow of the conversation. The great advantage of pre-caucusing is that it does not interrupt the positive flow of communication that may be established during the joint session. Furthermore, pre-caucusing probably reduces interruptions after the joint meeting has begun.

Free Time to Solidify Stance

The concern that caucusing permits one party time to further solidify her or his own stance while the other is engaged in caucusing is simply not an issue. In transformative mediation one of the roles of the mediator is to help disputants consider potential pitfalls. Mediators help contenders truly understand the problem and thus avoid quick, unworkable solutions.

CONCLUSIONS

Contention creates a sense of psychological distance between people, making even minute differences seem insurmountable. A tool of particular value is the caucus, in which the mediator meets separately with parties. The literature has shed light on both the positive and the negative contributions of caucusing. Positive aspects of caucusing include giving contenders an opportunity to tell their story and be heard, explore needs, and vent privately. Mediators may also take advantage of caucusing to coach parties and help them understand the tools that will help them become better negotiators in the future.

Interestingly, most of the criticisms associated with caucusing derive from a directive mediation approach. When caucusing is used within a transformative framework, most of the potential shortcomings disappear. In transformative mediation, the disputants remain the primary actors. Not only do the contending parties retain control over the outcome, but they are also equipped with many of the tools they will need to solve future problems: "A skillful transformative mediator can use caucuses in a manner that not only avoids the problem-solving pitfalls [found in the directive approach] but actually builds transformative momentum over the course of a session" (Bush & Folger, 1994, p. 270).

Although in the literature we find some allusions to the benefits of the pre-caucus, very little is said explicitly about it. When pre-caucusing is used with a transformative approach to mediation, the benefits of caucusing are multiplied, and the potential negatives are further reduced.

The main reason why pre-caucusing is effective is that the mediator affords each party the opportunity to be heard when he or she needs it the most. A conflict situation that calls for mediation, almost by definition, is a difficult one. Parties are most often focused internally and have little capacity to listen to someone else at the beginning of mediation. This internal focus tends to extinguish creativity by increasing negative emotion and defensiveness. A party who feels heard in the pre-caucus is better able to listen to the other disputant and to connect in a more positive way. The groundwork laid out during the pre-caucus allows parties to address each other with little mediator interference.

Mediation has the potential to do much good. Poorly carried out mediation, in which contenders feel they can exchange insults in a psychologically safe environment, can do more harm than other forms of neutral-party interventions. The pre-caucus affords mediators the opportunity to make difficult decisions as to whether to bring contenders into a joint session.

Sometimes the most productive approaches are the simplest, and this is certainly true with the pre-caucus. Caucusing as a mediation tool has been partially misunderstood and certainly has not been used to its potential.

APPENDIX II—REFERENCES

Billikopf, G.E. (1994). *Labor management in agriculture: Cultivating personnel productivity*. Modesto: University of California Agricultural Extension.

Billikopf, G.E. (2000).Ch. 13. Conflict Management Skills [On-line]. *Labor management in agriculture: Cultivating personnel productivity*. Modesto: University of California Agricultural Extension. http://www.cnr.berkeley.edu/ucce50/ag-labor/7labor/13.pdf

Blades, J. (March 1984). Mediation: An old art revitalized. *Mediation Quarterly*(3), 59, 78–79.

Brown, R. (1986). *Social psychology: The second edition*. New York: Free Press.

Bush, R. and Folger, J. (1994). *The promise of mediation: Responding to conflict through empowerment and recognition*. San Francisco: Jossey-Bass.

Butler, F. (1994). Questions that lead to answers in child custody mediation. In Kolb, D.M. (Ed.), *When talk works: Profiles of mediators* (pp. 17–58). San Francisco: Jossey-Bass.

Castrey, R.T. and Castrey B.P. (Summer 1987). Timing: A mediator's best friend. *Mediation Quarterly*(16), 15–19.

Covey, S. (1989). *Seven habits of highly effective people*. New York: Simon & Schuster.

Emery, R.E. and Jackson, J.A. (Summer 1989). The Charlottesville mediation project: Mediated and litigated child custody disputes. *Mediation Quarterly*(24), 3, 6–7.

Engram, P. and Markowitz, J.R. (June 1985). Ethical issues in mediation: Divorce and labor compared. *Mediation Quarterly*(8), 19, 24–25.

Fisher, R.; Ury, W.; and Patton, B. (1991). *Getting to yes: Negotiating agreement without giving in* (2nd ed.). New York: Penguin Books.

Folger, J., Marshall, P. and Stutman, R. (1997). *Working through conflict: Strategies for relationships, groups, and organizations* (3rd ed.). New York: Longman.

Hobbs, K.S. (November 1999). Attention attorneys! How to achieve the best results in mediation. *Dispute Resolution Journal*(4), 43–47.

Hohlt, E.M. (1996). Effective use of caucus, in Trachte-Huber, E. and Huber S. *Alternative dispute resolution: Strategies for law and business*. Cincinnati, Ohio: Anderson Publishing Co., pp. 335–337.

Keltner, J. (1965). Communications and the labor-management mediation process: Some aspects and hypotheses. *Journal of Communication*, 74. (In Moore, *The mediation process*, 1996).

Kressel, K. (1994). Frances Butler: Questions that lead to answers in child custody mediation. In Kolb, D.M. (Ed.), *When talk works: Profiles of mediators*. San Francisco: Jossey-Bass, pp. 17–58.

Lewicki, R., Litterer, J., Minton, J. and Saunders, D. (1994). *Negotiation* (2nd ed.). Bur Ridge, Illinois: Irwin.

Milne, A. (June 1985). Model standards of practice for family and divorce mediation. *Mediation Quarterly*(8), 73, 77.

Moore, C.W. (1996). *The mediation process: Practical strategies for resolving conflict* (2nd ed.). San Francisco: Jossey-Bass.

Moore, C.W. (Summer 1987). The caucus: Private meetings that promote settlement. *Mediation Quarterly*(16), 87–101.

Pruitt, D.G.; Fry, W.R.; Castrianno, L.; Zubek, J.; Welton, G.L.; McGillicuddy, N.B. and Ippolito, C. (1989). In M.F. Afzalur (Ed.), Ch. 15. *The process of mediation: Caucusing, control, and problem solving.* (pp. 201–208). NY: Praeger Publishers.

Rothman, J. (1997). *Resolving identity-based conflict in nations, organizations, and communities* (2nd ed.). San Francisco: Jossey-Bass.

Schlenker, B. (1980). *Impression management: The self-concept, social identity, and interpersonal relations*. Monterey, CA: Brooks/Cole Publishing Co.

Swann, W. (1996). *Self-traps: The elusive quest for higher self-esteem*. New York: Freeman.

Ting-Toomey, S. (1999). *Communicating across cultures*. New York: Guilford Press.

Volkema, R.J. (Winter 1988). The mediator as face manager. *Mediation Quarterly*(22), 5–14.

Welton, G.L.; Pruitt, D.G. and McGillicuddy, N.B. (March 1988). The role of caucusing in community mediation. *Journal of Conflict Resolution*, 32(1), 181–201.

Winslade, J., and Monk, G. (2000). *Narrative mediation: A new approach to conflict resolution*. San Francisco: Jossey-Bass.

2009 UPDATE

Two additional books that promote pre-caucusing have since been brought to my attention:

Umbreit, M.S. (1995). *Mediating interpersonal conflicts: A pathway to peace*. West Concord, MN: CPI Publishing.

Weeks, D. (1992). *The eight essential steps to conflict resolution: Preserving relationships at work, at home, and in the community*. New York: Tarcher/Putnam.

Index

A

Active listening. *See* empathic listening; listening
Admitting mistakes, 94–95
Advice. *See* prescribing
Affirmations. *See* positive feelings and comments
Aggression
　eye contact, 114
Agreements
　in joint session, 118, 120–125
　Negotiated Performance Appraisals, 228–230, 232, 257, 262–264
　See also Solutions
Alienation. *See* psychological distance

Amor propio (false self-esteem), 70
Analytical comments, 26
Analytical questions, 33
Apologies, making and accepting, 50, 58, 94–95, 101
　case study examples, 151–152, 177
　in joint session, 118, 296–297
Arbitration, 287
　mediators as arbiters, vii, 9, 104, 285
Argyle, M., 273, 275
Autoestima (self-esteem), 70
Attentive listening, 15, 59
　See also Empathic listening; Listening
Avoidance, 71, 72–73, 77

B

Banana story, 268–269
Bargaining, 71, 97
Benjamin, Alfred, 21–22, 28
Best behavior phenomenon, 105, 291
Billikopf, Gregorio
  "Contributions of Caucusing and Pre-Caucusing to Mediation," x, 283–303
  Helping Others Resolve Differences: Empowering Stakeholders, viii–ix
Blades, J., 299
Blaming, 44–45, 53, 86–87, 88, 152
Blind spots, challenging, 10, 41, 52–56, 59, 139
  delivering a challenge, 54–55, 231
  mediator's authority for, 41, 53–54
  pre-caucus example, 156–157
Body language. *See* nonverbal communication
Borker, Ruth A., 280
Boulware, Lemuel R., 88
Boulwarism, 88
Brown, Charles T., 47
Bush, Robert Baruch, 49, 120, 123, 125, 285–286, 287, 301

C

Case study. *See* mediation case study
Caucusing, as mediation tool, 284–303
  caucusing in mediation literature, 284, 285–287
  controversy and criticisms, 284–285, 297–300, 301
  deciding to bring parties together, 287–289
  educating parties on effective negotiation skills, 295–297
  exploration of needs and benefits of mediation, 294–295
  helping parties feel understood by mediator, 292–294
  opportunity to vent, 289–292
  positive contributions, 287–297, 300–301
  See also Pre-caucus entries
Challenging blind spots. *See* blind spots, challenging
Client-Centered Therapy (Rogers), 4, 14
Coaching. *See* pre-caucus coaching
Coin shifting story, 224
Collective bargaining, Boulwarism in, 88
Comments, 26
  empathic sayings, 32–33
Communicating Across Cultures (Ting-Toomey), 47, 280
Communications, 107
  conversational skills and styles, 76–78, 107, 280
  cultural differences, 280–281
  effective listening, 62, 67, 76
  improving through caucusing and pre-caucusing, 56, 58–59, 296–297
  Negotiated Performance Appraisals as tool for improving, 213, 236
  See also Listening; Negative communication patterns

Compensation, performance-based, 235–236
Competition
    competitive negotiation, 67, 70–71
    in conversations, 76
Compliments. *See* praise and compliments
Compromise, 73
Concessions
    mutual compromise, 73
    unilateral (yielding), 71, 89–90, 120
Confidentiality issues, 103–104, 299–300
Contention, 66–67, 283, 288, 300
    See also Interpersonal conflict
"Contributions of Caucusing and Pre-Caucusing to Mediation," (Billikopf), x, 283–303
Conversation
    cultural differences, 280
    skills for, 76–78, 107
Courting periods, 68, 291
Covey, Steven, 82
Creative thinking
    barriers to, 52, 67, 73, 83
    searching out creative solutions, 90–91
Critical incidents, 221–222
Crucial Conversations (Patterson, Grenny, McMillan, and Switzler), 45, 46
Cultural differences, x, 267–282
    focusing on commonality, 270–272, 281
    group participation, 277, 278, 280
    interpersonal communication, 280–281
    nonverbal communication, 273–275
    stereotypes and generalizations, 270, 272, 273, 277, 280–281
    subservience and submissiveness, 277–278

D

Dangling questions, 28
Deadlines, renegotiating, 92
Defensiveness, 45–46, 102, 301
    Negotiated Performance Appraisals, 219, 232, 258
Diagnosing, 15, 16, 23–26
    avoiding the presumption of evil, 85
    shortcomings of, 16–19, 22
Diagnostic questions, 23–24, 33
Directive mediation, vii, 9, 105, 284–285
    criticisms and shortcomings, 105, 298–299, 301
Distorted mirroring, 100
Domestic violence, 94
Dostoevsky, Fyodor, 70

E

Egan, Gerard, 33, 41, 53, 54
The Eight Essential Steps to Conflict Resolution (Weeks), viii
Emery, R. E., 289
Emotions
    controlling, 83–85, 290
    releasing, 11–13, 59, 294
    See also Venting

Empathic listening, x, 4, 11–42, 291
- authority to challenge blind spots and, 41, 53
- benefits of, 12–13, 26–27, 31, 38, 41, 59
- vs. diagnosing, 23–26
- disputants as empathic listeners, 14, 59
- empathic body language, 34
- empathic responses, 26, 28–34, 35
- empathy defined, 13
- empathy vs. sympathy, 21–22
- listener's role, 20
- online resources for, xi
- overviews, 11–15, 41
- pre-caucus listening phase, examples, 134–135, 141–145
- vs. prescribing, 16–22
- reconciling values, 37–41
- respecting pauses, 35–37
- vs. silence, 22
- techniques for, 28–37
- time needed for, 37

Empathic responses, 26, 28–34
- body language, 34
- dangling questions, 28
- empathic questions, 33–34
- empathic sayings, 32–33
- positive minimal responses, 28
- repetitions, 28–30
- seen as directive, 30

Empathy, vs. sympathy, 21–22

Empowering disputants, 6, 8, 106–107, 301
- conditions required for empowerment, 49, 59
- ownership of solutions, 87, 89–90, 285

Engram, R. E., 298–299, 300

Ethical issues, 37–41, 120, 299–300

Explaining our side. *See* self-justification

Eye contact, 276
- aggression, 114
- cultural differences, 273–275
- between disputants, 114
- with mediator, 114–115
- Negotiated Performance Appraisal sessions, 216

F

Facework, vii, 291–292

Facilitators
- vs. mediators, 283–284
- in Negotiated Performance Appraisals, 214–215, 223, 226, 229, 232, 264

Fault-finding. *See* blaming

Fears, 67
- presenting and discussing, 79–81, 102, 121–122

Feelings
- questions to stimulate discussion of, 24–25, 33–34
- *See also* Negative feelings; Positive feelings and comments

Finding fault. *See* blaming

Fish feeding story, 142

Fisher, Roger, *Getting to Yes*, 79, 121

Folger, Joseph, 286, 298
- *The Promise of Mediation*, 49, 120, 123, 125, 285–286, 287, 301

Forester, John, 125

Forgiveness, 95

Free advice story, 275

G

Gender differences, 270, 271
General Electric, 88
Generalizations, 99–100
    See also Stereotypes
Getting to Yes (Fisher and Ury), 79, 121
Giving advice. *See* diagnosing; solutions
Goodwill deposits, 39, 83, 102
    compliments as, 212, 220, 241
Greetings
    cultural differences, 271, 272, 274, 275
    as validation, 48, 75
Grenny, J., *Crucial Conversations*, 45, 46
Group participation, cultural differences, 277, 278, 280
Groups, conflicts among, 8

H

Half Dome story, 62
Heiken, Jill, 277
The Helping Interview (Benjamin), 21–22, 28
Helping Others Resolve Differences: Empowering Stakeholders (Billikopf), viii–ix
Hispanic culture
    nonverbal communication in, 270, 273–275
    stereotypic views of, 270
Honeymoon periods, 68, 291
Humor, 95–96

I

Identity projections and validation, 47–49
    See also Validation
The Idiot (Dostoevsky), 70
Integrity, maintaining, 91–92
Interest-based negotiation, 79–82, 108
    needs focus vs. positions focus, 79–81, 121–123, 124, 294
    potential failure of, 123, 125
    presenting needs and interests, 79–81, 102, 121–122
    traditional alternatives to, vii, 9, 80, 96–97
Interjections. *See* interruptions; positive minimal responses
International mediation, viii
Interpersonal conflict, 8, 62–73
    blind spots and, 52–53, 54
    contention, 66–67, 283, 288, 300
    effective listening and, 62, 67
    escalation of, 62–63, 65, 75, 83, 288, 289, 290
    facing directly, 68, 70, 72, 100
    factual vs. relationship issues, 162, 170
    identity validation and, 47–48
    Sam and Porter's story, 63–66
    seeking sympathy and support, 68–69, 98
    self-esteem and, 69–70
    self-justification and, 67
    sources and types of, 62–67
    weak conflict resolution methods, 67–73

Interpersonal negotiation skills, 61–110
　admitting mistakes, 94–95
　avoiding generalizations, name calling, and labels, 99–100, 104
　avoiding presumption of evil, 84, 85
　avoiding threats and manipulation, 55–56, 98–99
　being flexible, 96–97
　being patient, 97
　breaking down big issues, 86
　considering the worst alternative, 91
　controlling emotions, 83–85
　focusing on the problem, 87–89
　involving a third party, 103–107
　looking for creative solutions, 90–91
　maintaining integrity, 91–92
　moving away from blame, 86–87, 88
　online resources for, xi, 58
　overviews, 61–62, 107–109
　positive feelings and affirmations, 50–52, 54, 59, 95, 102
　preparing carefully, 98
　rejecting weak solutions, 89–90
　searching for interests, 79–82
　seeking to understand, 82–83, 102
　separating problems from self-worth, 98
　steps for confronting a person or problem, 100–103
　understanding time pressures, 92
　using humor, 95–96
　using pre-caucus to teach, 3–4, 296–297
　value of empathic listening, 14
　valuing others and oneself, 95, 102, 107
　weak negotiation methods, 67–73
　See also Apologies; Interpersonal conflict; Interpersonal relations
Interpersonal relations, 75–78
　conversations, 76–78, 107, 280
　courting periods, 68, 291
　See also Cultural differences; Interpersonal conflict; Validation
Interruptions, 26, 30, 72–73
　See also Mediator participation in joint session
Investigative questions, 23–24, 33, 123
Invitations to continue talking, 26, 28

J

Jackson, J. A., 289
Joint session case study, 173–208
　authority issue, 183–187, 195–201
　discussion of goals and solutions, 182–183, 201–202
　friendship issue, 187–190, 202–208
　lab assistant issue, 176–177

mediator participation, 175, 190, 192–193, 195, 197–200, 204
mediator's opening, 175
personal frustrations and miscommunication issues, 177–178, 180–182, 185–187, 189–193
sharing of positive comments, 175, 207–208
year-end report issue, 178–180, 193–196, 201–202
Joint sessions, vii, 3, 113–126
affirmations and positive comments in, 49, 50–52, 117, 119, 297
agreements, 120–125
allowing enough time, 113
covering all topics of dispute, 117, 125
disputants' anxiety about, 113
getting dialogue started, 117–120
location, 113
mediator participation in, 56, 117–118, 120–121, 125, 215
mediator's reduced role, 5–6, 106, 173
opening the mediation, 117
overviews, 5–6, 106, 125
parties' readiness for, 6, 52, 59, 139, 203
parties' readiness for, examples, 148–152, 161
preparing parties for, 10, 215, 287–289, 301
preparing parties for, examples, 138–139, 151–152, 171–172, 173, 175
riskiness of, 6, 287–288
seating arrangements, viii, 6, 106, 114–115, 125
steering parties away from weak solutions, 120–121
topic lists for, 44, 59
venting in, 289–290
See also Joint session case study; Negotiated Performance Appraisals

K

Kressel, Kenneth, vii, 289–290

L

Labeling people, 99, 104, 219, 231
Lee, Faye, 281
Linden, Jon, ix
List I, Negotiated Performance Appraisals, 215, 216, 218–225
discussion clips, 237–247, 255–257
List II, Negotiated Performance Appraisals, 215, 216, 226
discussion clips (pre-caucus), 247–251
List III, Negotiated Performance Appraisals, 215, 216, 218, 226–232
discussion clips, 251–253, 257–260
List IV, Negotiated Performance Appraisals, 216, 218, 232–234
discussion clips, 253–254, 260–264
Listening
attentive listening phase, 15, 16

diagnostic phase, 15, 16, 23–26
effective listening skills, 59, 62, 67, 76
prescriptive phase, 15, 16–22
selective hearing, 142
See also Empathic listening
Long-distance mediation, viii
López, Rodrigo, xiii, 237, 241–246
Losing face, vii, 290, 296
The Lost Art of Listening (Nichols), 17, 76

M

Maltz, Daniel N., 280
Markowitz, J. R., 298–299, 300
Marshall, P., 286, 298
McMillan, R., *Crucial Conversations*, 45, 46
Mediating Interpersonal Conflicts: A Pathway to Peace (Umbreit), viii
Mediation, appropriate situations for, 103
Mediation case study, 129–208
 introduction, 129–132
 joint session, 173–208
 Nora's first pre-caucus, 141–152
 Nora's second pre-caucus, 163–172
 Rebecca's first pre-caucus, 133–139
 Rebecca's second pre-caucus, 153–162
 See also Joint session case study; Pre-caucus case study

Mediation styles, 105–107, 284–285
 See also Directive mediation; Party-Directed Mediation; Transformative mediation
Mediator-directed mediation, vii, 9, 105, 284–285
Mediator neutrality, 9, 105, 106, 296, 298–299
Mediator participation in joint session, 117–118, 120–121, 125, 173
 Negotiated Performance Appraisals, 215
 Rebecca and Nora's joint session, 175, 190, 192–193, 195, 197–200, 204
 reduced role in Party-Directed Mediation, 5–6, 106, 173
Mediators
 as arbiters, vii, 9, 104, 285
 choosing a mediator, 103–104
 concerns about mediator power, 298
 confidentiality issues, 103–104, 299–300
 conflict escalation and control of joint session, 290
 as facilitators, 104
 vs. facilitators, 283–284
 in mediator-directed mediation, 105
 mediator values and empathic listening, 37–41
 neutrality, 9, 105, 106, 296, 298–299
 parties' relationships with, 291
 supervisors as, 103
 See also Facilitators; Mediator participation in joint session

Mirroring, distorted, 100
Monk, Gerald, 23, 44, 280–281, 286
Moore, C. W., 285, 288, 298
Moral issues. *See* ethical issues
Multicultural conflicts, vii, x

N

Name calling, 99
Narrative Mediation (Winslade and Monk), 23, 44–45, 280–281, 286
Needs-based negotiation, 79–82, 108
    incompatible needs, 123, 125
    needs focus vs. positions focus, 79–81, 121–123, 294
    presenting needs, interests, and fears, 79–81, 102, 121–122
    separating positions from needs, 124
    traditional alternatives to, vii, 9, 80, 96–97
Negative attribution, 85
Negative communication patterns
    assuming the worst, 85
    blaming, 44–45, 53, 86–87, 88, 152
    distorted mirroring, 100
    generalizations, name calling, and labels, 99–100, 104, 219, 231
    interruptions, 26, 30, 72–73
    joint session example, 190–192
    presuming evil, 84, 85
    threats and manipulation, 55–56, 98–99

Negative feelings
    creating distance from, 44–46
    empathic questions to expose, 33–34
    encouraging expression of, 292–293
    expressions of, in joint sessions, 154, 155, 177, 289–290
    finding constructive outlets for, 68–69
    venting in pre-caucus, 3, 12–13, 16–17, 289–292
Negotiated Performance Appraisals, 211–236, 237–264
    agreements and solutions, 226, 228–230, 232, 234, 252–253, 257, 262–264
    delivering negative feedback, 231–232
    delivering praise effectively, 220–222, 241–246, 248
    explaining the process, 216
    facilitator involvement, 214–215, 223, 226, 229, 232, 264
    features and benefits of, 212–215, 224
    follow-up meetings, 234–236, 253
    introducing at high organizational level, 214
    joint meeting, 218–234
    List I (complimenting subordinate), 215, 216, 218–225, 255–257
    List I discussion clips, 237–247, 255–257
    List II (subordinate's recent improvements), 215, 216, 226

List II discussion clips, 247–251
List III (subordinate's weak points), 215, 216, 218, 226–232
List III discussion clips, 251–253, 257–260
List IV (superior's potential for improvement), 216, 218, 232–234
List IV discussion clips, 253–254, 260–264
as model for preventive/alternative mediation, ix–x, 211–212
multiple joint sessions, 230–231
overviews, 215–218, 236
pre-caucus discussion clips, 237–254
pre-caucuses for, 215, 218, 226, 232
signs of success, 223
Negotiation skills. *See* interpersonal negotiation skills
Nichols, Michael, 17, 76
Nonverbal communication
cultural differences, 273–276
eye contact, 273–275, 276
in listening situations, 26, 30, 32, 33, 34
as stroking, 74–75
Nora and Rebecca's mediation. *See* mediation case study

O

Online resources, xi, 58
Orange story, 73

P

Parking story, 71
Party-Directed Mediation
appropriate situations for, vii, viii, 8, 107
controversy over, 3, 6
factors required for success, 116
inappropriate situations for, 38, 49
mediator's role, 5–6, 106, 173
Negotiated Performance Appraisals as alternative to, ix–x, 211–212
overviews, vi–viii, 3–6, 106–107
See also Joint session entries; Mediation case study; Pre-caucus entries
Patience, 15, 17, 25, 97
Patterson, K., *Crucial Conversations*, 45, 46
Pauses, respecting, 35–37
See also Silence
Performance appraisals. *See* Negotiated Performance Appraisals
Performance-based compensation, 225, 235–236
Personal space, cultural differences, 270, 275, 277
Pons, Macarena, xiii, 237, 238–240, 246–264
Positions, 67
having parties explain each other's positions, 122–123
positions focus vs. needs focus, 79–81, 121–123, 124, 294
separating from needs, 124

Positive feelings and comments, 95, 102
  eliciting and permitting in pre-caucus, 10, 49–52, 54, 59, 288–289
  eliciting and permitting in pre-caucus, examples, 135–138, 145–147, 158–161
  in joint session, 49, 50–52, 117, 119, 297
  in Negotiated Performance Appraisals, 215, 216, 218–225, 234–235
  sharing in joint session, examples, 175, 207–208
  sharing in pre-caucus, examples, 153, 160, 164
  See also List I; Praise and compliments
Positive minimal responses, 28
Power
  of mediator, vii, 9, 104, 285
  See also Empowering disputants; Superior-subordinate relationships
Praise and compliments, 218–225, 233, 234–235, 255–256
  delivering praise effectively, 220–222, 241–246, 248
  fear of praising, 224–225
  validation through, 49, 75, 220, 224, 225
  See also List I; Positive feelings and comments
Pre-caucus, vii, 3, 9–60
  controversy and criticisms, vii, 284–285, 298–300, 301
  effective uses of, viii
  explaining process to parties, 10, 133–134
  introduction and preliminary conversation, 10
  judging parties' readiness for joint session, 6, 52, 59, 139, 203, 215, 288–289
  listening portion, overviews, 10, 11–13, 41
  in mediation literature, 284, 285–287, 301
  mediator's role, 4
  multiple sessions, 171, 175, 215
  Negotiated Performance Appraisal discussion clips, 237–254
  for Negotiated Performance Appraisals, 215, 218, 226, 232
  overviews, 3–5, 9–10, 106
  transformative opportunities in, 49, 117, 120, 286–287, 296–297
  See also Empathic listening; Pre-caucus advantages and opportunities; Pre-caucus case study; Pre-caucus coaching
Pre-caucus advantages and opportunities, 9–10
  helping parties feel understood, 294, 301
  improved communications and problem-solving in joint session, 295, 296–297, 301
  preparing parties for joint session, 10, 288–289, 301
  reduced interruptions of joint session, 300
  venting and emotional release, 11–13, 291–292, 294
Pre-caucus case study, 141–162
  eliciting and permitting

positive feelings, 135–138, 145–147, 158–161
Nora's first pre-caucus, 141–152
Nora's second pre-caucus, 163–172
Rebecca's first pre-caucus, 133–139
Rebecca's second pre-caucus, 153–162
sharing of issues raised by other party, 139, 157–158, 162, 164–165
sharing of positive comments, 153, 160, 164
shuttle diplomacy, 139, 140
Pre-caucus coaching, 43–60, 301
creating distance from contentious feelings, 44–46
eliciting and permitting positive feelings, 10, 49–52, 54, 59, 288–289
examples, 135–139, 145–152, 156–162
improving communication skills, 56, 58–59, 166–167
overviews, 9–10, 43, 59
practicing through role plays, 56–58
preparing a topic list, 44, 59
sharing issues raised by other party, 55, 56
sharing positive comments, 50, 52
validating identity projections, 47–49
See also Blind spots, challenging
Pre-mediation, *see* pre-caucus
Prescribing, 15, 16–22
drawbacks of offering advice or suggestions, 18, 19–21
Preventive mediation, Negotiated Performance Appraisals as model for, ix–x, 211
Priming the pump, 25–26, 33
Problems
discussing in Negotiated Performance Appraisals, 226–232
introducing, in joint session, 102, 118
problem focus vs. solution focus, 87–89, 284–285
separating from self-worth, 98
See also Solutions
The Promise of Mediation (Bush and Folger), 49, 120, 123, 125, 285–286, 287, 301
Pruitt, D. G., 289
Psychological contact, establishing, 100–101
Psychological distance, 66–67, 292, 300

Q

Questions
dangling questions, 28
different interpretations of, 280
empathic questions, 33–34
to introduce a challenge, 55–56
investigative/diagnostic questions, 23–24, 33, 123
priming the pump, 25–26, 33
waiting for an answer, 72–73

R

Rebecca and Nora's mediation. *See* mediation case study

Refusal to speak, 77
    See also Silence
Repeating words or phrases, 28–30
Restorative justice mediation, viii, 6
Rogers, Carl, 4, 14, 30, 38
Role plays, 56–58, 98, 119–120, 151
    Negotiated Performance Appraisal example, 244–246
    real problems and suggestions as distractions, 20–21, 123
Rothman, Jay, 81–82
Russian banana story, 268–269

S

Saving face, vii, 291–292, 296
Seating arrangements
    directive mediation, 105, 115
    joint session, viii, 6, 106, 114–115, 125
    Negotiated Performance Appraisal sessions, 218
Self-esteem, 69–70, 139, 285
    amor propio (false self-esteem), 70
    autoestima (self-esteem), 70
    Negotiated Performance Appraisals and, 219, 220
    separating problems from, 98
Self-image. *See* identity projections; self-esteem
Self-justification, 45–46, 67
Seven Habits of Highly Effective People (Covey), 82
Shuttle diplomacy, 139, 140
Silence, 17
    vs. avoidance, 72–73, 77
    vs. empathic listening, 22
    respecting pauses, 35–37
    The Skilled Helper (Egan), 53, 54
Smoking in class story, 90
Soccer refereeing story, 46
Solutions, 118, 120–125
    avoiding focusing on, 87–89
    looking for creative solutions, 90–91
    in Negotiated Performance Appraisals, 226, 228–230, 232, 234, 252–253
    ownership of/control over, 87, 89–90, 285
    as positions, 67
    premature/unwelcome offers of, 18, 19–21, 87
    rejecting weak solutions, 89–90, 120–121
    solution focus vs. problem focus, 87–89, 284–285
    sustainability of, 102–103, 121
    taking proposals seriously, 88–89
    See also Agreements; Prescribing
Spatial behavior, cultural differences, 270, 275
Speech
    cultural differences, 280
    See also Communications
Stereotypes, 180–181, 270, 272, 273, 277
Stories and anecdotes
    banana, 268–269
    coin shifting, 224
    fish feeding, 142
    free advice, 18
    Half Dome climb, 62
    orange, 73

parking, 71
Sam and Porter, 63–66
soccer refereeing, 46
tetherball, 26
wine, 78
Yosemite driving, 275
Stroke exchanges, 74–75, 107
Stutman, R., 286, 298
Superior-subordinate relationships, ix–x, 212–213, 214
See also Negotiated Performance Appraisals
Switzler, A., *Crucial Conversations*, 45, 46
Sympathy, 16–17
vs. empathy, 21–22
seeking sympathy and support, 68–69, 98

T

Take-it-or-leave-it bargaining tactics, 88
Taking notes, 44, 102, 290
Negotiated Performance Appraisals, 219, 220, 223
Tannen, Deborah, 270, 280
Tetherball story, 26
Therapy, challenging blind spots in, 53
Threats and manipulation, 55–56, 98–99
Time pressures, understanding, 92
Ting-Toomey, Stella, 47, 280
Topic discussion, in joint session, 117–118, 125
Topic list preparation, 44, 59
Touch, cultural differences, 270, 275
Transformative mediation, 49, 120, 284, 285

key features and benefits, 296, 299, 301
mediator neutrality and, 299
See also Party-Directed Mediation; Validation; Valuing others
Trust, trustworthiness, 73, 74, 89, 90, 92, 96
acceptance of apologies and, 95

U

Umbreit, Mark S., viii
Ury, William, *Getting to Yes*, 79, 121

V

Validation, 47–49, 225
establishing psychological contact, 100–101
as motivator, 224
through positive comments, 49, 75, 220, 224, 225
through stroke exchanges, 74–75, 107
See also Positive feelings and comments
Values differences, finding common ground, 125
Valuing oneself, 95
Valuing others, 50–52, 54, 59, 95, 102, 107
See also Positive feelings and comments
Van Riper, Charles, 47
Venting, 3, 11–13, 50, 289–292
diagnostic and prescriptive responses to, 16–17

value of emotional release, 11–13, 294
See also Empathic listening
Verbal strokes, 75
Victim-offender mediation, viii, 6
Volkema, R. J., 286, 291, 298

W

Weeks, Dudley, viii
When Talk Works (Kressel), vii
Wine story, 78
Winslade, John, 23, 44, 280–281, 286
Withdrawal. *See* avoidance
Workplace violence and harassment, 99, 103
Worst alternatives, considering, 91

Y

Yielding, 71, 89–90, 120
Yosemite driving story, 275